Playing Smart

Playing Smart

New York Women Writers and
Modern Magazine Culture

Catherine Keyser

Rutgers University Press

NEW BRUNSWICK, NEW JERSEY, AND LONDON

Visit our Web site: http://rutgerspress.rutgers.edu

Manufactured in the United States of America

LIBRARY OF CONGRESS CATALOGING-IN-PUBLICATION DATA

Keyser, Catherine, 1980–
    Playing smart : New York women writers and modern magazine culture / Catherine Keyser.
        p.   cm.
    Includes bibliographical references and index.
    ISBN 978-0-8135-4786-2 (hardcover : alk. paper)
    1. American literature—Women authors—History and criticism.   2. American literature—20th century—History and criticism.   3. Journalism and literature—United States—History—20th century.   4. American periodicals—History—20th century.   5. Literature and society—United States—History—20th century.   6. Modernism (Literature)—United States.   I. Title.
    PS151.K49 2010
    810.9'9287—dc22

                                                                                2009048294

A British Cataloging-in-Publication record for this book is available from the British Library.

A book in the American Literatures Initiative (ALI), a collaborative publishing project of NYU Press, Fordham University Press, Rutgers University Press, Temple University Press, and the University of Virginia Press. The Initiative is supported by The Andrew W. Mellon Foundation. For more information, please visit www.americanliteratures.org.

THE
AMERICAN
LITERATURES
INITIATIVE

For my parents, Barbara and Les Keyser

Contents

ACKNOWLEDGMENTS

Dorothy Parker complained, "Why is it no one ever sent me yet / One perfect limousine, do you suppose?" Thankfully, I have ridden deluxe, so to speak, through every stage of this book's conception and execution thanks to the people with whom I have had the privilege to work and play. To my mentors, colleagues, family, and friends, I offer these acknowledgments like the "One Perfect Rose" that Parker disparages in her poem: a small token of my appreciation that cannot possibly live up to the limousine of their support, influence, and laughter.

Werner Sollors has been this book's champion and godfather; his brilliance, generosity, and humor inspire me and all those lucky enough to work with him. I owe a great debt to my graduate mentors at Harvard University for fostering with acumen and care my development as both literary critic and teacher. Marjorie Garber shared her keen editorial eye and passion for knowledge, Lawrence Buell his pedagogical dedication and unerring counsel, and Philip Fisher his aesthetic vision and intellectual rigor. Glenda Carpio demonstrated that one could be both a scholar of humor and a scholar with a sense of humor. Thanks also to Henry Louis Gates Jr., Douglas Mao, Louis Menand, Ann Rowland, Elaine Scarry, and Jason Stevens. I am deeply grateful to my friends from graduate school, especially Erin Minear, Nadine Knight, Melissa Jenkins, Josh Rothman, Pelagia Horgan, and Glynne and Akiko Walley, who always reminded me that delight and scholarship are not only compatible but crucial companions. Princeton professors lit the spark of intellectual inquiry for me while I was an undergraduate; I remember their classrooms fondly and their innumerable lessons with humble gratitude: Maria DiBattista, Diana Fuss, Claudia Johnson, Gaetana Marrone-Puglia, Lee Mitchell, Deborah Nord, Elaine Showalter, P. Adams Sitney, and D. Vance Smith.

Heartfelt thanks to my colleagues and friends in the English Department at the University of South Carolina for their intellectual and interpersonal generosity; I can't imagine a more supportive, dynamic, or inspiring group. Special thanks to Greg Forter for his unstinting mentorship, thoughtful counsel, and sage revision suggestions. Debra Rae Cohen and Brian Glavey each read sections of this manuscript, and I am grateful both for their sterling insights and their delightful friendship. Susan Courtney, Cynthia Davis, Nina Levine, Rebecca Stern, and Laura Walls shared time, expertise, and encouragement. Anne Gulick and Tara Powell cheered me on and provided necessary time away from my desk. Thanks also to Katherine Adams, Robert Brinkmeyer, Holly Crocker, Paula Feldman, Ed Gieskes, Leon Jackson, Ed Madden, Tom Rice, Sara Schwebel, David Shields, Scott Trafton, Susan Vanderborg, Qiana Whitted, and Gretchen Woertendyke. Research assistants Jamie Libby Boyle and Alisha Reid endured my flurries of inquiries with patience and aplomb. Their contributions enriched the content and ensured the accuracy of the book (any errors therein are attributable only to the author). Jeffrey Makala in Rare Books and Special Collections at the Thomas Cooper Library aided my research with expertise, insight, and wit. Mark Volmer and the ILL staff have also been unfailingly helpful. Thank you to my students in ENGL 429V: Sophisticated Ladies and ENGL 840A: Sass and the City; your insights and humor form a crucial part of this book, as they did a crucial (and delightful) part of my life during the spring of 2008.

Thanks to my editor Leslie Mitchner at Rutgers University Press for her belief in and enthusiasm for this project. The professional and responsive staff members at the Press, especially Rachel Friedman and Katie Keeran, made this process a pleasure. I am grateful to Tim Roberts, managing editor of the American Literatures Initiative, for skillfully shepherding my book through its final stages and to Lisa Jerry for her careful copy-editing. I extend thanks also to the anonymous readers of this manuscript for their eloquent encouragement and constructive revision suggestions.

The University of South Carolina English Department provided me with summer funding, research assistants, and licensing fees as I completed this manuscript. I am also grateful to the Mellon Foundation for its support of the American Literatures Initiative. The Jacob K. Javits Fellowship program supported my graduate work, which gave me the freedom to pursue independent research and develop serious intellectual goals. Thank you to the staff of the New York Public Library, Columbia University's Butler Library, Yale University's Beinecke Library, and the Schomberg Center for Research in Black Culture. I presented work in progress from this book on panels at meetings of the Modern Language Association, the American Literature Association, the Modernist Studies Association, the Northeast Modern Language Association, and the Midwest Modern Language Association. I offer many thanks to the panel participants and the auditors who made suggestions or asked questions at these presentations.

Portions of this book have appeared elsewhere, and I thank the original publishers for permission to reprint. Parts of chapter 1 appeared in "Edna St. Vincent Millay and the Very Clever Woman in Vanity Fair," in *American Periodicals* 17.1 (May 2007): 65–96. Copyright 2007 The Ohio State University. Reproduced with permission. Parts of chapter 2 were published in "'That's Why I'm Not So Well': Dorothy Parker, Macabre Humor, and the Female Body," in *Death Becomes Her: Cultural Narratives of Femininity and Death in Nineteenth-Century Literature*, edited by Elizabeth Dill and Sheri Weinstein (Newcastle: Cambridge Scholars Publishing 2008), 131–156. Published with permission of Cambridge Scholars Publishing.

Excerpts from and complete poems by Edna St. Vincent Millay— "Exiled," "The Penitent," "Daphne," "I shall forget you presently, my dear," "Thursday," "Love, for though you riddle me with darts," "To the Not-Impossible Him," "I think I should have loved you presently," and "III. Sonnet in Answer to a Question: To Elinor Wylie"—copyright 1921, 1922, 1939, 1948, 1950, 1967 by Edna St. Vincent Millay and Norma May Ellis. Reprinted by permission of Elizabeth Barnett, Literary Executor, the Millay Society.

Excerpts from poems by Jessie Fauset, "La Vie C'est la Vie" and "Here's April," which were first published in the July 1922 and April 1924 issues of *The Crisis*, reprinted by permission of the Crisis Publishing Company, Inc., the publisher of the magazine of the National Association for the Advancement of Colored People.

My friends and loved ones have both added to the book and freed me from it. Thanks to my supportive family (Bridges, Cheresnicks, Crattys, Famolaris, Keysers, McCans, Yarbroughs, and more) and especially to my grandmother Emma Yarbrough, the biggest bookworm of all and an

XII / ACKNOWLEDGMENTS

advanced professor of *joie de vivre*. To the Abrechts (Helen-Jane, Russell, Ryan, Chris, and Eric) and to the Baios (Aunt Mary and the clan) I am most grateful; they welcomed me into their families and shared their gifts for laughter and celebration. Thanks also to cherished friends: Jake Ruddiman and Kate Callahan, Alisa and Richard Freed, Kristin Wiley and David Backeberg, Caitlin and Kevin Joy, Tom Dent and John Castleman, Courtney Gerber and Chad Freeburg, Danielle Di Leo and Michele degli Esposti, Kate Minear, Felicia Leicht, Dan Cammisa, Eleni Delopoulos, Ryan Abrecht, and Jessica Rogers.

My beloved husband, Paul Famolari, has watched me eat, sleep, and breathe this book. His patience, insight, support, and laughter ring through every page. I owe him the world for his partnership and love, and instead, he gives me the world. I make out like a bandit in this bargain.

This book is dedicated to my parents, who educated me by example, not only in the study of literature but also in the art of life. I thank my father, Les, for his eloquence and empathy. My witty and wonderful mother, Barbara, read me "One Perfect Rose" instead of nursery rhymes when I was little. She painstakingly read every draft of this manuscript: Mom, I am sorry you will never get those years of your life back, but I am grateful you were willing to give them.

PLAYING SMART

Introduction

The December 1923 issue of *Vanity Fair* featured "A Very Modern Love Story" by Nancy Hoyt, sister of the poet Elinor Wylie. In this fable, a "young, fashionable, well bred, and rich" man laments that he has "found no maiden at all up to his standard."[1] He watches a beautiful modern girl, waiting for her to develop sufficiently to spark his interest. Like Goldilocks, the modern girl samples each cultural brew: lowbrow, highbrow, and finally middlebrow, the concoction—or confection—that is just right. First, the modern girl is too uncultivated: "noisy and raucous," singing a jingle for "'Booth's old-time gin.'" Then she is overly intellectual, "mus[ing]" and "hushed," "wistfully" reading Rupert Brooke. The young man longs for her to "grow just a little more cynical, a little more sad, a little more able to regard her past loves with her tongue in her cheek and through amused, sardonic eyes! To read authors who were flippant about serious things, and serious about flippant ones." Finally, the young man sees the sign he needs that "his every hope would be fulfilled; for, under one of her arms, she held the latest issue of *Vanity Fair.*"

This tale treats humor as seductive and nonthreatening. The man wants a woman to be "subtle" and "charming," but he does not want her to be "too serious" or "too heavily cultured." Bon mots and cynicism together convey the exquisite impression that she has "admired and passed beyond all the imbecilities of society," turning her worldliness into a status symbol for this young man with "his yacht and his motorcars." Lest fulfilling the prince's fantasy seem the fable's prescription for women, tongue-in-cheek narration tweaks the young man's perspective. He "look[s] disdainfully down on the jejune and flaccid pleasures of Bar Harbor." With "jejune and flaccid," Hoyt suggests that this pose of superiority is designed to ballast his sense of masculinity. This anxious modern man longs for "One Perfect Girl" and turns to the magazine to confirm this fantasy. The young girl, however, holds the magazine as one possible script, and she has inhabited at least two other cultural poses before adopting this sardonic persona.

This "Very Modern Love Story" could serve as an allegory for the waltz between consumer fantasies, gendered prescriptions, and tendentious irony in the pages of smart magazines like *Vanity Fair*. In fact, *Vanity Fair* is a good historical test case for the modern popularity of urbane humor. Its publication dates from 1914 to 1936 encompass the metropolitan outlook of the late 1910s, the fabled sophistication of the 1920s, and the waning of this zeitgeist in the early 1930s due to economic crisis and political upheaval. In Hoyt's 1923 fable, a daydream of luxury prompts instructions on how to be appropriately feminine. Thus commodity culture supports gender normativity and vice versa. But that is not the end of the tale. While the story names ironic distance as an appealing and appropriate feminine role, this same perspective turns the tables on the man who thinks it would be desirable. Humor can appear ingratiating even as it interrogates. According to Freud, jokes "are in a position to conceal not only what they have to say but also the fact that they have something—forbidden—to say."[2]

This book attends to the forbidden subject matter aired by the seemingly most conventional of writers, middlebrow magazine humorists, who found themselves in the unconventional position of being modern women in the public eye. I focus on the work of several influential New York writers lauded as urbane sophisticates in the decades between the two world wars: Edna St. Vincent Millay, Dorothy Parker, Anita Loos, Lois Long, Jessie Fauset, Nella Larsen, Dawn Powell, and Mary McCarthy. They published in wide-circulation magazines, such as *Vanity Fair*, the *New Yorker*, and *Harper's Bazaar*, that advertised an imaginary New York filled with tuxedoed men and daring (and darling) flappers and that advanced wit, epigram, and understatement as the modern lingua franca.[3] In their humor writing, these women writers respond to the fantasies generated by magazines and imagine their influence on the modern public.[4] As a feminist literary critic, I employ close reading and the attention it enables to irony, narrative perspective, and theatrical tropes to show how the marketable pose of the smart woman writer facilitated literary strategies that offered critiques of gender roles, mass media, and modernity.

Although humor provides methods of concealment and disguise, humor and its frequent comrade, irony, also derive power from revelation, from the conceptual and critical potential of unmasking. These women writers reflected on their own personae in their work by investigating the growing publicity culture of which they were a part and a symbol. Writing of the modern drama, Walter Benjamin defined irony as a technique that could expose the artificial form not only of the artwork but indeed of modern society: "an actor should reserve for himself the possibility of stepping out of character artistically" to reflect "the philosophic sophistication of the author who, in writing his plays, always remembers that in the end the world may turn out to be a theatre."[5] This self-reflexive pose is not simply the domain of the drama, and indeed in their fiction these writers accentuate the role of performance in everyday life and in print culture. By imagining the flippant "One Perfect Girl" in her "Very Modern Love Story," Hoyt reflects about her role in modern media culture as a magazine humorist. In such indirect reflections on their own cultural positioning, these modern women writers employ appropriative irony, "an irony that acknowledges the mediating system . . . [and] endeavors to use that system, with all the play the system allows, to produce different ends, that is, to change the products of the system."[6]

The public status of modern women led to profound situational ironies and cultural contradictions. These writers combined characteristics of iconic incarnations of the modern woman: celebrities, professionals, and flappers. Female celebrities, the beautiful objects of the mass media gaze, also dominated the public stage and manipulated their personae.[7] Women who entered the workplace were imagined as accomplished exceptions and at the same time were insistently pigeonholed. The historian Alice Kessler-Harris observes that the flapper role "was meant to guarantee only peripheral involvement in the task of earning a living: an extension of women's supportive functions in the male world without the threat of competition." Nonetheless, this safely secondary role provided a cover for new ambitions: "By masking women's real possibilities, the guise of the flapper enabled them to emerge from their homes and into the business world."[8] The modern woman in the public sphere occupied paradoxical roles that promised freedom yet delimited its possibilities.

As I argue in the following chapters, these humor writers found literary techniques to represent and even play with this doubleness. They establish both the confining contours of modern stereotypes and the liberating possibilities of rewriting these roles. Sometimes this doubleness emerges in their manipulation of genre. For example, Millay's light verse and her satirical prose, the two genres she published in popular magazines, together suggest the giddy possibilities and threatening instabilities of the reinvention of self. Fauset uses the didactic arc of the novel of passing to promote the sense of humor and its attendant individualism, even as the plot appears to chastise her heroine for those very qualities. Some writers used persona and narration to create a double perspective that illuminates cultural foibles or contradiction; for example, Parker compared her aging book reviewer body to the youthful flapper, and McCarthy allowed her third-person narrator to expose the hypocrisies of would-be radicals.

This literary approach of ironic juxtaposition reflects the doubleness of their cultural positioning as both successful magazine writers and also hesitant participants in the marketplace of gender roles. This approach also suggests the performances required to attain and maintain professional status as a woman. In her influential 1929 essay "Womanliness as a Masquerade," psychoanalyst Joan Riviere argued that humor could serve as a disguise for professional women. Riviere suggests that to avoid offending her male colleagues, the professional woman "has to treat the situation of displaying her masculinity as a 'game,' as something *not real*, as a 'joke.' She cannot treat herself and her subject seriously." Even so, humor expressed aggression and often appeared rude or disruptive: "she becomes flippant and joking, so much so that it has caused comment and rebuke." Riviere concludes that humor, a strategy initially adopted to make controversial ambitions unobjectionable, ultimately underscored the effrontery of ambition rather than erasing it, "enabl[ing] some of her sadism to escape, hence the offence it causes."[9] Riviere's reading of this double performance—humor adopted to palliate and then articulated to challenge—helps to inspire my reading of these worldly personae as both strategic disguises and mouthpieces for cultural critique. From within the magazine, these humorists interrogate the cultural impact of the modern magazine industry.

In this investigation, I extend the work of critics who have established the contradictions of the modern woman writer's role in print culture.[10] Nina Miller ends her book on modern women writers and the literary subcultures of New York by invoking "the modern woman writer's *"irony of embeddedness* deriving from a whole social matrix of tensions, to which there is no 'outside' and no end."[11] This idea provides the departing premise of my book, in which I treat humor as a form that dramatizes embeddedness and reflects on this social matrix of tensions. The anthropologist Mary Douglas argues that the humorist disarranges the tidy categories of hierarchy and binary; the joker "is one of those people who pass beyond the bounds of reason and society and give glimpses of a truth which escapes through the mesh of structured concepts."[12] Because the modern woman writer inhabited a symbolic cultural role of complications and contradictions, she was particularly well situated to express ironies that escaped tidy conceptual binaries. Simone Weil Davis considers the 1920s ad women: "The allusive impact of the wry dig becomes crucial to consider among women who were occupying a vexed, multiply identified position."[13]

The indirection and allusiveness of this humor writing makes it as pleasurable as it is trenchant. The sophisticated personae of these women writers conspire with the stylish language that they use to challenge readerly expectations and undermine the magazine's surface messages. Freud observes that play with language permits the critical aims of the joke to land without immediately alerting its target: "this façade is intended to dazzle the examining eye."[14] Thus, in Freud's view, humor employs style to hide aggression. Conversely, according to Henri Bergson, humor also strips the mask of style (social type, fashionable attire, intellectual pretense) from the people who would like their status to be taken most seriously.[15] The humorists I discuss dazzle with epigram and wit, but they also delineate the failures of purported sophistication, especially where that pose carries social, literary, or political weight. Each writer hints that behind her urbane feminine persona, so popular within the magazine, lay an ironic author who cannot be so easy defined or codified.

Modern New York humor magazines like *Vanity Fair* and the *New Yorker* have been dubbed the "smart magazines" by historian George H. Douglas.[16] These publications targeted a middle-class audience and presumed that this readership longed for luxury and elite social status. The smart magazines reflected this potent combination of hedonism and hierarchy in implicit promises of class mobility for urban professionals. They also treated the modern flapper as a status symbol for the sophisticated man, even though, ironically, the magazine industry was one arena where professional opportunities and public visibility facilitated the increased autonomy of modern women. As Eli Zaretsky observes, "the emerging world of mass production and mass consumption was a mixed-sex world."[17] Even as magazine caricaturists attempted to render the difference between men and women in indelible ink, the conventionality of the stereotypes that appeared in these magazines blurred the lines of gender roles by making them seem artificial and subject to parody. Given the gendered stereotypes and heterosocial topics the smart magazines addressed (the so-called war between the sexes, the flapper, and the sophisticated man), women writers for these magazines could emulate and emphasize these generic and gendered conventions to unsettle the seeming naturalness of the norms with which they played.

I argue that the female magazine writers could—and in the specific instances that I analyze *did*—play a double role. The magazine humorist could feign that she was the "One Perfect Girl" and at the same time could challenge the existence of such a figure with the literary tools of ironic juxtaposition, comic exaggeration, and self-conscious theatricality. The guise of the one facilitated the guile of the other. The word "smart," to which I return throughout my analysis, also plays a double role: first, as a prized value in middlebrow magazine culture and, second, as a facilitating tactic for these writers. Within the rhetoric of the magazines and their visual field of illustrations, advertisements, and cartoons, the ideal of smartness connoted a number of individual and coordinating qualities: wealth and elite social status, conversance with the latest trends, practical intelligence (especially when applied to shopping), a sense of humor, fashion sense, and sex appeal. To be smart, then, could mean to be feminine in very narrow terms—terms that emphasized woman's role as consumer, sex object, and charming companion. While the word smart tended to correlate with the modern (whatever was deemed smart was frequently also new), this ideal does not seem to depart much from a domestic vision of woman as helpmate, hostess, and shopper.

Through attention to the topography of the magazine and literary landmarks by women writers, I map smartness as a modern territory of feminine ideals that could be uncomfortably familiar and unduly confining, even though the magazine promised it was a new frontier. Smartness is thus the cultural field that throws the object of femininity into perspective. Exploiting this contrast, however, I also view smartness as a pose (distinguished by humor, urbanity, irony, worldliness, sexuality, detachment) deliberately adopted by these women writers. These humorists treated fashion as costume, sex appeal as a sign of autonomous desire, and humor as both mask and medium. In their work, the pose of smartness metamorphoses from the prescription of the periodical into a tactic that establishes modern subjectivity and enacts satirical critique of the surrounding field.

My primary aim is thus to establish the power of literary humor as women writers used it to reflect on specific problems of modernity: the influence of the new mass media and magazine culture, the instability of gender roles and the use of normative stereotypes to ballast them, and the public embodiment of celebrity women. By linking their work to the styles and stereotypes promulgated by smart magazines, I demonstrate how these writers adopted the deceptive air of triviality associated with these middlebrow publications to expose the anxieties riddling modern hierarchies of class identity, gender norms, and even literary reputation.

The Middlebrow, Modernism, and Irony

Suggestively, Freud and Bergson, two major theorists of humor, were also trying to understand modernity and its discontents. Freud used his essay on joking to extend his theories about aggression and society, instinct and sublimation. In essence he argued that humor was a way for people to live together in crowded spaces and competitive spheres without killing one another, a pessimistic take on urbanization's forced proximity and civilization's unrealized promise. When Bergson located humor in the mechanization of the world, he implied that humor was a symptom of modernity because the alienated individual felt stuck in systems beyond his control. Bergson's theories of *la durée* tried to set this individual free within the subjective perception of time. By contrast, his theories of humor drew attention to the rigidity of modern regimes and routines. Both Freud and Bergson treated humor as a necessarily inadequate method of coping with increased social regimentation that left traces of its failures and struck uneasy bargains with seemingly overwhelming systems.

The women writers I address certainly express frustration, aggression, and anxiety in their work, especially about the restricted roles imposed upon and sometimes embraced by modern women. But I argue that humor is not just symptomatic, as Freud and Bergson might speculate, but rather diagnostic. These women writers use humor and the traces it carries of failure and compromise to focus the reader's attention on the elements of modernity that produce these alienated responses. In this humor writing, one finds anxieties about mass duplication, celebrity, publicity, and bodily discipline. By generating friction between the magazines' smooth presentations of modernity and their own disruptive articulations of disbelief, these humorists call into being a counterpublic that can reimagine humor as critique rather than capitulation. Michael Warner defines counterpublics as "spaces of circulation in which it is hoped that the poesis of scene making will be transformative, not replicative merely."[18] The humor replicates while transforming, adopting a familiar frame (rhetorical, generic, social), and changing it just enough to expose its absurdity.

In this simultaneous responsiveness and resistance to the conditions of modernity, this popular humor intersects with literary modernism. Both draw attention to social performances, rhetorical texture, and individual alienation. Modernist writers often highlight artifice through syntactic experimentation, breaking apart the sentence and making it new in order to expose the conventionality of the old. The writers considered here instead use familiar language to describe an unfamiliar world, employing caricature and wisecrack to expose social convention, clichéd language, and gender stereotypes. Through ironic narration and internal monologue, they establish the friction between interior experience and external markers of status and identity. Thus, they share the mistrust of appearances and the ethos of cultural exposure characteristic of American modernists such as F. Scott Fitzgerald and Ernest Hemingway.

Today, these women writers, owing to their use of conventional rather than experimental literary styles, are more likely to be considered middlebrow than modernist. The term "middlebrow" gained currency in the 1920s because of the rapid and unprecedented expansion of print culture; it was "used by literary and cultural critics to describe the modern texts, readers, and print-culture institutions that they believed threatened a long-standing hierarchy of genteel and avant-garde literary value."[19] *Vanity Fair* and the *New Yorker*, magazines that popularized the innovations of literary and artistic modernism even as they promoted bourgeois status and consumer pleasure, represented such threats. So too did the prominence of women as popular writers and magazine readers.[20] In this way, understanding the modern and the middlebrow is a continuous rather than an oppositional enterprise; the technologies and conditions of modernity gave birth to the mixing of registers and the broad availability of cultural artifacts that became known as the middlebrow. While mass circulation magazines and popular women writers served as producers of middlebrow culture—mixing high and low culture, catering to a middle-class audience, embracing commercialism—they also served as symbols of modern change (mechanical reproduction, rapid communication and mass culture, shifts in gender roles, women's entrance into the professions and the public sphere).

Even as its expansion resulted in the invention of the middlebrow as a category, modern print culture destabilized the purported boundary between modernism and the middlebrow. Janice Radway points out that the titles included in the Book-of-the-Month-Club ran the gamut from "high modernist fiction" to "sea yarns, mysteries, and adventure stories."[21] Indeed, the term middlebrow referred perhaps more clearly to mass-market venues and middle-class audiences than to formal characteristics of literary style. Radway explains that the middlebrow flourished in "the liminal space of hybrid forms where . . . literature was . . . sold to anyone with a few extra dollars."[22] If we imagine middlebrow magazines as a liminal space of hybrid forms, we can see how these commercial vehicles allowed these writers latitude in self-presentation, literary experimentation, and cultural critique.[23] Indeed, smart magazines invited the combination of the accessible and the artful, the conventional and the trendy, and, as Elizabeth Majerus observes, "This multiple, inclusive context opened up more and different kinds of roles for women contributors: they could be modern without necessarily being modernist, and they could draw on modernism while still retaining other more traditional or mass-cultural elements in their work."[24] The persona of the smart woman pushed the boundaries of theatricality and irony while also providing the pleasures of epigram and punch line.

Often when contemporary literary critics refer to the middlebrow as a category of women's fiction, the term denotes sentimentalism or domestic fiction, an implication that befits neither the tone nor the milieu of the smart magazine writers. In *America the Middlebrow*, for example, Jaime Harker addresses domestic fiction as a vehicle for progressive politics, and in *The Feminine Middlebrow Novel, 1920s to 1950s*, Nicola Humble provides "the stylistic and thematic blueprints of the sort of literature that became seen as middlebrow—a particular concentration on feminine aspects of life, a fascination with domestic space, a preoccupation with aspects of courtship and marriage."[25] The female humorists in the smart magazines certainly made their femininity a central subject of their works and wrote extensively about heterosexual relationships, a topic through which they could articulate the tensions between the sexes in public and professional spheres.[26] But they employed wit and irony as distancing tools that could place the conventionality of gender in question rather than naming it as the solution to cultural anxiety, as Lauren Berlant argues middlebrow texts often do.

Although she warns against feminist overreadings that reflect the critic's desire to find political resistance and then obscure complicity and compromise in middlebrow texts, Berlant articulates the potential of culturally reflexive humor when she praises Parker's work: "the emphasis on convention secretly aims at making people sick of convention, releasing energies of radical critique."[27] Where Berlant reads sentimental middlebrow texts as compromises between discomfort and acclimation, refusal and bargaining, my readings treat literary humor as a theorization and indeed dramatization of being both outside and inside cultural norms and especially gender norms. These middlebrow writers take the ambivalence Berlant diagnoses in women's culture and channel it into formal techniques that promote simultaneity and paradox. Their texts display double perspectives, ironic narration, theatrical tropes, and stereotyped characters to undercut the naturalness of the identities sold by the mass media, commodity culture, and normative gender ideals. Through the boldness of its voice and its affection for digression, bragging, and controversy, humor facilitates self-invention and cultural commentary. Where Berlant focuses on "the female complaint," I take up the female quip and argue for its power.

These witty writers participated in a culture of publicity and a marketplace of class and gender ideals; they drew upon periodical conventions and familiar genres, *and* they adopted literary strategies of irony and persona to address the themes of alienation and masquerade. In this sense, their work exemplifies the critical dismantling of the modernist "Great Divide" between high and mass culture undertaken in the decades since Andreas Huyssen published his famous assessment of modernists' defensive posture against mass culture.[28] The postures of urbane magazine writing and literary modernism share several features: both are preoccupied with style, form, and surface; both are fascinated by the media and messages of modern culture; and both are drawn to irony as a literary vehicle for expressing alienation and disbelief. Even the cultural malaise often attributed to the high modernists affects the middlebrow writers of the smart magazines. Indeed, David Savran suggests that "Middlebrow cultural producers are . . . always uneasy about their own class positionality and their own tastes; always trying to negotiate between creativity and the exigencies of the marketplace, between politics and aesthetics, between an art that requires studied investment and the desire for untrammeled pleasures."[29] These negotiations reflect the divided cultural position of the modernist writer as well, what Robert Scholes calls the "paradoxy of modernism."[30] These modern women writers, perhaps because of the liminality of their professional and literary status, felt comfortable playing with and across this divide, while the writers commonly deemed modernist often attempted to obscure or resolve these tensions in the favor of high art.[31]

Because they did not claim to occupy an upper perch in the ladder of the arts, middlebrow writers were perhaps especially preoccupied with the questions of stratification and classification that characterized the modern moment and its proliferation of cultural artifacts and mass cultural goods. Was middlebrow culture art or commerce? Were urban professionals really the elite or just trying to get there? Were bourgeois men genuinely masculine if they were as preoccupied with the body, fashion, and taste as women were supposed to be? Were modern women emboldened flappers or protected little girls? Many of these identity questions arise implicitly and explicitly in the literary works that I analyze here. I argue that humor's embrace of muddle, liminality, and paradox provided an escape mechanism from the cultural fetishization of hierarchy. Mary Douglas proposes that jokes "connect widely differing fields, but the connection destroys hierarchy and order. They do not affirm the dominant values, but denigrate and devalue."[32]

In the following chapters I focus on the work of these women writers rather than compare them with more canonical American modernists, but I hope that my analysis of their tactics and personae suggests directions for further study of the connection between smart femininity and modernist anxieties about mass media culture. In *The Great Gatsby*, the duplicitous Daisy "laugh[s] with thrilling scorn and pronounces that she is 'Sophisticated—God, I'm sophisticated!'"[33] Nick Carraway explicitly connects the cynical Jordan, tennis celebrity, to magazine iconography: "She was dressed to play golf, and I remember thinking she looked like a good illustration, her chin raised a little jauntily."[34] With the tone and appearance of smart magazine copy, these women appear to Nick all brittle surface. Fitzgerald's pairing of glamorous Daisy and sardonic Jordan resonates with Anita Loos's characterization of Lorelei Lee and her friend Dorothy in *Gentlemen Prefer Blondes*, a novel published in the same year. Like Daisy, Lorelei plays the feminine fool for the men who want to own her, and like Jordan, Dorothy deflates her (and their) pretenses with punch lines. Both novels use the topic of sophistication to address the allure and emptiness of materialism, and through irony, they render dubious the self-presentation (and indeed self-promotion) of modern subjects. The kinship between middlebrow humor and American modernism should not, after all, surprise. Like Fitzgerald, himself a magazine writer and celebrity, the writers in these chapters recognized and commented on the middle ground on which they stood: between intellectualism and mass appeal, between (masculine) professionalism and (feminine) seduction, between popular snobbery and cultural critique. This divided stance makes them close cousins of American modernists who faced similar cultural dilemmas and circumstances. Indeed, in many cases, they were friends.[35]

The formal and thematic strategy that these smart women writers and the high modernists most obviously share is their prominent use of irony, a term I return to throughout this book as I discuss both the rhetorical texture of the works and their thematic focus on contradiction and paradox. As vexed as critical debates around irony's definition and effects can be—Wayne Booth called it "the mother of confusions"—most accounts agree that producing and recognizing irony requires "the ability to hold two contradictory realities in suspension simultaneously," an understanding of both the surface message and its undertones and counter-message.[36] Thus, reading irony becomes a potentially educative process "when we learn how to say *both-and*, not *either-or*, when we see that people and works of art are too complex for simple true-false tests."[37] Modern women writers, themselves a focal point of cultural contradiction, make such tensions their topic, and they show that there are no easy outs from a media culture that fetishizes feminine bodiliness and materialism and aligns irony with consumer passivity or professional cynicism. Linda Hutcheon aptly describes the challenge of parsing irony's effects, whether rhetorical or ideological: "If you will pardon the inelegant terms, irony can only 'complexify'; it can never 'disambiguate.'"[38]

The use of irony, semantic and thematic, by high modernist writers often marks a sense of loss. Alan Wilde contends that "the clue to ironic vision lies" in "those unbridgeable spaces that define as they disfigure the map of modern life." In this account of high modernism, the distance between the way things ought to be and the way things are, the distance between an imagined past and the fragmented present, are represented by the juxtapositions of irony. Wilde poignantly concludes that "modernism, spurred by an anxiety to recuperate a lost wholeness in self-sustaining orders of art or in the unselfconscious depths of the self . . . reaches toward the heroic in the intensity of its desire and of its disillusion."[39]

While the ironic perspectives of the women humorists in this book often express disillusionment, they seldom memorialize loss in this way, perhaps because of the liminality of their cultural positioning as middlebrow writers, perhaps because of the new opportunities of modern publicity and professional culture for women, perhaps because of comedy's emphasis on the on-going parade of human absurdity.[40] Whatever the source of their thematic tenor, they most frequently imagine irony as inquiry, self-reflection, and survival. Groping to learn about their world and survive in it, the self-conscious characters in these works bear witness to the gap between who they would like to be, who they pretend to be, and who the public thinks they are. Thus, Millay reminds us that the sexual voracity and independence that can serve as an emblem of the autonomous modern woman can also be co-opted and redirected by the sensuality of cosmetics and the allure of advertising. Parker derides the bodily woman in order to ally herself with ironic masculinity, but at the same time she dramatizes her inevitable embodiment in the public eye thanks to her gender. Fauset demonstrates that African American women can use humor to validate their autonomy and political observations, but she also satirizes the hedonism, myopia, and self-satisfaction that accompany the witty role of the white flapper. Powell depicts a wry magazine writer employed to promote the virtues of consumerism, corporations, and political causes, but she also indicates that these ironic sensibilities, when directed to private life, allow for honesty, skepticism, self-interrogation, and intimacy. The formal properties of rhetorical irony— resting in contradiction, illuminating the differences between surface and realities—contribute to the political properties of thematic irony. Living in the world requires a balancing act, and McCarthy posits that this feat could be educative if, instead of exculpating the subject, it forces her to maintain self-interrogation and laughter.

Though I argue for the playfulness and agency in this humor writing, these women writers use tonal shifts to mark the disturbing elements of the masquerades demanded in the modern marketplace. They may not imagine a lost past that was better, but they do mourn lost opportunities and alternative identities. Humor allows for tonal lability and the incorporation of modes like the Gothic and the grotesque. Both Millay and Parker write tales of entrapment, whether in the beauty salon's chair or in the corner at a party, and, while the incidents they describe and imagine may seem trivial, the emotional costs and the cultural implications of this imprisonment in the imperfect body are not. Both Larsen and Fauset acknowledge that smartness is an unfulfilled promise for women of the black bourgeoisie. In their novels the momentum of personal and racial cost often overtakes the possibilities of improvisation and banter. None of these writers is unaware that humor plays with serious stakes and hence that its failures threaten significant losses.

Mind and Body

Along with my argument for the formal and cultural complexities of this literary humor and its illumination of the interconnection between the middlebrow and the modernist, comes a focus on the relationship between mind and body manifested in the works of these women writers. They wanted to establish their intellect and ironic perspective but also to inhabit the embodied role of female celebrity. Repeatedly in this book, I address moments in this humor writing when female characters confront the cultural expectation that their intellect is limited by their femininity and physicality. These writers acknowledge the role of the phantasmal female body in the public marketplace, whether they emphasize their intellect and cosmopolitanism instead (Fauset), imagine themselves as invalids (Parker), or contrast their bodies with glamour girls (Loos).

In magazine rhetoric, the word smart implied the importance of being attractive, and it is symptomatic of the confusion of body and mind in feminine stereotypes and ideals, as it simultaneously alluded to appearance, fashion, and intellect.[41] The seamless unity of wit, sex, and chic wove a potent fantasy of impossible mind, body, and commodity accord. In her work on *Harper's Bazaar* in the 1920s, Sarah Churchwell observes that: "Smartness is ubiquitous in these advertisements, always imminent but out of reach."[42] In *Advertising to Women*, a 1928 guidebook on the rhetorical appeals that most effectively snare women's attention, Carl Naether writes of "the omnipresent 'smart'" that "without fear of being exaggerative, I may say that copy which is produced to promote the sale of woman's dress and which does not contain either of these terms [smart or smartness] is indeed rare." He explains that the word "smart" implies "individuality" and "taste," but he then denies female readers both: "How gullible, how dull, the feminine reading mind must be to accept month after month selling language so lacking in discrimination and finesse!"[43] For Naether, women are the passive consumers of vitiated language rather than the active producers of sharp, surprising, fitting words.

The connotations of the word smart evoke the mythologized traits of the modern woman as she enters the public sphere: her fabled consumerism, her scrutinized body, and her increased (and often threatening) agency. The ambiguities of smartness as a qualifier underscore the dichotomies of agency and passivity, intellect and embodiment deployed to define and sometimes restrict modern women. In a 1920 *Vanity Fair* article on "The Quality of Smartness: A Modern Idea and Some of Its Devotees in the Past," George Hibbard defined smartness as a precursor to feminine celebrity: "Pauline [Bonaparte] was the first of smart women, the first of the long line of celebrities who have succeeded her in France,

England, and America."[44] Pauline Bonaparte was famed for her beauty and her sex life; thus Hibbard's history signals the cultural conflation of femininity and bodiliness. The humorists I consider here emphasize the body's potential for pleasure and performance and its symbolic role as an avenue for self-invention and public presence. These women depict sexuality as a source of pleasure and autonomy, from Millay's voracious light verse to Fauset's connection of titillation and banter. They also expose the fragility and ephemerality of the mass media's body fantasies. Lois Long displays her phantasmal body and then highlights its vanishing act to remind her readers of the mass cultural obsession with female bodies. In novels of passing, Larsen and Fauset suggest the precariousness of the mass media fantasy that restricts wit and urbanity to white women. By first imitating and subsequently undoing the smart body, these women writers suggest the double binds of embodiment and intellect for women in the public sphere.

By humanizing and mocking the feeling of being stuck between body and mind, these women reflect critically on both categories as they are defined in modern cultural life. They challenge the pose of intellectualism as represented in popular culture, the literary canon, and even the world of politics. Thus, Fauset reimagines the potential of the Harlem Renaissance, not as masculine intellectual coterie, but as a gender-integrated movement defined by banter and play. McCarthy parodies the citadel of leftist thought through exaggerated gender metaphors that make the patriarchal underpinnings of ideological seriousness apparent. As I show in the following chapters, these writers look at such variously reviled and hallowed categories, the two sides of the divided human subject, body and mind, with irreverence and attention to their construction in the cultural imagination.

Imaginary New York

I have reflected on some major terms that define the output of these women writers: middlebrow, magazines, modernism, smartness, and especially humor. Along with these literary and historical categories, however, comes a defining location: New York. One reason for this focus is practical and historical: the smart magazines came out of New York during the magazine boom at the beginning of the twentieth century. Urbanity, supposedly achieved by way of Manhattan, was a major uniting pose for the middle-class readers all over the country who subscribed to these periodicals. The fate of *The Chicagoan: A Lost Magazine of the Jazz*

Age exposes the prominence of New York's version of urbanity, which eclipsed other regional attempts to define the smart. This magazine was only recently recovered and published, but neither *Vanity Fair,* the *New Yorker,* nor *Harper's Bazaar,* all magazines prominent during the Jazz Age, suffered the same fate and were thereafter lost.[45]

The smart magazines, especially the *New Yorker,* relied on a shared belief in what Thomas Bender calls "the metropolitan idea."[46] New York was imagined as a place where behaviors could be audacious, chic commodities and lifestyles could be easily obtained, and small town identity and constrictions could be abandoned. This belief in the freedom and anonymity of the city facilitated the self-invention celebrated and enacted by these women writers. McCarthy calls New York "a world that . . . looked magic," and Powell dubs it the "Happy Island."[47] Along with this sense of freedom and self-invention comes a combination of toughness and play associated with Manhattan. The hustle of urban life required an external veneer of imperviousness, while the pleasures of Broadway, Harlem, and even the Algonquin Round Table called for a susceptibility to and affinity for jazz, publicity, fame, crowds, intermingling, and quipping. This simultaneous detachment and engagement defines the humor writing that criticizes the mass media and the dislocations of modernity and yet revels in the individualism permitted by anonymity, professionalism, and urban subcultures.

Advocating detachment and individualism, these humorists also tentatively imagine connection through humor.[48] Sophisticated, worldly, and withering personae associated with imagined New York might initially seem to repel rather than attract affiliation, but recent critical work on worldly postures establishes their significance as both symbols of modern subjectivity and entrées for new coalition building. Joseph Litvak celebrates the pleasures (gustatory, sexual, attitidunal, and literary), the perceived excess, and the power of sophistication.[49] Rebecca Walkowitz proposes critical cosmopolitanism as a strategy of detachment from suspect forms of social cohesion (nationalism, racialism, imperialism) and investment in new forms of affiliation (friendship, sex, coterie).[50] Similarly, I see smartness as an alternative to smugness, wry asides as an alternative to press releases. Within the dominant discourse of the magazine, the smart woman winks at her audience and imagines affiliation based on wit rather than formal education, based on improvisation rather than income; indeed, she imagines another world where wisecracks rule, even if that other world is just a round table in a midtown hotel.

Each humorist whose work I examine in the following chapters published at least some of her work in middlebrow venues; these writers confessed their enjoyment of material attainment and bourgeois lifestyles; and they employed conversational language in popular genres: light verse, dialogue sketches, tongue-in-cheek monologues, book reviews, sentimental fiction, satirical short stories. They often dramatized their own bodies as part of their work's appeal. Their manipulation of celebrity and femininity has diminished their critical reception and in some cases (Parker comes to mind) has arrested their work in the popular imagination as wit turned into commercial jingles, cosmopolitanism turned to quietism and cocktails. I hope to demonstrate in my close readings of their work that these writers are smarter than such an evaluation suggests.

In chapter 1, I address the humorous personae of Edna St. Vincent Millay in her light verse and prose satires to suggest that this modern magazine celebrity used these popular genres to establish the advantages of artifice, the artifice of gender, and the modernity of both conventions. Riviere's "Womanliness as a Masquerade" provides a theoretical launching point for my consideration of Millay's flippant personae as a tactic for intervening in the public sphere and of masquerade as a destabilizing figure for gender roles and relationships. In the prose satires that she published under the pen name Nancy Boyd, Millay experiments formally with the possibilities of drag, repetition, perspective, and performance. In these sketches, the overt theatricality of modern femininity reveals the supposedly authentic posture of masculinity as unstable and performative. In the poetic corollary of this humorous unmasking, the transformations, disobedience, and fickleness that speakers of Millay's light verse espouse demonstrate the modern possibilities of self-invention and independently chosen affiliations as advantages of a posture of femininity.

In chapter 2, I turn to the inheritors of Millay's legacy—urbane female humorists in the *New Yorker* and *Harper's Bazaar*. With Parker as my chief example, I contemplate not ethereal metamorphoses and playful poses, as I do in the Millay chapter, but rather the problem of the intractable body. I argue that Parker and fellow magazine humorists Lois Long and Anita Loos exaggerate the presence of the flesh—in Parker's case, usually a Gothicized or grotesque body, in the work of Long and Loos, overly bodily glamour girls—and then project it elsewhere (onto another character, for example) to achieve dual aims. First, they point out distortions of the female body in modern mass cultural fantasies, and, second, they claim access to ironic sensibilities and professional status typically denied to the sexualized woman. If the body is supposed to be the ne plus ultra of feminine identity, they inhabit the "plus." Mary Russo writes of the feminine masquerade: "for a woman, a . . . flaunting of the feminine is a take-it-*and*-leave-it *possibility*. To put on femininity with a vengeance suggests the power of taking it off."[51]

In the transition from chapter 2 to chapter 3, I move from the first part of my book, presenting women of the 1920s who established the allure of the smart magazine writer, to the second part of my book, which considers women who alluded to this figure in their literary work of the 1930s. These later women writers criticize the prejudices and myopias of middlebrow magazine culture, but they also renovate the ironic posture and bantering woman for new purposes by retrieving value from a figure that had come to seem an unfortunate vestige of Jazz Age hedonism and superficiality. In chapter 3, I consider the novels of Harlem Renaissance writer Jessie Fauset, typically viewed as didactic and domestic, as a response to the urbane culture of sophistication surrounding the smart magazine industry. From the perspective of an editor and thinker ensconced in black periodical culture, Fauset both analyzes the shortcomings of the glib narcissism linked with the white flapper and advocates the individualism that a sense of humor permits black female speakers. I contrast her optimistic conclusions about the power of smartness with Nella Larsen's depiction of sophistication and white magazine culture in *Quicksand*, where Larsen treats this fantasy world as a dangerous delusion. Finally, I argue that Fauset uses irony as a technique within her novels to expose the political ironies of racial injustice and the hypocrisies of supposedly bohemian white New York culture. Fauset views what she calls in an essay "The Gift of Laughter" as an opportunity to publicly challenge the status quo.

Satirist Dawn Powell associates the status quo with a disturbingly mass-media-saturated public sphere. In her novels of the late 1930s and early 1940s, Powell alludes to magazine culture and depicts female celebrities whose sense of self has been eroded in this age of mechanical reproduction. In chapter 4, I argue that Dawn Powell at once magnifies the force of feminine glamour to establish its sinister collusion with political propaganda and corporate control, and she also amplifies the voice of the individual witty woman to speak up against such cultural loudspeakers. Thus Powell explores the role of magazines and celebrities in reinforcing the power of media magnates, and she also suggests that the sense of humor, however much associated with those publications, can send oppositional messages and establish thriving counterpublics that question dominant cultural values through banter and skepticism.

Mary McCarthy is also interested in the role that banter and skepticism can play in cultural critique. A participant in the Trotskyite left in the 1930s, McCarthy recognizes the contradiction between the bourgeois lifestyles of intellectuals and their proposed proletarian revolution. In chapter 5, I discuss her representation of the smart female magazine writer as a symbol of the hated middlebrow who exposes the politically committed New York intellectuals' entrenchment in elitism, consumer desire, and cultural pretense. In *The Company She Keeps*, McCarthy traces the strain after distinction and the gendered superiority that characterizes intellectual culture's failed efforts to differentiate from the supposedly debased and feminine middlebrow. Ultimately, I argue that McCarthy depicts irony as a lens shared by so-called smart and intellectual cultures and as a tool for complex, pragmatic political engagement and salubrious skepticism about ideological frames.

Ultimately, the humor writing of these modern women displays a deep and sometimes grim understanding that mass media visions and versions of femininity could be both reductive and seductive. The female magazine writer as a public figure promised the modern frisson of a woman taking her place on the urban stage and speaking (and mocking) in public. Nonetheless, the humor writers of smart middlebrow culture maintained their popular personae and witty tone by skating across the dangerous surface of snobbery, materialism, emphasis on feminine bodiliness, and celebration of consumerism. That icy surface, associated with the embarrassing bourgeois culture of acquisitiveness and solipsism, has often stopped critical inquiry into these women's work with an apology for the perceived brittle superficiality in their tones and themes. I view the analysis of humor as a way to plunge beneath that surface. In a culture still obsessed by "sex and the city," a literary-historical perspective on the emergence of the chic urban magazine writer as a feminine fantasy helps readers understand better not only the work of these writers but also some of our continuing cultural longings for slender sentences, lithe figures, and ample means.

1 / Thoroughly Modern Millay and Her Middlebrow Masquerades

In his introduction to the November 1921 issue of *Vanity Fair*, Donald Ogden Stewart celebrated a female humorist whose byline had appeared in the magazine since January. Like her contemporary Mae West who promised that too much of a good thing could be wonderful, Nancy Boyd vowed to her readers that one could "Sin without ostentation." In a poem called "I Like Americans," Boyd staked national pride on American excess: "they know that one roll does not make a breakfast. / Nor one vermouth a cocktail." Unfazed by the supposedly crucial negotiations of the marriage market, Boyd gave her readers practical instructions on how to reply to a proposal. Rejecting a hopeful suitor, she apologizes for misleading him and attributes their previous closeness to a rainstorm: "you were the only dry spot for miles around." Her proposed acceptance letter is hardly more sentimental: "I shall be able to dress twice as well as ever before; I look forward with eagerness to spending your money."[1]

Who was this unabashed, worldly, and wry magazine writer? Magazine subscribers, Stewart explained, sent "many letters asking if our distinguished contributor, Miss Boyd, were a withered spinster of forty or a sophomore at Rutgers." He assured his readers that the columnist in question was neither barren nor virginal, and he complimented her brassy tone. Boyd "may not be much on aesthetic stuff, and poetry," Stewart wrote, "but she sure writes great stories for honest-to-God he-men like you and I!"[2] As Stewart well knew, the actual writer behind the columns, Edna St. Vincent Millay, was better known for "aesthetic stuff, and poetry" than for these "great stories." Nonetheless the witty, worldly persona of Nancy Boyd intersects with the rebellious and self-transforming speakers of Millay's light verse to produce a legacy that combines the popular appeal of sophistication with a deeper level of tendentious humor and cultural critique.

Millay wrote twenty-two Nancy Boyd pieces for *Vanity Fair* between January 1921 and March 1923. In 1924, she collected these stories in the volume *Distressing Dialogues*. Millay wrote an arch preface confessing that she (Millay) was the *"author's earliest admirer"* and had *"a never-failing interest and delight"* in Nancy Boyd's work.[3] This pen name plays on "Nancy boy," derogatory slang for an effeminate man, and also forms an anagram of "Body." Named after the poet's great-grandmother, "Nancy Boyd" was born in Millay's potboilers for second-tier smart magazine *Ainslee's*, a popular *Smart Set* imitator. As Deborah Woodard notes, these typically overblown romances were set in an exaggerated bohemia.[4] Her *Ainslee's* stories contained some humor in the absurdity of their melodrama, but, when Nancy Boyd moved to *Vanity Fair*, she adopted a new tone of urbanity, sophistication, and flippancy.

Vanity Fair prized this worldly tone of the New York woman. They employed Dorothy Parker as the only female theater critic in New York from 1917 to 1920. In her first success at *Vanity Fair*, Parker wrote "Hate Songs" about all the men and women who frustrated her, from in-laws to bohemians to "glossies," pretentious urbanites. Elinor Wylie's light verse also appeared in the magazine. In one poem, "The Doll," Wylie wrote about crafting the perfect lover; the verse was accompanied by a drawing of a giant woman cradling a doll-sized tuxedoed man in her arms and feeding him a martini.[5] Wylie's sister Nancy Hoyt also supplied anecdotes and articles, including the modern fable described in my introduction. Anne O'Hagan penned essays about modern topics like women's careers and free love with wry titles, such as "The Doom of the Home: And What About Children? And Rubber Plants?"[6] Established humorist Carolyn Wells published stories in the magazine, as did then newcomer Anita Loos, whom I discuss in chapter 2. Ethel Plummer and Thelma Cudlippe (later Grosvenor) drew cartoons of the modern woman in her many stereotypic incarnations.

This catalogue of names should not mislead about the ratio of women to men writing for *Vanity Fair*: the majority of *Vanity Fair* writers were men, and women were far more likely to be stenographers than columnists on the staff. Nonetheless, in the excitement of cultural change and urban expansion, worldly femininity could be a hot commodity, as evidenced by the fame (and, indeed, notoriety) of the flapper, the movie star, and the blues singer. Magazine writers participated in a fabled world of professionalism, nightlife, sex, and independence. Though magazine writing was not considered *real* writing, cleverness took on a competitive edge for press professionals. Quick quips had commercial potential for a generation that claimed cynicism as its trademark and imagined an America that had come through a terrible war and found a devil-may-care attitude on the other side. At the same time that smart humor suggested rebellion, youth culture, and glibness, bon mots also betokened valuable cultural currency. Prosperity fostered a fantasy of class mobility, professional advancement, ethnic assimilation, and middle-class attainment that banter could bolster.

By infusing the everyday routine with the sparkle of wit, magazine writers could affirm that urban professionals were in the know instead of out to lunch. Nancy Boyd jokes in a story about two humor writers: "We never ordered a luncheon, or hailed a taxi, or bought a postage-stamp, but the air between us snapped with visible sparks. With no polishing or padding, and expurgating only the bad words, we could have sold our conversations at a dollar a syllable."[7] Nina Miller deems *Vanity Fair* of the 1910s and 1920s "the vanguard journal of the new sophistication" that promoted "wit and urbanity for New York and the nation as early as 1914."[8] If *Vanity Fair* spread the gospel of smartness, Millay was one of its most prominent apostles. In 1928, *Time* magazine declared that "for ten years smart young women have been trying to rival with their versification Edna St. Vincent Millay. But she eludes them all with her impertinent patter."[9] For Millay and her inheritors, this impertinent role allowed frankness about sexuality, intellectual competition outside the realm of formal education (an arena in which men still vastly outnumbered women), and direct traffic with the speed of modernity. Millay's candle burning at both ends promises to keep pace with the rapidly changing present.

To the benefit of Millay's reputation and place in literary history, feminist critics have reclaimed Millay's play with personae as a prominent achievement of her verse and prose.[10] Nonetheless, much criticism that describes Millay's masquerades and her magazine work focuses on restrictive versions of femininity that she could not escape.[11] By contrast, I argue that Millay's use of humor embraces the opportunities of professionalism and publicity, detachment and worldliness as sites of potential (if not always realized) agency. Thanks to irony's capacity to contain contradiction, Millay's humor actively holds multiple possibilities in suspension rather than resolving stereotypes into normative roles. Millay's poetic speakers and female characters are often adept at self-presentation and indeed self-transformation, and her male addressees and characters are on the verge of recognizing their own fleeting status and multiple poses. As I interpret the significance of Millay's comic personae and their voices, an implicit parallel should emerge between their abilities to change at a moment's notice and shock their fellow characters (or imagined reader) and Millay's skillful deployment of familiar magazine tones to do unexpected cultural work.

Millay's Personae

The illustration that accompanies Stewart's introduction of Nancy Boyd helps to establish the mystique of the smart magazine writer. A blonde with wavy bobbed hair, a Cupid's-bow mouth, and large eyes sits poised on an enormous armchair. Her accessories accentuate her seductiveness. Nancy Boyd is swathed in a pair of oversized men's pajamas, which the caption reports "are of Miss Boyd's own designing—after Poiret," a French fashion designer who claimed to have "released women from the tyranny of the corset single-handedly."[12] Though she appears to be at work on her latest *Vanity Fair* piece, her pose suggests sensuality. The neckline of Boyd's pajamas plunges behind the portfolio on her lap, and a long line, presumably her pen, extends from long fingers to puckered mouth. Above Nancy sits a cat, its head tilted at the same angle as that of its mistress. Though Nancy bends over her work rather than reclining, her low armchair and the pillow under her feet evoke the luxury and the languor of an odalisque's couch.

This cartoon creates an ideal of a worldly woman in her twenties or thirties, dressed fashionably and earning her living by her wits—though not by getting up early in the morning, putting on clothes, and heading to the office. (The potency of such a fantasy endures in contemporary cultural icon Carrie Bradshaw of HBO's *Sex and the City*. It is worth noting that Boyd wears high heels, even with pajamas.) This cartoon presents femininity as felinity, profession as seduction (and vice versa), and artistry as decadence—not to mention blonde as cover girl or pin-up. On one level, *Vanity Fair* insiders are mocking the idea that winsome Millay with her slender frame and famous red hair could be imagined as a voluptuous blonde bombshell. In another way, however, Stewart's article exposes a feature of the magazine. Women writers were expected to seduce their readers, if not directly then at least through their reportage of New York, romance, parties, banter, and (indirectly) sex. In the

"Christmas Dance: 1922," for example, Nancy Hoyt concludes her sonnet about "Chattering flappers" sporting "marcelled fluffs" with the couplet: "Sometimes I've heard, and hearing, have not seen / A stifled giggle from a parked machine" (lines 13–14).[13]

Joan Riviere's 1929 essay, "Womanliness as a Masquerade," provides a helpful contemporaneous view of the strategic potential these flirtatious authorial personae offered.[14] In this essay, Riviere elaborated the subterfuges employed by a modern intellectual woman, who dressed seductively and spoke flippantly to her male colleagues. Riviere views these moves—masquerading as hyperfeminine and adopting a flippant tone—as tactics to render inoffensive what might affront masculine authority. At the same time, Riviere acknowledges that in the humor, some of the impulse to challenge escapes control and is expressed. In her Nancy Boyd dialogues, Millay emulates *Vanity Fair*'s topical preoccupation with what Miller calls "modern love," the contretemps between couples, men and women who fit into comic types, whether fop or flapper, sheikh or sheba, but Millay uses these categories to reflect on the process of type-making, the creation and reproduction of norms in middlebrow culture.[15]

Millay's private writing suggests her self-awareness about the role of the mass media industry in producing attractive (and hence consumable) feminine roles. In a 1922 letter, Millay bragged to her sister: "Nancy is going strong in Vanity Fair, isn't she? Isn't she a blessing? Almost two years now the woman has been well nigh supporting me."[16] Sometimes, poems by Edna St. Vincent Millay and prose by Nancy Boyd appeared in the same issue. In a November 1922 column about visiting Paris, Nancy Boyd records her shock at witnessing the famous poet Millay eating sauerkraut and sausage in a café: "I had always imagined her so ethereal."[17] Millay was photographed for *Vanity Fair*, which praised her loveliness as well as her poetic skill, and she recognized the power of iconicity. Millay wrote to friend, fellow poet, and satirist Witter Bynner: "I am becoming very famous. The current *Vanity Fair* has a whole page of my poems, and a photograph of me that looks about as much like me as it does like Arnold Bennett."[18] (Doubtless her devoted public could tell the difference.)

In her letters, Millay does more than quip about her celebrity persona; she throws her voice to demonstrate two things: the instrumentality of playing feminine within the mass media framework and her ironic awareness of that role play. Millay brags in a letter to Allan Ross Macdougall: "Oh Lud! Have you noticed how Vanity Fair is featuring me of late. They just can't seem to go to print without me . . . Aint it wondafil?"[19] In this and other letters, Millay adopted dialect patterned after her beloved comic, *Krazy Kat*, about a cat in love with a mouse.[20] The cat's gender is famously unclear; E. E. Cummings wrote later that Krazy's "ambiguous gender doesn't disguise the good news that here comes our heroine." Cummings saw in this figure light-hearted opposition to societal norms: "The sensical law of this world is might makes right; the nonsensical law of our heroine is love conquers all."[21] Cummings's use of pronouns is suggestive here; he deems the humorous Krazy Kat who embraces nonsense a woman, and he associates law and reason with her compatriots, a mouse and a dog, both of whom he refers to as male. Play-acting Krazy Kat, Millay has not abandoned an adorably feminine role. At the same time, this voice allows her to assert her own "law," even when it does not fit what Cummings calls the "law of this world." For example, using the Krazy Kat voice in this letter, Millay jokes that legal contracts ceding away the rights to her work are "whereasinine."[22]

In this letter, Millay stresses her instrumental use of feminine fashions and attitudes and decodes the offensive implications of this role. Millay adopts a posture of surprised commercial triumph as she puts on the costume of the flapper, reporting her updated, bobbed-hair look: "Did you know, li'l' wisdim toot', that li'l' aingil had had her hair bobbed?" She flirts with her addressee Macdougall, naming him her "li'l' wisdim toot'"—Eve's dental corollary to Adam's rib?— and she smirkingly sums up her appeal as "'Sawful cute." When she returns to a formal register, Millay undermines the allure: "I look, when I am blessed with health, approximately twelve years old." In this letter that lists her commercial successes and new publications, Millay overtly comments on her ironic sensibilities: "perhaps, I am funny,—which is just possible." Humor allows her to reflect upon her personae and tones, and that ironic perspective keeps her slightly aloof from the thrill of her magazine popularity and the flapper fad.[23]

Her personal writing thus indicates Millay's awareness about the transformation of self into an authorial celebrity created for the public. Millay treats the artifice of these roles with relish and humor in her letters. In a letter to her mother and sisters Millay describes the cover of her latest volume of poems. In a postscript about the production process, she alludes to a nursery rhyme: "P.S. I have just finished numbering the pages. 'Lak a Mercy on me, this is none of I!'"[24] The line comes from the Mother Goose poem "The Old Woman and the Pedlar." An old woman "went to market on the market-day," and a dishonest peddler cuts her petticoats off at the knees. The final line of the poem expresses the old woman's astonishment at her transformation: "Lauk a Mercy on me, this is none of I!"[25] This nursery rhyme shares the topic of Millay's letter: marketing. Through her volume of poems, Millay has entered the market, a place where women wear short skirts and call themselves flappers. These poems are her "eggs" to sell at market.

The mystique of Millay's serious poetic persona was often more withdrawn, perhaps to preserve the aura of high art around that work and to disguise its entanglement with the market. In one poem that she published under her own name in *Vanity Fair*, Millay stressed her lonely estrangement from her preferred rusticity:

> Searching my heart for its true sorrow,
> This is the thing I find to be:
> That I am weary of words and people,
> Sick of the city, wanting the sea. (lines 1–4)[26]

This winsome longing for solitude is a far cry from Millay's sharp satirical persona. Indeed, Nancy Boyd may express the sentiment that she is "weary of words and people," even "sick of the city," but she channels exhaustion and malaise toward mockery. The exposure of popular hypocrisies and inconsistencies affords special pleasures and powers to the humorist, claims anthropologist Mary Douglas, who argues that "all jokes are expressive of the social situations in which they occur" because in them "a dominant pattern of relations is challenged by another."[27] Instead of withdrawing from the city, the joke-teller Nancy Boyd confronts the falseness of "words and people" that Millay's lyrical speaker mourns.

In her first person columns, Nancy Boyd celebrates her New York detachment. Even when Boyd admits Garbo-like that she wants to be alone, she quips that she will flee her crowds of fans by moving from "rural fastness to urban looseness." Boyd acknowledges her lack of emotion while immersed in the cityscape, not as a loss of "true sorrow" as the poet Millay does in the verse above, but instead as a tactic to evade manufactured relationships: "I fail to feel necessarily a choking surge of affection for the butcher, the baker, the gas-fixture-maker who happened to buy the house next-door to the house I rented."[28] Modern anonymity equips Boyd to shrug off sentimental poses. This confession of alienation, this confrontation of inauthentic bonds, whether between Gatsby's party guests or members of Nick Adams's family, is a crucial part of the ethos of American modernism, what Ann Douglas calls its "terrible honesty."[29]

Millay also created a popular poetic persona that was less terribly honest than wonderfully irreverent, and critics viewed this flippancy as an appropriately feminine pose. In an early poetry review grouping

Millay with her poetic peers, "Women of Wit," Mark Van Doren called this attitude "feminine, fearless, and fresh." Van Doren praises *A Few Figs from Thistles*, her 1920 collection of light verse, as having "sparkle in its passion, even a little smartness." The danger of being patronized for precocity and celebrated for sexiness is here apparent. While "sparkle" has its diamantine advantages, it is separated by a mere sequin's edge from superficiality. This very flimsiness and flashiness facilitated Millay's entrance into a middlebrow culture that celebrated amusement and distraction. Suggestively, Van Doren imagines humor itself as an appealing and flashy costume, "a harlequin-cloak of charming, irresponsible banter."[30] The smart magazine audience opened the pages of *Vanity Fair* each month to see slender Art Deco women draped in the latest fashions. Millay's various postures of detachment, seductiveness, playfulness, and glee fit within this world of swank and desirable femininity, but they also open up strategies for its undoing.

Van Doren praises Millay's "smartness" in her verse, and this moniker helps to indicate the attunement of her literary personae to her magazine context. In its columns, photographs, caricatures, ads, features, and articles, *Vanity Fair* praised "smartness" as an attitude, an acquisition, an image, and an aspect of New York daily life. A golf suit, Newport beaches, a Buick, the audience at a boxing match—all could be (and were) deemed "smart."[31] An advertisement for *Vanity Fair*'s shopping service proclaimed that the magazine's "function in life was to keep *en rapport* with the best and smartest things that people buy, wear, use, or admire."[32] One article even called Alexander the Great "smart" because "what he did was the chic thing to do—it was *épatant*, and he did it."[33] The smart could conquer the world, it seemed, or could at least conquer the past and embrace the modern. The pages of the magazine became a crucial testing ground for what the modern might mean, especially as it concerned gender roles. "Smartness" could also refer to a sense of humor, the wiseacre sensibility that took all surface messages with a grain of salt. Through the doubleness of smartness, both fashionable ideal and irreverent play, Millay found a tactic to introduce wiseacre iconoclasm to her chic posture.

Who Is Smart Now? Men and Women in *Distressing Dialogues*

In establishing its modernity and smartness, *Vanity Fair* mocked the sob sisters of both then (the nineteenth century) and now (its early twentieth-century periodical peers). One column noted that "all the contributors to *Harper's Magazine* are women with three names," while in contrast "*Vanity Fair* is invariably up on the latest thing in fashion, art or literature."[34] (In fact, both *Harper's Magazine* and *Vanity Fair* published many poems by the three-named "Edna St. Vincent Millay.") An early issue declares, "*Vanity Fair* is by no means to be a woman's magazine."[35] In spite of these words, *Vanity Fair* sought to appeal to a female readership, and the tone of an early editorial patronizes in its promise to address this group: "For women we intend to do something in a noble and missionary spirit, something which, so far as we can observe, has never before been done for them by an American magazine. We mean to make frequent appeals to their intellects. We dare to believe that they are, in their best moments, creatures of some cerebral activity."[36] This editorial recruits female readers through their desire to be mentally superior to the herd. At the same time, the magazine often depicted women as anti-intellectual and primarily sexual and hedonistic. In one dialogue in the magazine, a girl rejects a man who reads George Bernard Shaw because "I'm not going to risk getting one of those cerebral or epigrammatic kisses."[37]

Often in *Vanity Fair*, the modern woman's slang and clichés provided a comic foil for ironic and laconic male narrators. In "The Lost Art of Conversation," St. John Irvine juxtaposes the sublime and the banal: "I felt the awful meanness of men in the presence of mountains, and trembled slightly when I heard the trees swaying with the soft noise of music played on muted strings . . . [ellipses in the article] until I heard that lady say, with incredible banality, 'It's awf'lly nice, isn't it?'"[38] Another columnist laments the modern woman's new access to education: "her voice . . . will rise to shrillness. She will talk faster, and she will talk more. She will acquire ologies, isms, and ics."[39] When the magazine celebrates the bantering modern girl, its rhetoric is dismissive in its very appreciation. In "In Defense of Debutantes," George S. Chappell celebrates "the 1921 model. She is a form of mental and physical exercise, violent perhaps, but far more enlivening than pulling literary chest-weights with dull high-brows who can hardly lift their own chins." The modern woman is light in every sense of the word. The columnist jokes of this "lissome young lady" that her "dress was a poem—a short poem, to be sure, but still a poem."[40] Feminine sexuality displaces literary accomplishment.

The sexuality of these modern girls throws into relief the educated rationality of the male. A 1923 ad for Goode & Berrien, Advertising Counsel, jokingly suggests this contrast by picturing a voluptuous naked Eve and an overdressed head-rubbing Sir Isaac Newton together. According to the ad, they are "the greatest pair in the history of the apple! To the same appeal, his response was intellectual; hers, emotional."[41] In spite of its type-casting of Eve the emotional, the firm recruits copywriters of both sexes. Playing up her supposed kinship to the emotional female consumer could have its advantages for a female ad writer, as Simone Weil Davis recounts in *Living Up to the Ads*.[42] The increased presence of women in the workforce meant a new symbolic reliance on the seductive capacities of Eve as she herself might author them.

The comparison of professional women to the fallen Eve exemplifies the problematic equation of women's minds and bodies. Eve possesses carnal knowledge, and for some the idea of women in public, even in the professions, necessarily implied seduction. *Vanity Fair*'s "Success Editor" (an invented title for this parody) urged "Bright Ambitious Girl[s]" to abandon intellect and embrace attractiveness. The Success Editor observes that many girls do not become stenographers because they "are not able to write good English or spell correctly" but assures the magazine readers that women do not have to "have a 'highbrow' education to succeed, and time after time have the laurels in stenographic work gone to the poor uneducated girl with a kind heart and a Ziegfeld Follies face." The article continues in mock ruefulness: "I have seen so many perfectly beautiful girls spoiled by the possession of a brain that, if I had my way, all female institutions of learning would be dynamited tomorrow."[43] *Vanity Fair* separates the smart, professional woman from the brainless, glamorous girl in this article, and, while it ostensibly applauds the latter, its backhanded compliments encourage education and ambition. Nonetheless, the essence of the joke relies on the perceived dubiousness of female intellect and the centrality of feminine attractiveness to women's public success.

Millay recognized the cultural tendency to dismiss feminine potential for intellect and ironic poise and to focus on feminine embodiment. In a July 1922 *Vanity Fair* story called "The Barrel," Millay, writing prose under her own name, rewrites the tale of Diogenes the Cynic, living alone, ascetic and contented, in his barrel. A woman invades the barrel, and he finds her presence intolerable. This story describes a newly and uncomfortably shared space, perhaps a metaphor for the periodical industry or even the magazine itself. Within this space, cynicism, a pose of superiority and irony, provides the reigning virtue. While they are packed together in the barrel, Diogenes and the woman struggle against one another. He thinks of her as pure body and finds her attitudes and ambitions untenable. She may be "young and beautiful," Diogenes muses, but she has "a hateful expression on her face." He reads her flapper frame like a magazine cartoon establishing the brainlessness of this stereotype: "She is broad in the buttock and narrow in the chest, and the back of her head is much too near the front." Bobbed hair emphasized the shape of the female head. (In 1925, Emily Post reminded the female readers of women's magazine *McCall's* to "remember that the classic proportion of the head is one-eighth of the height of the body. And the ideal is a trifle less. If you are small-boned and slim, your head ought to be small and slim in proportion."[44]) Criticizing her skull size, Diogenes moves on to decry her mental weakness: "She is incapable of abstract thought."[45]

Though Diogenes circumscribes woman's access to intellectualism, he admits the necessity of cooperation: "he has not yet devised a way of doing without her . . . she is as his left hand, inefficient but useful." Millay thus tweaks her generation's begrudging capitulation to the newly gender-integrated workplace and alludes to the association of women with secretarial work and stenography. Millay's Diogenes fantasizes wordily about a day when women will no longer be necessary: "'The day after tomorrow she will be as his caudal appendage, shriveled up, dropped off and forgotten. And man will go on the more merrily without her,'" while the woman drily responds: "'You don't say,'" undermining the force of his melodramatic predictions. The woman in the barrel protests Diogenes' subordination of her gender and insists that they can share this space: "'There's plenty of room for two in this barrel.'" She defends her intellectual capacity: "'I'm just exactly as smart as you are! I just haven't had a chance!'"

Diogenes' prejudices are untouched by such protests, but, tellingly for Millay's vision of the power of humor, when the woman jokes, he hears her claims to equality and her criticisms of his supposed superiority. The woman ridicules his habit of taking a lamp out during the daytime to find honest people, and the erstwhile self-satisfied Diogenes is embarrassed. In her description of the woman's amusement, Millay allegorizes the power of humor: "As soon as he was out of hearing, she began to laugh, the sweetest merriest laughter that had been heard in this valley for a thousand years . . . 'Oh oh!' squealed the woman again and again. 'Aren't men *funny*? Aren't they funny?' . . . And after a while the barrel began to laugh, too. It swelled and puffed its big sides until it seemed it would burst its hoops entirely."[46] A comic female perspective on gender is something new, a voice that has not been heard "for a thousand years," and it almost "burst[s] the hoops" of its containing medium (in this case, the barrel; in Millay's case, the magazine). This word "hoops" recalls nineteenth-century feminine fashions and the outdated gender prescriptions they reflected. Humor allows women to reinvent themselves as modern and to reshape the magazine through their laughter. In the end, the woman and Diogenes collaborate in the project of finding an honest man, and the woman lights his lantern in spite of its futility. Perhaps the sexes could cooperate after all.

In her volume of collected satires, *Distressing Dialogues*, Millay depicts the negotiations, both petty and profound, required for men and women to share the public stage. Millay indicates that the problem with such cooperation is not just the competitive spirit but also deeper anxieties about gender identity. Who is the modern woman in the eyes of the modern man if she is no longer simply a "caudal appendage," as Diogenes has it, or a romantic object? Could these roles shift, and would that inevitably mean disenfranchisement for men? The characters Millay describes in her "distressing dialogues" are always in danger of (or possess delightful potential for) veering off script. Millay exploits the generic looseness and relative brevity of magazine humor to experiment formally with the representation of gendered performances. Many prose pieces in this volume are short scripts or sketches, and Millay emphasizes social performances through stage directions and stylized speech. In *Distressing Dialogues*, men and women clash over intellect, body, profession, and art as Millay depicts fights between lovers, married couples, even a male hairdresser and his female customer.

In "Two Souls with But a Single Thought," Millay places tension between the sexes directly into the modern context of professional journalism and humor writing. In this sketch, Nancy Boyd the magazine writer describes her marriage to Cecil, a newspaper columnist and humorist. According to Boyd, their friends thought "'How perfect! The wedding of the cap and the bells! The comic sock and mask!'" Indeed, the pair imagined their lives "brought to a riotous close by our simultaneous dying of laughter."[47] This imagined climax (*la grande mort* instead of *la petite mort*) devolves into competition and mutual theft when they sell one another's jokes to their respective publications. They evolve from bringing "out each other's best, for the sake of the act" to "watch[ing] each other as a mouse watches a cat" (179, 182).

Like characters from Ben Hecht's *The Front Page*, later adapted into the Howard Hawks film *His Girl Friday*, professional identity dominates their lives: "we settled down to work, which for Cecil meant being funny once a day, and for me being twice as funny once a month" (180). Much like the disgruntled Diogenes wishing he could stay alone in his barrel, the husband and wife begrudge one another the limited resources of humor and fame. This rivalry precipitates the death of banter: "not a word is uttered in our house. You might think us a pair of undertakers instead of a pair of humorists." Abandoning productive dialogue, the pair engages in "covert scribbling" (183). The female magazine writer jousts with the male newspaper columnist for cultural dominance. Boyd is not cowed by wifely duties into marital obeisance; it is clear at the end of the story that she will persist in her career, the priorities of private life shunted into (at best) second place, where divorce looms as a distinct possibility.

In pitting these wits against each other, Millay dramatizes the confrontation in magazine culture between the cosmopolitan man and the smart woman—ever harder to differentiate and hence ever more strenuously defined against one another. An early article on "The Quality of Smartness" in *Vanity Fair* stressed that Pauline Bonaparte "instituted smartness," while Napoleon Bonaparte, though he had "almost all aptitudes in connection with worldly affairs," "never became smart."[48] Perhaps it was too risky for a man to be fully "smart" because smartness entailed an articulacy, fashion sense, and cultivation that American culture eschewed in the taciturn, rough-and-tumble ideal of virile manhood. *Vanity Fair*'s column "For the Well-Dressed Man" aired these latent insecurities: "The American man has always been a little ashamed of appearing smart . . . [because of] a sort of Puritan suspicion that it is immoral to dress well."[49] This allusion to shame and immorality suggests the fear of homosexuality and effeminacy that increasingly characterized middle-class culture in the modern period. George Chauncey observes that "the scorn heaped on overcivilized men established the context for the emergence of the fairy as the primary pejorative category against which male normativity was measured."[50] The fairy, Chauncey explains, "embodied the very things middle-class men most feared about their gender status" because "the boundaries between the she-man and the middle-class man seemed so permeable, despite men's best efforts to develop manly bodies and cultural styles."[51]

Millay gives the dandy a starring role in "Ships and Sealing Wax," a Nancy Boyd dialogue between the walrus and Alice in Wonderland. The walrus serves as articulate hero in this conversation while Alice's slang and impatience betoken her dullness. In this modern Wonderland, Alice focuses on maintaining her appearance as a modern flapper: "Alice had begun feverishly to scratch about in her vanity-bag, and the clatter set up by a hand-mirror, a silver shoe-horn, several loose nickels, some safety-pins, a platinum cigarette-case, a cork-screw, a wrist-watch with a broken strap and a bunch of wardrobe-trunk keys, was nothing short of deafening. 'Can I look for my powdapuf or can't I?' snapped Alice. And producing the article in question, she proceeded to encrust her counte- nance with a thin layer of white lead."[52] This "vanity-bag" (like *Vanity Fair* itself) sets up a "clatter" of objects—a cigarette-case, a cork-screw, a wardrobe box—that together produce the impression of flapperdom. The deafening commotion of this clatter, however, indicates how much noise accompanies the role. Alice's snappish voice is neither appealing nor ar- ticulate, and her face becomes a toxic mask. Perhaps the flapper role is not a promising vehicle for the modern girl's self-expression. The walrus, by contrast, takes pleasure in his dandyish exterior. He "turn[s] his cuffs" and suggests that "Men's Bathing-Costumes!" should replace "Women's Bathing Costumes" as a modern conversational topic. Modern men, Millay suggests, are also preoccupied with the presentation of the body. Millay describes the walrus's flipper as a "flappish hand," which con- notes flapper envy and stereotyped effeteness (278). The walrus's wish to talk about "Men's Bathing-Costumes" evokes the ad copy of *Vanity Fair*. One advertisement for bathing suits in "*smartly quiet styles*" promises "The Swimming Suit *you would like to wear*" and pictures symmetrical, shapely, mustachioed men reclining on the beach.[53]

The appreciation of swim clothes verges on the appreciation of the male body, and Chauncey notes that "the very celebration of male bodies and manly sociability" in modern middle-class culture "required a new policing of male intimacy and exclusion of sexual desire for other men."[54] Suggestively, the walrus asks that sex remain private: "'sex is a very use- ful commodity, and one that no home should be without. But there is a time for all things'" (275). His insistence on privacy suggests closeting, and he stumbles while trying to get beyond this topic: "'In place of the subject of sex I would suggest as a topic of conversation—' said the Wal- rus, and was silent" (277). Leaving Alice inarticulate and sulky, Millay renders this Wildean walrus the dialogue's sophisticated star, perhaps hinting that homoerotic desire should be discussed with pleasure rather than pathologizing rhetoric. The walrus decries pop Freudianism as color-by-numbers psychology: "'You have heard, perhaps . . . of Mr. S. Freud, author of the popular ballad entitled *Tell Me What You Dream and I Will Tell You Want You Want?*'" Resisting such prescriptions of desire and consequence, the walrus concludes: "'I should like to kick his corduroys'" (274).

Similarly averse to sexual prescriptions and definitions, Millay once answered a psychoanalyst's queries with quipping equanimity: "'Oh, you mean I'm homosexual! . . . Of course I am, and heterosexual too, but what's that got to do with my headache?"[55] In her personal life, Millay treated masculinity as a masquerade, choosing her middle name, "Vincent," as a favored nickname. She uses the trope of drag in her Nancy Boyd story, "Powder, Rouge, and Lip-Stick," in the context of heterosexual domesticity to unsettle the seeming stability of masculinity. In this dialogue, a married couple, Gwen and Bob, get into an argument while preparing to go out for the evening. Bob claims that Gwen's time-consuming application of make-up is unnecessary: "It's just a habit, I tell you."[56] Bob grotesquely exaggerates her regimen on his own face: "*two apoplectic cheeks, a nose like a tomb-stone, and the morbid eye-sockets of a coal-heaver*" (117). This macabre make-up implies essential masculinity; he is "wrong" inside this costume. But Millay undoes this illusion of authentic masculinity; his wife Gwen recognizes that other rituals of self-maintenance and self-presentation contribute to his illusion of suave masculinity. Gwen offers to give up make-up if Bob will give up shaving, and he insists that "It's not the same thing at all" (118). Bob wants to defend his total separateness from his wife's theatrical self-presentation, her making-up. He mocks her alarm by imitating her voice: "Where's the eyelash dirt? If I can't have my eyes looking like a couple of star-fish, I won't go a step" (117). He treats mascara as taint and diminishes the celebrity "star" to a "fish." Bob exalts his own (masculine) authenticity in the face of her degrading (feminine) masquerade, and he accuses Gwen of having "an awfully dirty face" even while he himself is wearing make-up (118).

Millay once again introduces the power of humor to expose hypocrisy and undermine self-satisfaction. Bob's confidence in his authority crumbles when he becomes ridicule's object rather its source. Bob is uncomfortable when Gwen begins to laugh at him: "Oh, Bob, you look so funny! HE (*uncomfortably, from behind a fatuously indulgent smile*): That's right, dear, laugh" (119). Bob meant to burlesque Gwen's performance of femininity and hence to control and direct it, but perhaps he has exposed his own desires more than her foibles, as he "*lovingly finger[s] the eyebrow-pencil*" (118). After further bickering about the wearing (or not) of lipstick, order is restored, and Gwen wears the make-up, while Bob plays the cave-man: "*savagely, seizing her in his arms*" (121). But this rapprochement rings hollow, as Gwen and Bob engage in self-conscious conversation, the conventionality of which Millay underscores by repeating the stage direction "*in the accepted manner*" four times:

SHE (*in the accepted manner*): Have I kept you waiting?

HE (*in the accepted manner, rising*): Not at all. Not at all.

SHE (*in the accepted manner, pouting*): You might tell me that I look well.

HE (*in the accepted manner*): Charming, my dear. (121)

Bob has become uncomfortably aware that they are quoting scripted gender roles. His masculinity is not generated authentically or spontaneously as he might have imagined when he pooh-poohed his wife's valuation of gesture and costume. Gwen's canniness about performance conquers Bob's belief in his own mastery: "SHE: Mind the paint! (*She whispers in his ear*) Whose little girl am I now? HE (*ruefully, and in a low voice, snuggling his head upon her shoulder*): Bobby'th" (122). This argument over make-up has exposed the role-playing in both genders, and this revelation leaves Bob, not Gwen, vulnerable. Gwen is used to the business of self-transformation and indeed self-performance. Bob, however, must learn that masculinity is a performance, or as the subtitle to the dialogue puts it: "*Handsome is as Handsome Does*" (111).

Not only do Millay's male characters become uncomfortably aware of the constructed nature of their supposedly authentic masculinity, but they also see that their fantasies of feminine roles are surprisingly conventional or retrograde. Just as Bob was "*suddenly seized by a cramp of Let-Us-Lead-the-Simple-Life*," as the stage directions of "Powder, Rouge, and Lip-stick" wryly report, so too could the modern intellectual who praised bohemian rebellion turn into a petty drawing room patriarch (111). In "The Implacable Aphrodite," a Nancy Boyd dialogue, Mr. White, a violinist, attempts to woo Miss Black, a graceful sculptress; at first he praises her refusal of conventional feminine roles and ultimately condemns her insufficient desire to minister to him or for that matter to marry him.

In this dialogue, as in "Powder, Rouge, and Lip-stick," the New Woman adeptly treads the boards of the modern stage, while the New Man fumbles his lines. Miss Black exerts confident control over her body and image, while Mr. White is "a man of parts, but badly assembled," according to the stage directions.[57] Miss Black moves deliberately and seductively, "*rising sinuously, and dusting her hands, which seem to caress each other*" (45). She "*leans back wearily*," "*expos[es] a long and treacherous throat*," and "*turns her head slowly*" (44, 46). Her exaggeration of casual movements resembles Isadora Duncan, Sarah Bernhardt, or a practitioner of the Delsarte method of dramatic movement, which assigned each emotion a gesture. Miss Black wears a "heavy, loose robe" that "clings to her supple limbs," like the costumes women wore in modern dance meant to imitate, according to *Vanity Fair*, "the essential spirit of Greek art."[58] At one point, Miss Black stoops underneath a lamp, which illuminates her face: "*The sleeves fall back from her lifted arms; her fine brows scowl a little; her vermilion lips are pouted in concentration*" (44). Clearly, Miss Black has chosen the spotlight.

Uneasy with such surface glamour, Mr. White tries to lay claim to Miss Black's interior, authentic self: "It is your beauty which attracts them [other men], your extraordinary grace, your voice, so thrillingly quiet, your ravishing gestures. They don't see you as I do." His effusive language reveals the effectiveness and indeed titillation of her performance. Much to Mr. White's arousal and consternation, Miss Black reveals that she creates her nude sculptures by copying her figure in the mirror: "I—am my own model. You notice the two long mirrors?" She jokes about the profitability of this endeavor—"so economical!"—much as Millay saucily celebrated Nancy Boyd's commercial successes (44). Suggestively, Miss Black names her sculpture "Daphne" after a nymph who turns herself into a laurel tree to escape Apollo's advances. (Later I consider Millay's light verse poem "Daphne" as an example of her depictions of modern women's virtuosic self-transformations.) The doubleness of Miss Black's role as both artist and model parallels Millay's roles as poet and celebrity. Mr. White is flummoxed by Miss Black's sexual and artistic self-promotion. Distracted by the body of the artist, Mr. White's sexual excitation increases, even as he repeatedly insists that he sees her "unparalleled genius" rather than her beauty (46). Miss Black's intellectual powers free her from gender into genius, Mr. White opines, and he does not hear the inconsistency of his insistent mentions of her femininity: "Woman though you are, you stir me more deeply by your genius than ever a man has done" (47–48).

Mr. White wants to define her according to the appealing feminine types he already knows. The stage directions betray that in his thoughts, Mr. White transforms the bohemian Miss Black into a housewife: "*He draws his pipe from his pocket and fills it, gratefully, meanwhile watching her. She is cruelly slicing a lemon, by means of a small dagger with which a Castilian nun has slain three matadors; it strikes him that she looks gentle and domestic. A great peace steals over him. . . . [She] delicately pois[es] in her hand a sugar-tongs made from the hind claws of a baby gila-monster*" (50). This bizarre catalogue of castrating instruments eclipses Mr. White's comforting pipe. But these weapons with which a nun could slay three matadors do not jolt Mr. White out of his daydream of domesticity. Mr. White superimposes a tame image on Miss Black's theatrical body and her props, torture devices as a tea set. From a bohemian man of parts and a cosmopolitan violin player, Mr. White regresses into a conventional bourgeois suitor, coaxing Miss Black to marry him and turn her career into a mere hobby: "A man's wife *ought* to have some little thing to take up her time." She refuses him, and his feelings of powerlessness prompt misogyny: "He (*wildly*): You're a lying woman!" (52).

In this dialogue, much as in "Powder, Rouge, and Lip-stick," the performing woman faces with equanimity and even valor the insecure man's breakdown. She is prepared to compose herself in both senses of the word. As she answers Mr. White's accusations, Miss Black writes over him, black ink on a white page. She banishes him: "She (*rising, white with the fury of the righteous unjustly accused*): Will you be so good as to go? He (*laughing boisterously, then in a subdued and hopeless voice*): Very well. Of course I'll go if you want me to. But my heart I leave here," and then she deflates his romantic pretensions: "She (*languidly*): Pray don't. I have room for nothing more in my apartment" (52). Miss Black reduces his sentiment into one more object that can be refused—a far less tempting object than exotic gila monster tongs. Miss Black prefers autonomy to romantic fidelity, much like Millay's poetic speakers in *A Few Figs from Thistles*. Mr. White's fury indicates that his dream of genderless cooperation disguises the barely submerged ideal of domestic and wifely femininity. Early in the scene, he told Miss Black that she had "an intrepid mind" that could "see beyond . . . into a world, a cosmos, where men and women can understand each other, can help each other, where barriers of sex are like a mist in the air, dissipated with the dawn" (42). Even in seemingly dismissing this barrier, he invokes it.

Modern women like Miss Black are more elusive and self-determining than Mr. Black's fantasy of simplicity, nurturance, and domesticity acknowledges. Breaking off this affair, Miss Black embraces her artistic and romantic independence. In Millay's light verse, the speaker's espousals of liberty—cast as they are in the context of sexual relationships and private life—can also be understood as public declarations of the power of feminine performance.

"To Heel, Apollo!": The Power of Feminine Poses

During the 1910s and 1920s, many women poets published light verse in popular venues such as *Vanity Fair*, Franklin Pierce Adams's column

"The Conning Tower" in the *New York World*, and later the *New Yorker*. Light verse, as the name implies, was not viewed as significant literature. In fact, Edmund Wilson, who served as managing editor for *Vanity Fair* in 1920 and 1921, dismissed his friend Millay's light verse in *A Few Figs from Thistles* as "merely cute feminine pieces that had something in common with the songs that the sisters made up for their own amusement" and "easier lyrics that reflected the tone of the women's magazines."[59] In their 1934 anthology of American women's humor writing, *Laughing Their Way*, Martha Bensley Bruère and Mary Ritter Beard echo the association of light verse with feminine performance and literary embarrassment: "Like an apologetic pirouette by a lady in flounces the trend began."[60]

The February 1922 issue of *Vanity Fair* parodies light verse by women in a poem entitled (with deliberately prosy inelegance) "Rhymed Extracts from My Diaries: Unabashed Comments on Some Suitors I Might Have Accepted—But Luckily Didn't." Accompanying the poem is a cartoon of a smiling slender woman with a large boa, plumed hat, and high heels. A dapper gentleman with a bowler kisses her hand. The poem reports that "the intimate confession / Has become a smart obsession," and the speaker proceeds to describe a series of disappointing or disappointed suitors.[61] Women's writing is trendy and commercial, and the only aesthetic transformation required between personal, sexual experience and the page is the use of rhyme. Modern women's sex lives made them, this column implies, accidental poets of the moment. Light verse itself is still sometimes imagined as analogous to the form of the female body. Russell Baker writes in the introduction to *The Norton Book of Light Verse*: "The very term 'light verse' suggests inferiority, for in the Anglo-Saxon world at least, lightness is considered contemptible, except in the female figure."[62] More than one critic has observed that Millay's famous light verse poem, "First Fig," about her candle burning at both ends implies the shape of the poet's body. For posing as feminine, light verse seemed an apt form—syntactically slender, verbally pleasurable, and reassuringly unassuming.

To view light verse as diminutive rather than daring because its form was popular is, however, to overlook the opportunities of indirection. Ludic and scattershot rather than authoritarian and sententious, lightness could disguise tendentious humor and could communicate energy, iconoclasm, and rebellion. Light verse appropriated forms for children like nursery rhymes and lullabies and old-fashioned forms like triolets and ballades and applied them to surprisingly adult and modern topics.

Though the *Vanity Fair* column implies that these topics were exclusively romantic and gossipy, some women writers turned these familiar forms to overtly political ends. Alice Duer Miller, for example, wrote a column called "Are Women People?" in the *New York Tribune* from 1914 until 1917. She collected some of these poems in *Are Women People? A Book of Rhymes for Suffrage Times* (1915). In "Many Men to Any Woman," Miller adopts a patronizing antisuffrage persona:

> If you have beauty, charm, refinement, tact
> If you can prove that I should set you free,
> You would not contemplate the smallest act
> That might annoy or interfere with me . . .
> Why then, dear lady, at some time remote,
> I might consider giving you the vote. (lines 1–4, lines 13–14)[63]

Miller's title suggests that patriarchal social prescriptions enforced the feminine ideal of the lady. Promoting "beauty, charm, refinement, [and] tact," the men imagined in Miller's poem hope that ladies might forget their bid for independent voice and political agency in their pursuit of private charms.

In her light verse, Millay also suggests that among the most influential powers restricting women's opportunities is the internalization of behavioral norms. Her speakers flout narrow prescriptions of appropriate feminine behavior and affect. In "The Penitent," Millay's speaker fails at contrition:

> And, "Little Sorrow, weep," said I,
> "And, Little Sin pray God to die,
> And I upon the floor will lie
> And think how bad I've been!"
> Alas for pious planning—
> It mattered not a whit! . . .
> To save my soul I could not keep
> My graceless mind on it. (lines 3, 5–11, 16–17)[64]

Rather than excoriating her lack of discipline, the speaker revels in her freedom from regret: "'if I can't be sorry, why, / I might as well be glad!'" (lines 23–24).[65] Millay plays with a nursery rhyme voice, but rather than correct bad behavior, as an instructional child's verse might, she encourages it. On the surface, this speaker may seem acceptably feminine in her frivolity and flirtatiousness; after all, she "puts a ribbon in her hair / To please a passing lad" (lines 19–20). This façade, however, enables her transition from private shame to public participation, leaving her "room all damp with gloom" to go out into the street (line 3). Allegorically, the modern woman leaves the realm of nineteenth-century domestic senti- ment and "pious planning" for a sexual and public world of shameless experimentation. The discipline enjoined upon the speaker matters "not a whit!" when her wit provides an escape; instead, her "graceless mind" embraces play and improvisation.

These joint emphases on improvisation and transformation may be Millay's most important thematic contributions to reimagining women as subjects of modernity rather than passive consumers, objectified im- ages, or uncanny symbols of mechanical reproduction. Women's self- transformation and artifice were often vilified in the literature and philosophy of modernity, as their perceived ease with performance was often condemned or at least mistrusted.[66] In her poem "Daphne," first published in smart magazine *Ainslee's* in November 1918, Millay treats her speaker's ability to transform herself with exuberance rather than fear:

> Why do you follow me?—Any moment I can be
>   Nothing but a laurel-tree.
> Any moment of the chase
>   I can leave you in my place
>   A pink bough for your embrace.
> Yet if over hill and hollow
>   Still it is your will to follow,
>   I am off; to heel, Apollo![67]

While Millay depicts this transformation in mythological terms, the poem implies that the modern woman can outpace her male competitors in performing multiple versions of the self. Women can extend, when needed, the "pink bough" of blossoming femininity, what Riviere calls womanliness as a masquerade. Self-transformation in Millay's imagin- ing is neither tragic nor terrifying, but rather playful, strategic, and even triumphant.[68] Apollo will now be "at heel" rather than in the lead.

Where Nancy Boyd stories depict dialogue theatrically, Millay's light verse implies conversation but only allows one side of the story—that of the speaker. Millay thus exalts the sexual independence and appetite of the modern woman while she patronizingly consoles the modern man on his obsolescence. In one sonnet, the speaker assures her lover that "I shall forget you presently, my dear / So make the most of this, your little day." Moreover, she reminds him in the closing couplet that "Whether or not we find what we are seeking / Is idle, biologically speaking."[69] The modern woman is more blasé about the terms of sex and romance than the modern man who is reduced to a passing experiment. In "Thursday," Millay's speaker feigns surprise at her lover's expectation of monogamy. She tutors him like a child learning the days of the week:

> And if I loved you Wednesday
> Well, what is that to you?
> I do not love you Thursday—
> So much is true.
> And why you come complaining
> Is more than I can see.
> I loved you Wednesday, yes,
> But what is that to me?[70]

The speaker claims her own inconsistency as erotic triumph and dismisses man's dependence on monogamy. Millay acknowledges yesterday's love with a "yes" cordoned off by dashes, but that admission is not the end of the story. The simple rhyme scheme, monosyllables, and syllogism convey her incredulity that he would assume that she would—or could be held to an outmoded romantic standard.

Each of these poems casts sexual self-determination as a challenge wittily issued by the modern woman to her would-be partners, competitors, and lovers; she asks if they can possibly keep up. This challenge is not only a question of modernity and adaptability—changing along with the times—but indeed one of virility. Because Millay's speakers are willing to articulate their desires, the threat of their dissatisfaction looms as large as these verses render their lovers small. The sestet of this Petrarchan sonnet deflates masculine sexual sovereignty after exaggerating it:

> I, that have bared me to your quiver's fire,
> Lifted my face into its puny rain,
> Do wreathe you Impotent to Evoke Desire
> As you are Powerless to Elicit Pain!
> (Now will the god, for blasphemy so brave,
> Punish me, surely, with the shaft I crave!)[71]

Millay shows off her own insouciance with the extended double entendre and the admittance of "blasphemy so brave." The titillating posture of the "bared" speaker seduces, and the poet-speaker steals the thunder of the godlike man and his "shaft." The potential victim of his arrow becomes an Atalanta who bears wit's arrows. The speaker's power is initially disguised, and thus her pretense is (at least) double: first, she plays the seduced maiden, and then she questions her addressee's potency to provoke him into seducing her. Her final couplet reveals that her desire dominated the encounter the whole time. Millay literally gives her speaker's craving the last word.[72] Within her essay on the masquerade, Riviere proposed that the woman could steal the phallus (figuratively speaking) if she actively displayed her lack of one by flaunting her feminine sexuality. Rhetorically, Millay is doing something like that here—pretending to do obeisance to the "god" and then claiming sexual sovereignty. Apparently, it worked. Wilson read the poem when it was published in *The Dial* under the title "To Love Impuissant." He "immediately got [it] by heart and found [himself] declaiming in the shower." This persona both titillated and challenged Wilson who "felt . . . [he] might be worthy to deal the longed-for dart."[73]

The speakers in Millay's light verse present a seductive and modern exterior through sexual innuendo; after all, as Alice and the walrus acknowledged in Boyd's sketch "Ships and Sealing Wax," sex was the modern topic of conversation. At the same time, this tantalizing topic masks deeper concerns with agency, mobility, and autonomy for women, a set of subjects of which Alice Duer Miller would have been proud. Millay's poems about switching sexual partners espouse a democratic ethos of participation, experimentation, and choice. As Millay writes in "To the Not Impossible Him," which appeared in *Vanity Fair* in September 1920:

> How shall I know, unless I go
> To Cairo and Cathay,
> Whether or not this blessed spot
> Is blest in every way? (lines 1–4)[74]

Like Millay's "Penitent" unsatisfied with cloistering, this speaker embraces adventure as the explorer and cartographer of a new modern landscape both literal and figurative. In her verse and prose, Millay often wrote about travel, and *Vanity Fair*, naming her an official correspondent, funded her first prolonged trip to Europe.[75] Metaphorically, Millay's speaker travels from bed to bed:

> The fabric of my faithful love
> No power shall dim or ravel
> Whilst I stay here, but oh, my dear
> If ever I should travel! (lines 9–12)

Her punch line, the concluding line of the poem, undermines monogamy as a literary and a social ideal. Millay writes a modern literature of change, not just in the exterior details of romance, but also in identity. If the personality is a series of successful gestures, as Fitzgerald's Nick Carraway would have it, then Millay's speaker is going to try as many of these poses as she can. Rather than accept received values, the modern woman chooses her own affiliations, breaks them if she wants, and explores her options. There is nothing "light" about such possibilities.

The Risks of Smartness

Thus far, in this chapter I have explored Millay's adoption of an urbane persona to reflect on publicity culture and its artifice, to challenge masculine authority and establish the theatricality of gender roles, and finally to celebrate sexual autonomy as part and sign of the modern women's courageous self-assertion. Each achievement makes modern freedoms out of characteristics of modernity that were sometimes deemed its curses. If the self could be viewed as multiple masquerades rather than a monolith, one could consciously strike a pose. If sexuality could be cosmopolitan, then who was to say that deeper forms of affiliation and cultural connection were not as mobile? Millay's contemporaries in the magazine industry also noted the potential of sophisticated humor to articulate political freedoms and to espouse individualism. In his *Vanity Fair* article defining smartness, Hibbard called it "the expression and triumph of democracy. It is the assertion of the individual. In a way, it is the declaration of the main principles of freedom."[76]

The categorization of banter and charm as feminine traits could, to the contrary, provide a pretext for the continued privatization of women's gifts and curtailment of women's agency. John Peale Bishop complained in a *Vanity Fair* editorial, "The Art of Living as a Feminine Institution: Expressing a Vague Hope that the New Amendments Will Not Do Away with the Old Amenities," that "Scott Fitzgerald apparently has a monopoly on the witty flappers of the country; I have not met them except in his novels."[77] Bishop argued that women should improve their conversation before entering the political sphere; he thus denied modern women the wit that is their literary emblem. Bishop's easy move from criticizing lackluster cocktail conversation to condemning women's suffrage suggests that humor was already central to the debate over gender equality. Not only was wit a tone through which a bid for equality could be voiced, but it also raised the subject of subjecthood, whether in public voice or intellectual aptitude. Witty women ought to improve the quality of private life, Bishop proposes, or they might transform the basis of public life, Millay implicitly replies.

Vanity Fair, Riviere, and indeed Millay herself associate the pleasures of humor with the pleasures of the sexual (and sexualized) female body. Millay realized that the unpredictable perspective of the reader or spectator could render this association a double-edged sword. Would her readers, like Edmund Wilson, imagine themselves lovers who could "deal the longed-for dart," or would they attend to the modern woman's social potential as well as her sexual audacity? This hesitation about wit as a medium that could distract from the message, a corollary of the sexualized female body, comes across in Millay's verse. In a sonnet from *A Few Figs from Thistles*, the speaker recalls the "words [she] flung in jest" to a former lover.[78] She offers him the titillating proposition that, if they had remained together, she might have "Spread like a chart my wicked little ways" (lines 2 and 8). Using language that evokes nudity as well as frankness, the speaker imagines that "Naked of reticence and shorn of pride," she would have subjected herself fully "beneath your gaze," but then she retracts that fantasy. The speaker realizes that the Pygmalion she addresses would prefer a Galatea to the flesh and blood of a bantering woman. The speaker leaves him in the couplet with only a memory: "A ghost in marble of a girl you knew / Who would have loved you in a day or two" (lines 13–14). The scopophilic spectator who would have relished the speaker's confessions is distracted by silent images of the female body and misses the power of her voice.

As this poem implies, Millay is not always convinced that humor will provide a liberating voice for women. It can correspond too neatly with a culture of smartness that fetishizes the female body over the mind. If the smart woman alluded to in many *Vanity Fair* ads is the woman who turns to Elizabeth Arden or indeed the magazine itself for help, then the witty woman could easily be imagined as helpless. For example, in Nancy Boyd's satirical sketch "'Madame A Tort!,'" a French hairdresser insists that "*Madame a tort!*" when the narrator asks for a simple haircut, and the stylist gives her a full (and painful) makeover instead.[79] The agonized narrator falls in love with this transformation and sacrifices her career. Millay exaggerates the powers of the *friseur* into those of Gothic sexual predator: "'*Madame a tort*,' he replied with calmness, and reached for the irons. I was helpless in his hands. I dared not move, for fear I should be branded. I sat fearfully still and let him have his way" (171). The rape metaphor renders him ridiculous and foppish; he wields a curling iron rather than the phallus.

Ultimately, however, the stylist's silliness is not the subject of the tale. A fracture opens up between the narrator's consciousness of her plight and her persisting addiction to the process that has undone and transformed her. At the beginning of the tale, her narration is clear, straightforward, unrepetitive, and devoid of overstatement, and her appearance is simple: "I bathed regularly, with plain soap and a stiff brush, cleaned my teeth twice a day, washed my hair before it needed it, and kept my nails filed to the ends of my fingers. I dressed simply, and fairly well. I came and went about my business exciting no comment" (164). By the end of the story, her glamorous nails prevent her from sculpting, her former artistic calling: "one glance at my nails, so rosy, so roundly pointed, so softly bright, so exquisite from the loving care of years—and I know that I shall never work again" (174). The hairdresser has vanished altogether, his transformation to a villain secondary to the narrator's transformation into a beauty.

Millay's fragmented narration reflects the distraction encouraged by consumer culture and indeed by the magazine's format. Millay separates each stage of the narrator's makeover with a space on the page and also, more significant, by a break in her narrator's consciousness and volition: "a wave of perfume broke over me," "I was seized and borne off to another part of the establishment," "I have no recollection of leaving this room and returning to the other" (167, 169, 170). Products also proliferate in the opening pages of the story. Once in the salon, the narrator is variously subjected to: "Shampoo," "an anti-calvitique," "an atomizer . . . with scented water," "Camomile," "a fat bottle . . . of perfume," "a bowl of boiling soap," "white paste and red," "a bottle marked *Lait du Citron*," "a cream smelling of almonds," "cool water scented with roses," and "a grease reeking of camphor" (165–170). The specificity of these noun phrases only throws into relief how hazily the narrator perceives the action of the day. She abdicates her ability to narrate: "It would be useless as well as harrowing to prolong the story of that fatal afternoon." Objects overwhelm the subject and her voice: "I sobbed aloud, but made no comment" (171).

The climax of Millay's story launches an absurd accumulated catalogue of these products. The narrator lists the new cosmetics that she purchased and had delivered to her hotel room while she was unconscious: "Paste of Almonds, Milk of Lemons, Sugar of Peaches, Water of Roses, Lotion of Oranges, Cucumbers' Blood; scalp-tonics, skintonics, preparations to remove hair, preparations to promote its growth; bleaches, dyes, rouges, powders, perfumes, brilliantines, water-softeners, bath-salts; sponges, plasters, brushes, pads; eye-brighteners, wrinkle-eradicators, and freckle-removers" (172). This last item recalls Millay's famously freckled countenance. The catalogue loses coherence in the pleasures of pure description and sound. The list's parallel constructions—a seemingly logical form of syntax—draws out the nonsense of the siren song pitched to the cosmetics consumer: the natural pretensions of artificial products (the names drawn from fruits and flowers), silly sounds ("scalp-tonics, skin-tonics") and paradoxical aims ("to remove hair . . . to promote its growth"). Her list parodies the ad pages of the magazine (*Vanity Fair*) in which she originally published this story.

Though she mocks the language of marketing, hence suggesting its pervasive contemporary influence, Millay implicates the speaker who falls in love with the evidence that she can be decorative and settles for that limited aspiration. This claustrophobic incursion of products erases individual volition: "I am a slave to the most exacting of tyrants" (173). At the same time, Millay's double role as magazine columnist and cultural satirist generates uncomfortable friction in this tale, as Millay's ironic debunking of the grooming process implies having undergone it, and thus her wit and stylishness seem interrelated. This sketch begins to ask what limits have been accepted and what opportunities sacrificed in adopting a chic persona for the smart magazine.

In another Nancy Boyd sketch entitled "Knock Wood," Millay elucidates more explicitly the risks of the marketing of types, including that of the witty woman. In this story, a dinner party brings together characters each defined by a single superficial characteristic, such as the Only Woman in Black and the Man with the Wrong Kind of Tie. These characters outline the various superstitions to which they half-heartedly subscribe. Finally, the "Very Clever Woman in her low, ironic voice to which everyone listens," explains the practical bases for each: "Thirteen does not divide up into bridge, into tango, into tennis, into twosing on the stairs. . . . That it is taking one's life in one's hands to walk under a ladder there is no denying. Any pedestrian who commits this particular piece of folly well deserves to receive upon his somewhat undeveloped head an avalanche of shingles, a bucket of paste, or a Polish labourer."[80] The hypnotic quality of the "low, ironic voice" that has a universal audience makes this Very Clever Woman a prescriptive speaker, much like a witty magazine columnist.[81] Millay's shallow labels for these characters suggest the illusory nature of that distinctiveness.

Indeed, sophistication is not a banner of individuality in this story; it is a badge of caste. The Very Clever Woman defines the leisure activities promoted in *Vanity Fair*, such as cards, dance, tennis, and golf. She differentiates the group's intelligence and discrimination from other "undeveloped" individuals and offers taste as a basis for class distinction and even American citizenship. The reader is no "Polish labourer." While appearing to make jokes on common ground—the basis of superstitions is received wisdom, shared aphorisms, and cultural taboos—the Very Clever Woman in fact creates and markets that common ground. Her jokes generate the anxiety that one might be outside of this circle, that one might own the "Wrong Kind of Tie." The Very Clever Woman's prescriptions are all the more effective because she is the only member of the party whose identifying characteristic, being "Very Clever," seems immanent; the others relate to possessions, appearance, or social circumstance. Her appeal to "common sense" assumes that others long to know and follow the expectations of a narrow clique and elite social class (192). This move recalls the strategy of address in modern advertisements. Roland Marchand observes, "Advertisers assumed that their audience craved vicarious participation in displays of class standing and that it gladly imbibed the frank portrayals and discussions of the class hierarchy."[82] Intelligence and wit become extensions of elegance and elitism. Common sense and cleverness, masquerading as first principles, are in fact goals uniting the characters and the readers in social aspiration.

The Very Clever Woman's monologue is the climax of the sketch, and Millay confirms the power of "her voice to which everybody always listens" when her theories go uninterrupted. A knowing consumer and the center of cocktail party conversation, she defines social standards for those around her. Millay explicitly associates these standards with advertisement. The Very Clever Woman calls superstition, the category she sets out to define in her monologue, a form of "circuitous, underground advertising" (192). Her wit could also be described as circuitous, underground advertising; her sense of humor makes materialism and bourgeois pastimes sound good. Even as the Very Clever Woman seems poised to conquer, Millay introduces another female speaker to complicate this monologue of glamour and turn it into a skeptical dialogue. In a parenthetical aside, the narrator, "the Woman Quite Without Jewels," introduces herself: "(That is I, gentle reader; I never wear them; the chambermaid will tell you why)" (187–188). Her presence surprises; this narrator is both peripheral (her identity only communicated within the protection of parentheses) and frequently silent. When the narrator does speak, she offers not unmarked objective descriptions but remarks in quotation marks, presented in dialogue with the other characters. Thus, she seems to disown her priority and power as narrator to dictate and gloss the scene.

Through the unassuming first person voice of The Woman Quite Without Jewels, Millay gives us a sotto voce critical perspective on the exchange at the dinner party. This narrator openly lacks the wealth that the Very Clever Woman assumes they all share. When she appeals to the "gentle reader," the narrator obviously presumes that to be Quite Without Jewels might be a situation with which her reader could sympathize. The Woman Quite Without Jewels unravels the Very Clever Woman's vaunted common sense by troubling the surface of the social tableau. The narrator refuses the force of superstition that sustains the advertisement fantasy, a genre that relies as superstition does on symbol and anxiety. The narrator sees bad faith in capitulating to superstition even after admitting its irrationality: "half-beliefs are all we have today. We live by them. And we live for them" (188). The modern cynic's half-beliefs maintain a veneer of skepticism that provides a sop to the conscience of those immersed in material pursuits. The narrator implicates herself in this use of urbanity and detachment to disguise materialism and pretension: "We twitch at our chiffons, adjust our shoulder-straps and slink fawning from the room" (198). The costume of the smart set does not seem to fit comfortably, and the narrator mourns the loss of commitment in the face of studied insouciance: "'of course we would not die for them [half-beliefs]. All the martyrs were martyred years and years ago'" (188).

In lieu of the physical and moral suffering of the martyrs, the modern woman presents her body for appreciation, not flagellation. In the Very Clever Woman's seductive performance of advertisement, her skilful use of the brain is sexualized, and lithe language suggests lithe limbs. Millay alludes to the confusion of body-mind categories in labeling her character "Very Clever." The dominant definition then and now is "ready to use . . . [the] brain readily and effectively," and this mental quality derives from the word's earlier physical sense that was still in use as late as 1888: "lithe of limb," "well-made," "handsome," or "skilful in the use of the limbs or in body movements generally."[83] *Vanity Fair* underscores the material rewards of a seductive feminine exterior in advertisements that feature drawings of chic urban women and captions pitched to "smart" or "clever" female consumers.[84]

In essence, by encouraging "cleverness" and "smartness," the magazine suggests that the female mind should be used to approach consumption rather than abstraction. Millay differentiates "cleverness" from intellectualism when another character, the Woman Who Wears

No Powder temporarily halts discussion by awkwardly raising the topic of "mathematics" (188–189). The clever woman, then, is appealingly cosmetic, opposed to the socially awkward academic. The Woman Who Wears No Powder may know numbers, but she is neither consumer-savvy nor physically appealing, and the consumerism of the Very Clever Woman is part of her sexual appeal. Her "low, ironic voice" is seductive, sensual, the immediate purr of felinity/femininity. Could magazine writer Millay/Nancy Boyd seem similarly complicit with a marketing agenda, thanks to her topics of seductive women, middle-class mores, and bourgeois pastimes and her tone of worldly detachment?

Vanity Fair is conceived of as a marketplace. The magazine's title draws upon allegorical roots in Bunyan and satirical descriptions in Thackeray, and the editorial pages quote these two sources to establish the magazine's allure and the affluence of its readers.[85] But does that make a woman poet selling her wares in *Vanity Fair* a Becky Sharp whose lyrical flights disguise commercial ambition and whose body, literary and otherwise, will degrade into courtesanship? Does smartness, or "Sharp-ness," represent not a liberating engagement in a democratic discourse, but rather a capitulation to a restrictive feminine pose promoted by the smart magazine? In her Nancy Boyd stories, Millay evokes this endeavor's potential cost. Even after Miss Black has demonstrated her verbal superiority over Mr. White in "The Implacable Aphrodite," she confesses to unconquerable "restless"-ness.[86]

In *"Madame a tort!"* and "Knock on Wood," Millay's tonal combinations began to probe inward, asking how smartness of tone could attest to the smartness of pain. Indeed, in "Madame A Tort," Millay suggests that to ignore the pain of beauty regimens and the psychological pain of striving to meet modern beauty ideals is in itself a kind of blindness: "'The serviette will protect the eyes,' he said, placing in my grasp a towel, which I clutched with gratitude, and applied to my smarting vision" (167). The question of whether the woman writer could preserve her sharp cultural vision while observing the stylish conventions of urbane humor fascinated Millay long after she left formal magazine work. In 1938, under the impending shadow of World War II and fourteen years after bidding farewell to Nancy Boyd and the pages of *Vanity Fair*, Millay composed a verse in memory of fellow poet and *Vanity Fair* alumna Elinor Wylie:

Oh, she was beautiful in every part!
    The auburn hair that bound the subtle brain;

> The lovely mouth cut clear by wit and pain,
> Uttering oaths and nonsense, uttering art
> In casual speech and curving at the smart
> On startled ears of excellence too plain
> For early morning!—*Obit. Death from strain;*
> *The soaring mind outstripped the tethered heart.* (lines 1–8)[87]

Even here, Millay's appreciative account of wit and smartness asks whether women's minds and accomplishments have been restricted, not only by their audience's underestimation of their literary purposes but also by their own adopted (sm)arts. Millay's appreciation of "art / In casual speech" and the cutting turn of phrase that would "smart / On startled ears" anticipates the aesthetic of Dorothy Parker, whose reservations about the "strain" of femininity on the "soaring mind," explored in her heralded magazine work, were in part the result of her admiration and emulation of Millay.

2 /   "This Unfortunate Exterior": Dorothy Parker, the Female Body, and Strategic Doubling

In magazines of the 1920s, Art Deco representations of the modern woman rivaled New York City's rising skyscrapers in height and symbolic glory.[1] One ad for stockings featured a drawing of a giant woman tiptoeing through the New York grid at Park Avenue and Fifty-seventh Street.[2] The October 1926 issue of *Vanity Fair* featured a portrait of "The New York Girl," her garters and petticoats exposed by her billowing skirt as she stood atop skyscrapers in high heels. The caption writer rhapsodized that "toward her serenely frivolous body yearns fiercely and perpetually an entire, amorous, upward city—incarnation and epitome of the vivid and ferocious age in which we live."[3] The frivolous New York Girl was the symbol not simply of the city but indeed of modernity and its promise. Dorothy Parker, the poet of broken promises, the ferocious narrator of modern foibles, knocked this symbol from her pedestal. As she explained in a *New Yorker* book review: "I know those girls. I've seen them. That's why I'm not so well."[4]

A cultural icon associated with Manhattan even today, Parker might seem a candidate for representative New York Girlhood; she lamented that she "was cheated out of the distinction of being a native New Yorker, because I had to go and get born while the family was spending the Summer in New Jersey."[5] In spite of, and indeed because of, her potential resemblance to the New York Girl, Parker burlesques the prevailing stereotypes of modern women with her skeptical tone, ironic juxtapositions, and emphasis on their excessive embodiment. After all, a female body the size of a skyscraper could seem a threatening King Kong instead of a lovely Fay Wray, if one looked through the right lens. In her humor Parker provided that lens. For example, in a 1923 poem that appeared in *Life*, then a humor magazine and, not coincidentally, John Held Jr.'s first venue for his famous flapper caricatures, Parker treated the flapper's body as a modern threat:

> Her girlish ways may make a stir,
> Her manners cause a scene,
> But there is no more harm in her
> Than in a submarine. (lines 5–8)[6]

In Parker's reimagining, the flapper's body becomes enormous and mechanical as she plows through the modern scene. Parker's irritation with the flapper's girlish ways reflects her reservations about feminine roles that substitute a cult of the body for intellectual development and narcissism for ambition. In a 1927 *New Yorker* book review, Parker bemoaned the chic feminine persona in popular fiction: "She is always cool and wise and epigrammatic. In short, the sort of woman about whom my happiest day-dreams centre. I love to lie and think of dropping a girder on her head."[7] The magazine's tendency to flatten both body and mind into superficial feminine stereotypes vexes Parker, so she proposes flattening that imaginary woman herself.

While many may have thought of Parker herself as cool and wise and epigrammatic, Parker deliberately stresses her authorial persona's failure to fit popular feminine roles in order to ensure that she would not be conflated with brainless flappers or superficial sophisticates. In magazine fantasies, the flapper is flighty and sexy, slangy and imprecise in a verbal looseness that corresponds with implied sexual looseness. She is, in short, significantly more body than mind, and Parker refuses that ratio. In a book review, Parker quotes a popular romance novel that deems its heroine as "'fresh and bright and sparkling as the fresh bright sparkling March morning itself.'" Parker rejects such surface sparkle and responds: "Now fun's fun, and all that, but how is one who is only flesh and blood, after all, to keep that up?"[8] Stereotypes that cast modern girls as upbeat, beautiful, energized creatures ignore the inevitable limitations imposed by money, resources, time, and physical condition. Parker reminds her readers of those reality principles. In so doing, she emphasizes her own labor as a professional journalist and establishes her distance from the sexualized female bodies represented in the illustrations and advertisements of the magazine.

The expansion of the New York magazine industry in the 1910s and

1920s shaped Parker's career just as middlebrow humor conventions shaped her aesthetic. Lauren Berlant connects Parker's use of familiar poetic forms with her self-conscious reflections on normative gender roles. Arguing that both poetic conventions and gender roles are "forms that bind," Berlant concludes that "ironic formalism is the normativity of the middlebrow author, who can have her sex and hate it too."[9] Parker's career trajectory made her particularly aware, if uneasily so, of how central her femininity was to her role in professional journalism. Parker entered the magazine world as a caption writer for Edna Woolman Chase at *Vogue*. In an interview Parker later recalled that feminine gentility reigned in the *Vogue* offices, a stark contrast to the modern style of this high fashion kingdom: "Funny, they were plain women working at *Vogue*, not chic. They were decent, nice women—the nicest women I ever met—but they had no business on such a magazine. They wore funny little bonnets and in the pages of their magazine they virginized the models from tough babes into exquisite little loves."[10] Parker moved on to *Vanity Fair* in the late 1910s where she could be a "tough babe" in her Hate Songs, poetic catalogues of the various categories of people she despised, and in her scathing theater reviews.

By the time she was fired from *Vanity Fair* in 1920, Parker had become part of a now-famous coterie of humorists and magazine writers, the Algonquin Round Table, and was treated as the exceptional woman in that circle. Friend and fellow Algonquinite Alexander Woollcott famously deemed her an "odd blend of Lady Macbeth and Little Nell," part femme fatale and part innocent child.[11] This oft-quoted description inadvertently reveals the role of feminine stereotyping in the reception of modern women writers, especially celebrities like Parker.[12] When Harold Ross and his wife Janet Grant founded the *New Yorker* in 1924, they listed Parker on the editorial board. Parker wrote for the *New Yorker* as a book reviewer, short story writer, and poet. In her *New Yorker* writing, Parker both exaggerated her femininity and satirized feminine ideals.

In her book reviewer persona as the *New Yorker*'s Constant Reader, Parker nominates herself as a representative for the limited body and exhausted resources. In one review, Parker pronounced that she was "One Hundred and Forty-six." (In fact, the *New Yorker* humorist was thirty-five.) She describes her "haggard cheeks" and "withered frame" draped "with garments selected from the Junior Misses' department." This outfit is in "so extreme a style that they gave me a doll's tea-set with it."[13] Decades before *Whatever Happened to Baby Jane?* Parker dresses, grimly and uncannily, as a baby. This reversal provides a funhouse mirror reflection of the youthful flapper type. In another review, Parker substitutes the popular preoccupation with the exterior of the female body with the anatomization of the interior. The Constant Reader reads a book on appendicitis "embellished . . . with fascinatingly anatomical illustrations" and describes the "'Front View of Abdominal Cavity'" as though it were a portrait of a woman: "It may well turn out to be another 'Whistler's Mother' or 'Girl With Fan.'" Like the withering *Vogue* caption writer she had been, Parker finds the organ's presentation of femininity lacking: "my feeling is that it is a bit sentimental, a little pretty-pretty, too obviously done with an eye toward popularity."[14] Parker's absurd evaluation of the abdominal cavity implies the omnipresence of popular representations of the female body. The surface of the body may present a glamorous veneer (if the subject of the picture is a movie star, debutante, or celebrity), but internal organs provide an unlikely (indeed off-putting) source of stimulation.

Having thus done away with the "pretty-pretty," Parker exalts her professional identity through a microbial allegory. Parker explains that this anatomy book caught her attention by describing "the love-life of poisonous bacteria" that reproduce by division. If she were a poisonous bacterium, then, Parker could flee private life and romance: "Think of it—no quarrels, no lies, no importunate telegrams, no unanswered letters." While she spends "quiet evenings around the lamp," Parker could assure herself that budding bacteria with "16,772,216 little heads . . . [were] carrying on the business." This vision of mass duplication mirrors the effects of the modern press. Writing, labor that Parker performs during quiet evenings, finds its way into print, and the magazine reproduces the authorial persona in its many issues. This fantasy also allows Parker to envision invading spaces that she could not normally enter, a stealthy penetration that parallels women's gradual entrance into the professions.[15]

In both of these examples, dressing as a flapper and invading the body's interior, Parker presents her Constant Reader persona as a foil for glamorous exteriors in popular culture. In another book review, Parker uses her attention to her own body to establish her mental superiority. In an August 1928 book review, the Constant Reader reports that she was away from her post thanks to an appendectomy. Parker reports that the surgery was "Only fifty minutes on the table, with a good song ringing clear," and the results are equally harmless, just "the stitches (those stitches wrought, doubtless for auld lang syne, in purple silk, for the surgeon was a Williams graduate)."[16] Her voice and rhetoric exaggerate the femininity of her passive body. Parker's fifty minutes on the table burlesques defloration, though this "First" is surgical rather than sexual. Parker's flowery archaisms ("wrought" and "auld lang syne") and treatment of a scar as a keepsake ("purple silk" stitches) associates femininity with nostalgia and collected souvenirs of lost loves, wounded pasts, and romantic illusions. The clinicalism and sterility of an appendectomy clash with this imagined domestic, sentimental feminine world.

In this review, Parker imagines her body becoming text, but she places that transformation in private life and memory rather than public life and the magazine: "Baby's First Appendectomy can go into the memory book." Through this startling juxtaposition of intimacy and memory with anatomy and anesthesia, Parker heightens the artificiality of sentimental language and the nostalgic feminine role. She indicates her own ironic detachment, both tonal and topical, by exaggerating a voice that personalizes everything. The Constant Reader has put her body on the examination table, and she seems estranged from the experience of being inside it, reporting no pain or discomfort. Of course, this detachment is perfectly appropriate when the body is just a representation of the body, the illusion of self just an authorial persona. Just when she seems to be giving us the body most directly in an account of surgery and stitches, Parker reminds us of its textuality and the ephemerality of magazine fantasies of the body. The readers of the Common Reader's columns cannot access her body, only her ironized image of her abdomen.

Capitalizing on this rhetorical control, Parker turns her marked body into a token of her own experience, knowledge, and superiority. She is not carried away by the same myths of modernity's amusements and style to which others succumb.[17] For example, Parker complains that her surgery has kept her from the New York high life. She describes the activities that her glamorous friends still engage in—drinking, riding in taxis, "mucking about at night clubs." Meanwhile, Parker casts herself as the boring spinster: "It doesn't seem quite fair to invite your soul, and then provide no entertainment for it. Sometimes I wish I had a magic lantern. Or, again, I wish I had an electric train. Hell, while I'm up, I wish I had a couple of professional hockey teams. I could read, of course." Parker pretends to covet the allures of modern urban life: its spectacles, hubbub, activity, distraction, and motion. She lacks the magic lantern of the movies and the high speed of the electric train. The one symbol of modern experience that she does possess is a scar. Developed at the end of the nineteenth century, the appendectomy gained wide clinical acceptance in the 1920s. This procedure serves as a metonym for the modern, Parker's red badge of urban courage.

With this scar, Parker establishes herself as a knowing veteran of the modern age rather than a susceptible audience for its wonders. Parker's surgical recovery may prevent her participation in Jazz Age fast living, but Parker implies that this aloofness demonstrates her active intellectual life. She seems to lament her isolation and inactivity: "See how salubrious this is, just resting comfortably, speculating about Gomorrah?" However, her sarcasm reminds us that she is sitting home thinking (and thinking sharply). Parker might enjoy the decadence of Gomorrah more than speculating about it, but her discomfort emphasizes the cherished cost of her professional engagement as she pens this review. Parker rejects the feminine roles of timorous virgin, reckless night-clubber, and perky popular writer (one of whom she mocks in the review that immediately follows her appendectomy description). She proudly reports the flaws that differentiate her body from these seductive fantasies: "The scarless have no opportunities to broaden their minds this way. I'm a pretty lucky girl, I am." With misleadingly self-deprecating humor, Parker champions her alienation by insisting that she, like the modernist writer rather than the cover girl, retreats from the street into the mind.

The body-mind divide ultimately exalts the ironic stance of Parker the *New Yorker* reviewer as she manipulates her audience's fascination with the physical and subverts expectation through stressing age, ailment, anatomy, surgery, and scar. Parker communicates her awareness of her audience directly in her *Harper's Bazaar* short stories, which also use the opposition of exterior and interior to suggest the deceptions of the magazine fantasies of feminine glamour. *Harper's Bazaar* was primarily a women's fashion magazine with a literary bent. In her ironic stories for this publication, Parker suggests that popular magazine genres and celebrity icons manipulate the desires of middlebrow female readers who long for advice and escape. The female bodies associated with magazine features (in these stories that of advice columnist and of Broadway star) provide the target for exposure. Parker employs omniscient narration to direct the satiric gaze at the serene exterior of female bodies, and she ruptures this illusion of feminine glamour.

For example, in Parker's 1933 story, "Advice to the Little Peyton Girl," Miss Marion, an elegant lady, dispenses romantic counsel like an advice columnist. She tells Sylvie, the Little Peyton Girl of the title, that she made a mistake allowing her beau to see her emotion and that aloofness will win him back.[18] Parker begins the story with impossible similes describing Miss Marion's artificial loveliness and serenity: "She looked as white and smooth as the pond-lilies she had set floating in the blue glass bowl on the low table." This appearance creates the illusion of comfort and succor: "Miss Marion's voice was soothing as running water, and Miss Marion's words were like cool hands laid on her brow" (184). Parker associates this porcelain perfection with magazines, which have a similarly sleek surface: "Miss Marion moved slowly about the gracious room, touching a flower, moving a magazine. . . . She opened a large and glistening magazine, but turned no pages . . . her white brow was troubled" (189). Miss Marion's consternation disturbs her narcissus-reflection in the glistening pool of the magazine.

Parker uses her surveilling narrator who can see Miss Marion in private as well as in public to reveal Miss Marion's hypocrisy in championing the implacable surface, a form of emotional and physical blankness that conforms with glamour.[19] The narrator reveals that Miss Marion has shown none of the composure she enjoined upon her young protégée, and instead she keeps begging a man to take her back. Parker's description of Miss Marion in solitude destroys her physical composure: "Slowly her shoulders sagged, and her long, delicate body seemed to lose its bones" (189). Parker figuratively filets Miss Marion and her delicate body. Marion's voice also breaks when deprived of the melody of euphemism: "Words jumped among the moans in her throat" (190). Parker treats a popular genre of magazine writing (the advice column) and the dream of feminine elegance as cooperating deceptions. The advice column imparts to the reader (as it does to the Little Peyton Girl) an impossible ideal of comportment and emotional discipline, just as the iconography of feminine elegance inspires an impossible ideal of a static and contained body.

In "Glory in the Daytime," another *Harper's Bazaar* story, Parker focuses on debunking this ideal in the form of the female celebrity.[20] As the story opens, Parker sets up the celebrity as the object of middlebrow women's fantasies and projections. Her narrator addresses these readers in a gossipy, intimate voice: "She actually knew an actress; the way you and I know collectors of recipes and members of garden clubs and amateurs of needlepoint." But while she posits a connection between "you and I," Parker immediately presents a contrast in women's lives between domesticity and hobbies on the one hand and celebrity and careers on the other—the latter closer to her authorial allure than the former. The actress in question, Lily Wynton, attends a tea thrown by a would-be bohemian who "walk[s] at ease among the glamorous" (218). Picturing Wynton in hues that recall the silver screen, fans rhapsodize about her as "tall and slow and silvery" and "the pale bride of art" (218, 222).

Imagined thus, she is the incarnation of glamour and escape, married to her calling rather than to an unsatisfactory and uncaring husband as is mousy Mrs. Murdock, one of the guests at the tea.

The doubled perspective in the story establishes the friction between escapism and actuality. On the one hand, Mrs. Murdock tries to sustain her flagging belief in her idol, Lily Wynton. On the other, the impersonal narrator focuses an unsparing and even vindictive eye on this character. This narrator wastes no time contrasting the publicity photo and theatrical performance with the actress's physical frame: "There she stood, one hand resting on the wooden molding and her body swayed toward it, exactly as she had stood for her third-act entrance of her latest play, and for a like half-minute" (223). Wynton is both inebriated and inauthentic, betraying her private imitation of her onstage role through imprecision and automation. Rather than immediately acknowledge this awkward duplication, the flickering aura of Wynton's stardom, Mrs. Murdock focuses on the familiarity of this performance and the intimacy that her recognition implies. After all, recognition and intimacy are two promises of identification that celebrity culture offers fans, what P. David Marshall calls "the fantasy of intimacy and the reality of distance."[21] Mrs. Murdock clings to this familiarity: "You would have known her anywhere, Mrs. Murdock thought." But Parker's extension of Mrs. Murdock's thought undermines its vigor: "Oh yes, anywhere. Or at least you would have exclaimed, 'That woman looks something like Lily Wynton'" (223). The real Lily Wynton seems a poor imitation of her celebrity aura. Mrs. Murdock's initially earnest perspective is overtaken by the ambiguity of an ironic tone, as her final observation could be read straight as a correction of her first thought, or it could be read as a withering quip worthy of (or even coming from) the skeptical narrator.

Parker plays with at least two sets of doubles here: Mrs. Murdock's thoughts and the third-person narration, Lily Wynton's celebrity image and her grotesque body. Stripped of the veil of celebrity, she undergoes a ghoulish transformation: "Her figure looked heavier, thicker, and her face—there was so much of her face that the surplus sagged from the strong, fine bones." Parker includes an orgy of synonyms for excess— "heavier," "thicker," "so much," "surplus,"—suggesting the too-much-ness of the female body.[22] Lily Wynton also seems distressingly mortal, baring the skeleton beneath the skin rather than the ethereal glow of her star self. This body possesses too much flesh, but it also has too little coherence; the component parts of the face seem ready to fall apart: "And her eyes, those famous dark, liquid eyes . . . seemed to be set but loosely, so readily did they roll" (223). The real body spoils the illusion of wholeness provided by Mrs. Murdock's cherished pictures of and interviews with Lily Wynton.

Parker uses doubled perspective in her narration to taint the worship Mrs. Murdock formerly directed at this idol. While Mrs. Murdock maintains polite if halting conversation with the actress, this narration is ambiguous. Is the narrator detailing Lily Wynton's flaws, or is the allusion in this description to the actress's "famous dark, liquid eyes" an indication that this portrait comes from Mrs. Murdock's perspective, that this fan is checking each feature against a list of her heroine's beauties in her mind? This narrative ambiguity renders Mrs. Murdock's disillusionment inextricable from the narration's cruelty. This connection implies that one psychological effect of celebrity culture and its fetishization of glamorous surfaces is the unconscious revilement of female flesh—imagined as too heavy, too liquid, and too loose—by the fan, viewer, or reader. Preferring the fantasy of femininity that technological reproduction can offer, Mrs. Murdock no longer wants the reality of physicality and its flaws.

Propelling this disillusionment, Lily Wynton's own voice exposes the unpleasant interior of her body: "'Gas,' said Lily Wynton, in the famous voice. 'Gas. Nobody knows what I suffer from it'" (225). She further complains about her failing teeth: "'I have to go to the dentist tomorrow. Oh, the suffering I have gone through with my teeth. Look!' She set down her glass, inserted a gloved forefinger in the corner of her mouth, and dragged it to the side. 'Oogh!' she insisted. 'Oogh!'" (227). The "famous voice" of the glamorous celebrity vocalizes bodily complaint. Her identity has shifted from being a product of magazine scopophilia and celebrity iconography ("Look!") to issuing from her own utterance, the primal mammalian grunt ("Oogh!"). The demands of the body thus conquer the impenetrable visual fantasy. Her elegant glove is now presumably stained by saliva. Dental decay and flatulence disturb the celebrity aura of shining perfection and contained dignity.

Parker thus dishevels the glamorous body of the celebrity and leaves the middlebrow woman with few options for identification and emulation. Mrs. Murdock enjoys the pleasures of fandom like a form of religious transport: "always she had done her wistful worshiping, along with the multitudes, at the great public altars," but Parker suggests that celebrity worship is in fact a form of childish escapism, a magazine-generated Neverland, as Mrs. Murdock, repeatedly called "tiny," admires Maude Adams and Peter Pan (218). Adult life offers few avenues for such adventures. Because her husband dismisses her words, Mrs. Murdock imagines friendship with Lily Wynton as an opportunity for connection: "She heard her own voice in future conversations" (220). Reading magazines helps to inspire and sustain the dream of possessing a voice.

Parker contrasts this fantasy of having a voice with the reality of literary production. Lily keeps calling Mrs. Murdock a clever writer, though Mrs. Murdock is a housewife and no writer at all. Lily imagines that cleverness can be physically recognized rather than verbally manifested: "'What a clever little face,' said Lily Wynton. 'Clever, clever little face. What does she do . . . I'm sure she writes, doesn't she? Yes, I can feel it. She writes beautiful beautiful words. Don't you, child?'" (224). Even in this fantasy of a professional life, Mrs. Murdock appears to be a child. Eventually Lily nicknames Mrs. Murdock: "little Clever-Face" (227). While Mrs. Murdock longs for such a mask of cleverness, she is painfully shy. The label "Clever-Face" is one more case of misrepresentation based on fantasy and desire. These characters can achieve the ideal of neither a clever voice nor a beautiful exterior.

Parker emphasizes the compensatory properties of celebrity fantasies when Mrs. Murdock strains to extend the myth of Lily Wynton beyond the moment of disillusionment. "'Lily Wynton . . . is not a movie star. She is an actress. She is a great actress,'" she tells her scornful husband after her disappointing afternoon tea (229). These avowals of belief dissipate as the story concludes with Mrs. Murdock in solitude "wearily" facing her humdrum life (230). Parker's narrator does not comment directly on the disappointments of women's culture as defined by middlebrow genres, celebrity identification, and feminine glamour.[23] In these two stories, Parker dramatizes dichotomies that paradoxically define feminine roles: ideal bodies and monstrous ones; serenity and distress; sympathy and cruelty; cleverness and inarticulacy (to name just a few). Through these clashes, Parker exposes the contradictions meant to wake her readers from the lovely dream world generated by magazines like *Harper's Bazaar*. Mrs. Murdock's melancholy reminds the reader that these illusions can disappoint and constrain rather than transport and liberate.

What Men Love: Lois Long and Anita Loos

Parker's concerns as a professional journalist about the consequences of feminine embodiment and middlebrow fantasy were shared by other magazine writers. This hesitation did not always precipitate the eschewal of the glamorous body. Anita Loos and Lois Long flirtatiously present themselves as sexy sophisticates, and, at the same time, they deliberately

separate their authorial personae from the cult of the body and emphasize the physicality of other absurd figures surrounding the mentally superior "I." They render their bodies tantalizing and withdraw them from
public view. They play the seductive siren only to acknowledge through
humor that she is a fantasy.

Long signed her *New Yorker* restaurant and nightclub reviews "Lipstick," a name that betokened her feminine poses. As historian Kathy
Peiss observes, lipstick "connoted the come-on, a sexually assertive, public pose that trifled with bourgeois conventions."[24] This characterization
fit Long's professional and personal reputation. Her colleague Brendan
Gill reported that editor Harold Ross thought of Long as "the ideal *New
Yorker* writer, to say nothing of the ideal *New Yorker* reader" and "the
embodiment of a glamorous insider."[25] In his popular history of the flapper, Joshua Zeitz devotes a chapter to Long, quoting a peer's assessment
of her as "Miss Jazz Age."[26] Like Parker, Long began her career at *Vogue*,
and then she took over Parker's position as drama critic at *Vanity Fair*.
Moving to the *New Yorker*, Long wrote a restaurant and nightlife review
column, "Tables for Two," and a fashion and shopping guide called "On
the Avenue." In these articles, she not only evaluated New York estab-
lishments but also accentuated the excitement of the modern woman's
nocturnal activities.

In a 1931 *New Yorker* article about modern men, "Doldrums: the
Hunted," Long teasingly alludes to her audacious reputation: "I write
this as an interested onlooker, of course. I know nothing about men at
all, being a modest, retiring type."[27] Modest and retiring, however, would
not be the appropriate words to describe the seductive vision of the female body that Long proceeds to detail: "I know only that they [men]
all love black lace over pink; they adore long, sheer black silk stockings,
plain pumps without buckles or straps, and long eyelashes." This rhetorical move would seem sheer flirtation if it weren't for the ironic indirection of Long's catalogue. She privileges the costume and illusion
of femininity rather than its presence; she lists the component parts of
the tantalizing ensemble. While Long hints that she wears long, sheer
black silk stockings, she also suggests that men desire objects that sym-
bolize femininity and sex. This commodification of sex turns men into
consumers. In what category of sexuality does the male desire for lace,
stockings, plain pumps, and long (fake?) eyelashes fit?[28] The doubleness
of Long's humor keeps both messages—flirtation (female columnist with
the male reader, the celebrity with the public) and exposure (of modern
man's fetishism)—in play.

This strip-tease allows Long both to flirt and to vanish behind the costume of femininity. In crafting her public persona, however, Long insists on her professionalism rather than simply her stylishness. She breathlessly begins one restaurant review: "Just before staging a complete collapse, with definite indications of rigor mortis, galloping Charleston, and chronic mirages of a quiet home in the country, I wish to go on record as saying that, everything considered, this HAS been a week!"[29] This litany of physical symptoms inspires envy about the excursions and indulgences that produced them. Like Parker's Constant Reader forever unsatisfied at the material she is asked to review, Long disparages the night club performance she viewed: "at twelve-thirty, some awful smart boys and girls [were] puttin' on a dern good show, including singin', whistlin', jigs, an' other capers." Long's imitation of a rustic voice marks her urbane superiority to it. She distinguishes herself from this undifferentiated mob of mass culture cuties in order to establish her individuality as a middlebrow celebrity. Compared to these pseudo-smart performers and their strenuous jigs and capers, the female columnist is still, reflective, even serious. She leaves them with the bodiliness and claims the mind for herself.

Long's relationship to the body and to cultural stratification, however, is more complicated than a simple rejection of the physical and the lowbrow. Long hints at the role of the body and popular pastimes in her own cultural performances as she belittles "two feeble attempts at a Charleston" in the nightclub act "by young women who apparently don't know that anyone who does the Charleston now must do it exceptionally well." This self-confessed dancer of the "galloping Charleston," implies that she plays her flapper role "exceptionally well," so well that imitators come off badly. This role is not just a private performance of womanliness for the benefit of lovers, friends, or even colleagues. Long's *New Yorker* flapper persona has generated acclaim, money, and public stature.

Long signals through humor that she sells these feminine ideals rather than being sold on them or by them; she adds a postscript warning in bold to her review: "WARNING! Certain well dressed young women have been posing as 'Lipstick' and demanding free tables from guileless restaurateurs in my name. Know that the original model is a short, squat maiden of forty, who wears steel rimmed spectacles." Long treats "well dressed young women" as awkward pretenders who assume that Lipstick's stylish writing reflects her stylish looks. There is only one Lipstick, even if there are many would-be contenders for that role. Here, much as she does with the chorus line, Long reminds her reader of her singularity and celebrity and betrays anxiety about what it means to find fame through mass cultural duplication and circulation. The magazines sell, after all, in part because readers (and possibly advertisers and editors) imagine that they could successfully imitate these roles that they appreciate.

Undermining her chic role, Long declares herself a girl who wears glasses, to paraphrase Parker's famous poem "News Item." Long uses this unprepossessing description of herself to hint to her reader that she is physically attractive (neither short, squat, nor bespectacled). At the same time, this warning vaunts that the real Lois Long is nowhere in view.[30] "Lipstick" the persona is a tool like actual lipstick that decorates a surface and exaggerates femininity. Long thus exposes the artifice of the persona and flaunts her control over it. In this column, Lipstick's dual role as artist and seductive yet inaccessible model resembles Miss Black from Millay's "The Implacable Aphrodite" ("I am my own model," Miss Black confesses). Her ironically doubled role, as she plays both the girl who wears glasses and the flapper who can Charleston exceptionally well, allows Long to comment on the columnist's profitable and intangible vampdom.

Anita Loos takes this doubleness of persona a step further by inventing a fictional character rather than a nom de plum. Loos is most famous for giving voice to that most dippy of blondes, Lorelei Lee from *Gentlemen Prefer Blondes: The Illuminating Diary of a Professional Lady*. Though Loos was primarily employed as a screenwriter in the 1910s and 1920s, she also pursued magazine work. In her autobiography, *A Girl Like I*, Loos recalls that her first publications were "humorous anecdotes about life in New York" that she invented "undeterred by the fact that I had never been there."[31] When in New York rather than California, Loos moved in smart magazine circles. In the 1910s, Loos met the urbane Frank Crowninshield, the editor of *Vanity Fair* who published an early story of hers; in the 1920s, she mingled with the Algonquin Round Table, whom she would memorably belittle in both *But Gentlemen Marry Brunettes* and her memoirs. In 1925, *Gentlemen Prefer Blondes* was serialized in *Harper's Bazaar* and became a cultural sensation and later, when published as a book, a bestseller.

When Loos reflected upon her novel and its genesis, she described her desire to revenge herself on a glamorous blonde. The inspiration for Lorelei Lee, Loos claimed, was a buxom blonde who wanted to be a movie star: "Now this girl, although she towered above me (I weighed about ninety pounds) and was of rather a hearty type, was being waited on, catered to and cajoled by the entire male assemblage. . . . Obviously there was some radical difference between that girl and me. But what was it? We were both in the pristine years of early youth; we were of about the same degree of comeliness; as to our mental acumen, there was nothing to discuss; I was the smarter. Then why did that girl so far outdistance me in feminine allure?"[32] In spite of her professed insecurities, Loos uses this anecdote to glorify her own small body, her collegial camaraderie with male peers (instead of the "catering and cajoling" of flirtation), and her mental acumen. This description of the towering blonde recalls representations of glamorous women as Art Deco skyscrapers in modern magazines. (Indeed, in a Hollywood memoir, Loos conjectured that "an Art Deco type of blondeness . . . may have inspired . . . the Chrysler Building."[33]) Loos topples this monument by implying the superiority of a diminutive body and formidable brain. While her tone is self-deprecating, the effect is self-promoting: "I was the smarter." "Feminine allure" seems like a meager and even deceptive quality by contrast.

For Loos, the blonde emblematizes a culture obsessed with the body and sex and fueled by narcissism. In *Gentlemen Prefer Blondes*, the sexy blonde Lorelei Lee confuses surface for depth, or, perhaps more accurately, prefers surface to depth. A lover buys her "a whole complete set of books for my birthday by a gentleman called Mr. Conrad. They all seem to be about ocean travel although I have not had time to more than glance through them. I have always liked novels about ocean travel ever since I posed for Mr. Christie for the front cover of a novel about ocean travel by McGrath because I always say that a girl never really looks as well as she does on board a steamship, or even a yacht."[34] The acquisitive approach to high culture ("a whole complete set of books" recalls the book club fad that began in this era) threatens to vitiate literary value as the cover girl conquers Conrad. In a culture of marketing that tantalizes consumers with female bodies, Lorelei Lee—thus renamed, she tells us, by a man who compares her to a Rhinemaiden—discusses her desire to improve her mind only to fall back on the established resource of her looks.

Though Loos might seem to warn of Lorelei's seductions, her use of humor and irony conveys a more complicated account of feminine masquerade. Lorelei, shaping her body and her persona to fit the desires of the men who support her, baldly reports the contradictions of those desires: "Gerry does not like a girl to be nothing else but a doll, but he likes her to bring in her husband's slippers every evening and make him forget what he has gone through." This intellectual lover purports "to like me more for my soul" and not to want Lorelei Lee to "dress up," but Lorelei, practiced in the art of self-presentation, realizes his self-delusion: "I really had to tell Gerry that if all gentlemen were like he seems to be, Madame Frances' whole dress making establishment would have to go out of business." Like Mr. White in Millay's "The Implacable Aphrodite," Gerry only "seems" to be different on this point. In fact, he prizes the decorated female body and resents evidence of women's intellectual and political engagement. He derides Boston bluestockings for their homeliness and admits that he has never loved his wife, a suffragette. In spite of his pretenses to intellectual abstemiousness and sincerity, Gerry is entranced by surfaces too: "Gerry says he has never seen a girl of my personal appearance with so many brains."[35]

As Gerry's remark implies, Lorelei relies on her "personal appearance" for economic power over men. Lorelei betrays her own awareness of this performance when she argues with the wife of a wealthy lover: "So then she [the wife] said she would drag it into the court and she would say that it was undue influence. So I said to her, 'If you wear that hat into court, we will see if the judge thinks it took undue influence to make Sir Francis Beekman look at a girl.'"[36] The pleasure of "looking at a girl" provides the basis for all kinds of sales, from fashion to sex, from marriage to magazines. Women don hats (and feminine roles) to close those sales. At the same time that she diagnoses the shortcomings of this scopophilic and objectifying approach to the female body, Loos associates the manipulation of femininity with women's entrance into the professions and the public sphere. Lorelei Lee is variously a spy, movie actress, and best-selling author in the two novels that feature her. In her memoir *Kiss Hollywood Good-by*, Loos reflects on the connection between feminine poses and early careers for women: "All over the nation girls started to earn their own money. Gold diggers, whose lives had been the most tedious, readily took to exciting jobs as mannequins, models, and cover girls. Those with sufficient talent went on the stage. Nontalented beauties got jobs in Hollywood, and the nonbeauties went into offices."[37] In her depiction of Lorelei and her physical appeal, Loos indirectly comments on the sexism of the professional world. The display of the female body is lucrative (mannequins, models, and cover girls—oh my) in a culture preoccupied with the gaze.

Loos undermines the potency of the gaze by establishing the primacy of narrative voice. The reader is given few cues to envision Lorelei's body through her first-person narration. Her loose and baggy syntax, malapropisms, euphemisms, and misspellings obscure both her body and the events she describes. Autobiography provides Lorelei with comic revisionist agency; we can never know the "real story." Lorelei sees herself as an artist and a professional: "I am to [sic] busy going over my senarios [sic] with Mr. Montrose, to keep up any other kind of literary work."[38] While Loos's deliberate misspellings poke fun at Lorelei's lack of education and her membership in what H. L. Mencken would call the "booboisie," Lorelei triumphs in both discourse and plot over judgments that would designate her a courtesan, traitor, murderess, or even flapper (each an accusation leveled at Lorelei by other characters in the book).

While Lorelei Lee persists in the contemporary popular imagination as the voluptuous Marilyn Monroe, her body is elusive in *Gentlemen Prefer Blondes* and its 1928 sequel *But Gentlemen Marry Brunettes*. Lorelei's euphemisms and circumlocutions veil her body even as she enumerates her romantic (and presumably sexual) successes. At the beginning of *But Gentlemen Marry Brunettes*, Lorelei tantalizes her husband to persuade him to move: "when Henry came home from the banquet, I slipped into his bed room in my new pink neglijay, and I finally got him to promise that we would live in New York, where our life could be more mental."[39] Like Gypsy Rose Lee, Lorelei shows us her negligee, only to teach us to attend to her sense of humor. Henry may think he wants life to be "more mental," but his susceptibility to physical persuasion suggests otherwise.

In both novels, Lorelei uses the appeals of her body to ensure that her professional ambitions and personal desires come to fruition. Loos implicitly criticizes the insistent characterization of women as seductive sirens and the corresponding feminine masquerades this obsession with sex and body produces. Lorelei plays up the strip-tease because she knows it appeals to her audience. This cultural criticism extends beyond the bedroom. As her success in the movie business and in the courtroom (as the accused, not as a lawyer) suggests, Lorelei is an expert in feminine publicity. In *But Gentlemen Marry Brunettes*, the Algonquin Round Table grants Lorelei exalted status, not because of her Dorothy Parker wit (which she lacks) but for her seductive looks: "he turned and addressed the whole Round-Table, and said 'Gentlemen, you are always discovering a Duse, or a Sapho or a Cleopatra every week, and I think it is my turn. Because I have discovered a lady who is all three rolled into one.'"[40] Lorelei appears to be an actress, a writer, even a queen simply because of her appearance, not because of her accomplishment. This easy slippage between seduction and success doubtless troubled Loos who was marketed as a seductive and feminine celebrity. In the October 1928 *New Yorker*, an ad for Cutex nail polish featured a photograph of Loos.

The ad's caption proclaimed that "Gentlemen Prefer Flattering Hands."[41] Loos's coquettish praise of the product—"It flatters the hands, and I love flattery"—accompanies the endorsement of a "winsome blonde of Washington society." The ad implicitly equates sharp nails and sharp wit. Instead of opposing glamour and wit, as Loos does through the distance between narrator and implied author in *Gentlemen Prefer Blondes*, the advertiser turns Loos into the equivalent of a flirtatious, fashionable society girl. This celebrity persona brings Loos commercially close to Lorelei Lee.

As unlikely as it might seem, Parker's persona also risked flapperization. In the October 1927 *New Yorker*, an ad appeared next to one of Parker's book reviews. This ad promoted "Laddergrams," a collection of word puzzles in which a player changes one four-letter word into another by altering one letter at a time. The ad's slogan invokes Parker's pessimism: "As Dorothy Parker would say 'Shot to Hell Again.'" While this attitude is the opposite of the chirpy opportunism associated with Lorelei Lee, the advertising copy treats Parker's cynical persona as an equally chic posture for the modern woman: "LADDERGRAMS are a great solace to a disillusioned lady. They show the inevitable mutation of anything to anything else. (What was that?) Before you know it, Love changes to Hate, and Flame to Ashes. But LADDERGRAMS are Here to Stay (get that one?) as the newest and best of the pencil-destroying diversions. Now that you've worked this one (and very clever of you) there are fifty more all ready for you . . . GET IN THE GAME!"[42] Like the Laddergrams word puzzles, Parker's poetry substantiates the cleverness of the female reader, and her disillusionment is an attainable status symbol that can confirm the reader's desired worldliness. By equating word puzzles and light verse, this ad turns Parker's tonal reversals into mere rearrangements of letters and belittles her literary achievement.

To add visual insult to verbal injury, the ad's illustrations depict two short-skirted brunette flappers. One flapper stands atop the ladder, balancing a Valentine heart on her nose as a seal might balance a ball. The second flapper, at the bottom of the ladder slaps her cheeks in stylized shock at the broken hearts that have clattered to the floor. This shock only brings out the Cupid's bow of the cartoon's mouth. These Parker-like flappers, cartoons by Dick Spencer, imply that even pain can be adorable and disillusionment marketable. Such condescending marketing strategies, treating women writers as either flirtatious or cute, help establish a central reason that these writers employed humorous doubles in discussions of the female body and feminine roles. The authors were already replaced by publicity doubles of themselves, feminine celebrity roles that privileged attractiveness and whimsy over cultivation and wit. It is little wonder that in her *New Yorker* monologues that referred to her famous name, Parker made a bid not for membership in this sorority of flirtatious magazine vixens, but instead for the urbane status of the *New Yorker* Little Man.

The Waltz between Femininity and Masculinity

In each example addressed thus far, the female magazine writer uses shades of the other woman to establish the luster of the authorial persona. In her book reviews, Parker infects and dissects the female body to suggest its insufficiency to publicly represent her gifts. In her *Harper's Bazaar* short stories, Parker turns the icons of feminine glamour into agents of decay and collapse. Long and Loos establish the singularity and superiority of their wit and professionalism at the expense of the brainlessness and sexuality of bombshells. Not surprisingly, the divide between men and woman, so crucial to modern hierarchies of literary and professional status, also provides a symbolic vehicle for depicting the mind-body struggle. In Parker's monologues, her first-person speaker feels affirmed by her sophisticated male compatriots or befuddled by the bodiliness of muscle men. In either case, an escape from the sexualized female body provides the crucial first step toward proving professional and intellectual attainment.

Parker was acutely aware of the cultural tension between professionalism and femininity. In a 1924 essay for *Life* magazine, she mulled over the controversy of her career: "And what do you do, Mrs. Parker? Oh, I write. There's a hot job for a healthy woman. I wish I'd taken a course in interior decorating. I wish I'd gone on the stage." Parker connects being ornamental, whether decorating a room or decorating oneself, with being a "healthy woman." Pursuing this association, Parker contrasts her unadorned body with the bejeweled bodies of other women. She longs for: "Just some decent clothes, and maybe a string of pearls. Oh, God, those pearls in Cartier's window!" In spite of her lament, Parker elevates her professionalism over the consumerism and glamour that give other women status, and she underscores the contrast between their excess and luxury and her deprivation and hard work: "A dollar a line, and like it. Fat you'll get doing that." Diamonds are not Parker's best friend; her best friend is a pencil: "Just a common, ordinary, wooden pencil."[43] Once Parker dismisses the glittering allure of showroom window femininity, she claims her place at the office desk along with the boys: "Nothing but work; that's me. And no play. I'll be a dull boy, first thing you know."[44]

The aspiration to be a dull boy is a difficult ambition to fulfill as a woman constantly under the scrutinizing gaze of the public. In her 1928 *New Yorker* story, "The Garter," Parker places her speaker in an embarrassing situation: while she is at a crowded party, her garter snaps. This narrator, who refers to herself as Dorothy Parker, does not embrace her outsider status, as Parker does in her book reviews and *Life* essay. In "The Garter," the narrator fears the public exposure of her fallen stocking, and the whirl of the modern nightlife threatens to leave her behind in fatal stillness: "Tell the orchestra for God's sake to keep on playing. Dance, you jazz-mad puppets of fate, and pay no attention to me. I'm all right. Wounded? Nay, sire, I'm healthy."[45] Her wounded posture evokes the passive female consumer whose well-being relies on the well-chosen object. Her narrator's embarrassment betrays the social importance of impressing strangers, a priority stressed by advertising rhetoric.[46] Parker cites these feminine norms projected by magazine copy and communicates their force through exaggeration and morbid reflection, only to debunk this limited social role and to exalt her own professionalism as a magazine writer.

In this story Parker uses several strategies of doubling to establish the gap between attractiveness and insecurity, success and failure, survival and decay. First, Parker juxtaposes the female body as a decorative object with a vision of the living corpse. The speaker jokes that her body will become an ornament for the hosts' home: "I'll probably live a long time; there won't be much wear on my system, sitting here, year in, year out, holding my stocking up. Maybe they could find a use for me, after a while. They could hang hats on me, or use my lap for an ash-tray." Parker quickly blasts this antiseptic vision of the female body as object: "I wonder how they'll be able to tell when I'm dead. It will be a very thin line of distinction between me sitting here holding my stocking, and just a regulation dead body. A demd, damp, moist, unpleasant body" (100). "Damp," moist," and "unpleasant" could describe an unattractive woman, and indeed "damp" and "moist" suggest a discomfort with the wetness of female anatomy. Overtaken by anxiety and embarrassment, the narrator realizes that she cannot escape her body; her aspirations to loveliness are spoiled by her inadequacies. Public scrutiny makes her intensely aware of the divide between her desired self and her surface appearance: "All they can see is this unfortunate exterior. There's a man looking at it now" (101).

The narrator's body seems fatally feminine in this sequence, and indeed she compares herself to the sexually barren and moldering Miss Havisham from *Great Expectations*: "I expect my clothes will turn yellow, like Miss Havisham's." Spinsterhood and isolation seem the only ways to cope with the antipathy that the narrator feels toward her own body. Humor transforms the threat of this belittling comparison into an opportunity for self-advancement; the speaker fantasizes that she and Miss Havisham could be featured in a series of adventure books as the "Frustration Girls": "The Frustration Girls on an Island, The Frustration Girls at the World's Fair, The Frustration Girls and Their Ice-Boat, The Frustration Girls at the House of All Nations" (100). Parker thus redeems the female body and rewrites the Victorian spinster into the modern single girl. She and Miss Havisham, however unlikely a pair of popular heroines, are ready for cosmopolitan adventure and for success in the literary marketplace.

In another pointed intervention that links gender roles and profitable performances, Parker alludes to a second Victorian double for her modern woman—an emotive man. The phrase "demd damp moist unpleasant body" comes from *Nicholas Nickleby*. In this novel, a comical minor character, Mr. Mantalini, persuades his practical wife, a professional dressmaker, to grant him an allowance. When she hesitates, he claims that he will drown himself for her, a process that would leave him "'a demd damp moist unpleasant body.'" His strategically pathetic pose wins the day; Madame Mantalini gives him the money he wants.[47] By employing this allusion, Parker draws an implicit parallel between this character and her first-person narrator. Like Mr. Mantilini, Parker garners financial rewards by complaining and comparing herself to a corpse. Like Mr. Mantilini "drawing out his pocket-handkerchief" and letting out a "dismal moan," Parker fantasizes about bursting into tears: "Oh, if I only had the use of both my hands, I'd just cover my face and cry my heart out."[48] Mantilini and Parker share a flair for drama, exaggeration, and self-promotion in the guise of self-deprecation. While these tactics may seem like stereotypically feminine strategies for influence and control, Parker's allusion to *Nicholas Nickleby* indicates that excess has no fixed gender.

After establishing that both men and women employ overt emotionalism and bodily exaggeration to pursue their financial objectives, Parker grabs her opportunity to criticize the misogyny that the professional woman writer faces. She imagines the thoughts of her fellow partygoers: "Dorothy Parker? What's she like? Oh, she's terrible. God, she's poisonous. Sits in a corner and sulks all evening—never opens her yap. Dumbest woman you ever saw in your life." This dialogue suggests that women must both attract and charm, or they fail in their social and professional duties. As a female celebrity, Dorothy Parker must produce witty banter or fall out of public favor. Furthermore, as a professional journalist, she is a usurper; the party guests gossip about a male writer victimized by her success: "They say she pays this poor little guy, that lives in some tenement on the Lower East Side, ten dollars a week to write it and she just signs her name to it. He has to do it, the poor devil, to help support a crippled mother and five brothers and sisters" (101). Parker appropriates masculine professional privilege, and the looming figure of this female celebrity reduces the male writer to a "poor little guy."

In another ironic twist, this anecdote about modern women seizing professional prerogative from deserving men comes from the narrator's point of view rather than the actual voices of the critical public. The narrator is imagining what the other people at the party might be thinking of her; she has internalized the sense that she has done something wrong by publishing at all. Parker's use of doubles thus arrives at its pointed conclusion: the celebrity woman writer lives suspended between two potential sources of self-criticism—her failure to embody feminine glamour and her success at earning professional status and financial independence, previously male domains. Fortunately, at just the moment when the narrator begins to despair of her ability to rejoin the party, Parker sends in reinforcements; a man wearing Brooks Brothers enters her isolated corner, and Parker's narrator imagines the possibility of partnership: "Maybe he'll turn out to be one of Nature's noblemen" (101). Parker concludes the story with her conversational gambit (*"Listen, what would you do if you were I"*), a question that invites the suave man to identify with her plight. With this gesture, Parker hints that the modern urban world might permit heterosocial cooperation—perhaps even collegial collaboration—and that friendship and camaraderie might trump the resentment of change.

This hopeful conclusion of "The Garter" extends the dream of gendered cooperation in the professional sphere. This appeal to a professional fraternity characterizes Parker's ironic postures in her *New Yorker* monologues. Although Parker does not precisely impersonate masculinity, constantly thematizing her feminine vulnerability, she aligns her persona with the beleaguered passivity of the modern Little Man. In so doing, she confirms that she belongs in a professional and intellectual sphere dominated by men. *New Yorker* humorists such as Robert Benchley, E. B. White, and

James Thurber perfected a style that contemporary critics call "Little Man" humor: absurd, self-deprecating narratives from a man's point of view about the overwhelming forces of modernity. In these stories, the modern woman embraces bureaucracy, control, and efficiency, while the monologist proves his individualism and intellect through his whimsy and distractibility.[49] The sense that the Little Man should possess patriarchal authority (but doesn't) only exacerbates his feelings of disempowerment. In a 1926 *New Yorker* story called "Getting Through," E. B. White's narrator bemoans his corporate responsibilities: "When they gave me voice in the management of the company, I began to have trouble getting through the day."[50] White contrasts his narrator's difficulties with the efficiency of his secretary. In a 1930 *New Yorker* story, "The Noon Telephone Operator," Benchley sympathizes with the substitute telephone operator, a man, who is left "a nervous wreck" by the female phone operator's absence during her lunch hour. In a 1931 *New Yorker* story, Thurber's narrator hits upon an improbable solution to his daily intimidation; he must find "A Box to Hide In." Defeated in this as in all pursuits, he abandons his quest when overwhelmed: "I tried several other groceries and none of them had a box big enough for me to hide in . . . I didn't feel strong."[51] The feeling of faiblesse exalts these individual Little Men over the vitality and anonymity of the modern bustle.

In Parker's famous monologue, "The Waltz," her narrator is similarly resigned to her unpleasant fate as the dance partner of a boor (and bore): "I guess I'm as well off here. As well off as if I were in a cement mixer in full action. I'm past all feeling now."[52] In "The Waltz," Parker emulates several tactics of Little Man humor: a descent into the physical, bewildered passivity, flights of fancy, and absent-mindedness. Physical passivity grants Parker the mental freedom to reflect ironically and critically on her overwhelming and chaotic context. Parker narrates "The Waltz" with a double voice; the narrator's appropriately polite responses to her partner stand in italics, and her true thoughts dominate the monologue. Parker's humor resembles Little Man humor in this emphasis on the divide between interior life and external mandates.

Much like the Little Man who defines himself against the efficiency and hustle of the modern woman, Parker sets up her bluff male dance partner in "The Waltz" as the foil for her urbane and sophisticated narrator. In both, the divide between the sexes symbolizes the split between the mind and the body. In Little Man humor, men possess the power of reflection and speculation, while women act as efficient automatons. In "The Waltz," the narrator balks at the omnipresence of her partner's active and clumsy body. This physicality demotes his cultural and intellectual status; the speaker speculates that he might be from "the hill country, and never had no larnin'" (210). His physicality renders him bestial: "He has a heart of a lion, and the sinews of a buffalo." Like an athlete, her partner rushes into action; he attempts a waltz step that Parker describes as "Two stumbles, slip, and a twenty-yard dash." To him the urban nightlife is just another football game to be won through fearless tackles. (This approach does not bode well for his sexual finesse.) This hypermasculine dance partner prefers mindless activity to reflection and planning: "Look at him—never a thought of the consequences, never afraid of his face, hurling himself into every scrimmage, eyes shining, cheeks ablaze" (211).

Parker plays with the figure of the dumb muscle-bound man much as Loos exaggerates the figure of the ditzy blonde. Parker's waltz partner serves as a repository for the regrettable gravity of human flesh that limits the airy ascent of ironic wit. This figure of the muscle man also reflects and criticizes the physical regimens marketed to middle-class men. As early as "Men: A Hate Song" in the February 1917 *Vanity Fair*, Parker mocked:

> the Cave Men,—
> The Specimens of Red-Blooded Manhood.
> They eat everything very rare,
> They are scarcely ever out of their cold baths,
> And they want everybody to feel their muscles. (lines 19–23)[53]

The cult of body-building served as one response to the modern crisis in masculinity. Bernarr MacFadden published a popular magazine called *Physical Culture*, which promoted healthy living and body sculpting for men.[54] This bulky fantasy of the physical culture man was the obverse of the Little Man with whom Parker identified. In her description of her oafish waltz partner, Parker draws attention to his masculinity: "how effete the other dancers seem, beside him" (211). Here the insult of "effeteness" becomes an indirect compliment, however, implying admirable suavete next to her partner's gaucheries. In a January 1931 essay for the *New Yorker*, Lois Long similarly establishes the mental superiority of the female sophisticate against physical prowess. She fears the next generation will take up regrettably good habits: "they will be rosy-cheeked, big-chested young bores, eternally flexing their muscles in our weary faces," and she warns that "The Bernarr Macfadden age is what we are in for." Fragility and even fragmentation become signs of superiority, experience, and worldliness: "We will be bits of broken crockery, wobbly and weak but preserved forever in alcohol."[55] In "The Waltz" Parker also prizes her wounds and breaks as symbols of mental provenance rather than servitude to the merely physical: "What's it to me if I have to spend the next couple of years in a plaster cast?" (211).

Indeed, Parker turns her narrator into an ailing and decadent foil for the muscle man's hulking Frankenstein monster. She gothicizes her appearance to show how far she has strayed from the composure of the glamour girl and the vitality of the muscle man: "I bet I'm awfully effective when you look at me. My hair is hanging along my cheeks, my skirt is swaddled about me, I can feel the cold damp of my brow. I must look like something out of 'The Fall of the House of Usher'" (211). In the Edgar Allan Poe story, Madeline Usher, the twin of aesthete and artist Roderick, suffers from an illness characterized by "a settled apathy, a gradual wasting away of the person."[56] In the context of New Yorker sophistication, "settled apathy" becomes worldly cynicism, and "wasting away" becomes urban ennui. By claiming Madeline Usher and, by extension, Edgar Allan Poe, as literary ancestors, Parker embraces her own decadence as a sign of cultural and intellectual superiority.

After aligning herself with the living dead of the past, Parker longs for a peaceful future in the grave. This prospect would free her from the claims of the body. Parker's narrator looks for a deus ex machina or a Grim Reaper to rescue her from this disaster: "being struck dead would look like a day in the country, compared to struggling out a dance with this boy" (209). Parker considers action herself, "kill[ing] him this instant, with my naked hands," but then resolves that this would not merit the effort: "Maybe it's best not to make a scene. I guess I'll just lie low, and watch the pace get him." The sophisticate does not dirty his (or her) hands—just surveys the ground. Parker depicts herself as a reluctant player striving to escape notice like the urbane Little Man who also wishes to "lie low." While her partner drags her along in the dance, she is aloof from the killing pace of modern life. This detachment correlates with her intellect and attitude. Parker underscores her rationality as she measures the predictable limits of her partner's life span: "He can't keep this up indefinitely—he's only flesh and blood." She matches this analysis with tones of aggression and imperiousness: "Die he must, and die he shall, for what he did to me" (210).[57] Parker also conveys an impression of worldliness and experience when the speaker declares that she is dead already: "I'm dead, that's all I am. Dead, and in what a cause!" (211).

In "The Waltz," Parker chooses dignified death over mortifying life, detached mind over dancing body, urbanity over rusticity, alienation over conformity within an economy of gender roles that legitimate or deny access to intellection. In this case, her male dance partner is both mindless and culturally destructive. Parker compares him to Mrs. O'Leary's cow, the creature fabled to have caused the Great Fire in Chicago. In keeping with this joke about the potentially fatal consequences of his ineptitude, Parker describes her waltz with this shoddy partner as a "*danse macabre*" (212). His eagerness and vigor, she hints, will just about kill her. In medieval paintings of the danse macabre, unwilling victims are led, cavorting and jigging, to their ultimate demise by the skeleton death. Parker is led by the physically robust man into the intellectually feeble scene of modern courtship, and she seems decidedly and proudly out of place.

Suggestively, in an early issue, the *New Yorker* used the figure of the danse macabre to caricature and vilify urban women and their sexual influence on unlucky men. In 1925 and 1926 cartoonist and poet Hans Stengel wrote a *New Yorker* series, "Our Sermons on Sin," in which he parodied regional newspaper headlines through cartoons and light verse poems. Riffing on the headline "Dairy-Man Dies, Loss of Fortune Blamed," Stengel shows the corruption of an innocent man by urban harpies.[58] A fat farmer dances at a nightclub, while a thin woman with bobbed hair watches. In the next frame, the same woman, her eyes outlined in sinister black, shares his table. The subsequent picture shows him surrounded by "unholy hussies" who "hover / like so many birds of prey," and the final frame shows his tombstone (lines 17–18). This tongue-in-cheek fable warns that "the City's dance macabre / will exact its fearful price" (lines 7–8). Much like the poisonous Dorothy Parker who beats up on the "poor little guy" in "The Garter," the modern woman in this cartoon is a vampiric predator who steals from the abundance (physical and monetary) of the unsuspecting man.

This cartoon expresses anxiety about women's successful command of the public sphere, much as Loos's representation of Lorelei Lee's excessive sexuality establishes the uneasy status of the career woman. "The Waltz" also dramatizes the posture of the woman in public, but, rather than treat her as a villain, Parker hints that she is a sage (if weary) professional, even in these awkward social circumstances. She acknowledges the attrition of experience with ironic detachment: "The only way I can tell when he steps on me is that I can hear the splintering of bones." Parker's humor (Bergson called humor "a momentary anesthesia of the heart") produces self-protective intellectual apathy on the one hand and dramatic self-pity on the other: "after the first thousand years, I suppose nothing will matter then, not heat nor pain nor broken heart nor cruel, aching weariness" (212).[59] This combination reflects the numbness and melancholy articulated by the Little Man narrators, bored by office bureaucracy, and this pose in turn supports Parker's professional role in public life.

At the beginning of the story, the narrator complains of her partner's ignorance: "Why, he scarcely knows my name, let alone what it stands for. It stands for Despair, Futility, Degradation, and Premeditated Murder, but little does he wot" (209). This comment refers to the newness of their acquaintance but also implies that he might know the name Mrs. Parker if he read the *New Yorker*. Her urbane wit, colored by "Despair, Futility, and Degradation," is a magazine sensation and a literary accomplishment. Her dancing partner is left out of both of those worlds. While he pays the band to continue, she earns her keep by generating stories of her misfortunes: "There was the time I was in a hurricane in the West Indies, there was the day I got my head cut open in the taxi smash, there was the night the drunken lady threw a bronze ash-tray at her own true love, and got me instead, there was that summer that the sailboat kept capsizing." Through her grumbling celebrity persona, Parker conquers the gravity of mere embodiment (and the indignities of modern dating) with the acrobatics of wit: "I think my mind is beginning to wander" (212).

By 1933 when she published "The Waltz," Parker had seen almost two decades of smart magazines from the inside. Economic depression and the rumblings of war abroad left her increasingly dissatisfied with her role as urban sophisticate, an uneasiness not quelled by her professional status. Her authorial persona's combination of wit and femininity risked, in her mind, narcissism and inconsequentiality, even given her popular success; in fact, these fears were likely exacerbated by that success. In a 1939 address to the American Writers Congress, Parker declared the era of light verse over, and she condemned sophistication: "I don't think that any word in the English language has a horrider connotation than 'sophisticate,' which ranks about along with 'socialite.'" This equation of "sophisticate" and "socialite" connects witty magazine writing with both snobbery and femininity. Furthermore, Parker associates sophistication with deception and inauthenticity: "The real dictionary meaning is none too attractive. The verb means: to mislead, to deprive of simplicity, to make artificial, to tamper with, for purpose of argument; to adulterate." Parker's techniques of doubling, exaggeration, and irony all enhance the impression of artificiality and complication, and here Parker condemns that effect as politically divisive. Parker explicitly blames sophistication's ascendance on women writers, and she laments their literary immaturity: "We remained in the smarty-pants stage—and that is not one of the more attractive stages." It is telling that Parker's criticism of an aesthetic failure collapses into a social or even sexual failure. These women writers were not duly "attractive."[60]

After expressing the familiar 1930s refrain that the 1920s were misguided, that the time for flippancy was in the past and the time for earnestness in the present, Parker erases women writers in favor of a communal voice gendered male: "[Writers now] know you cannot find yourself until you find your fellow man—they know there no longer is an 'I,' there is 'we'—They know that a hurt heart or a curiosity about death or an admiration of the moon is purely a personal matter. It is no longer the time for personal matters—Thank God! Now the poet speaks not just for himself but for all of us—and so his voice is heard, and so his song goes on."[61] After Parker delineates the weaknesses of "light verse writers—especially the ladies among us," the male pronouns in this passage arrive pointedly. She sets up a dichotomy between masculine authorial voices that could be straightforward, pared down, unironic, and a feminine authorial voice that was morbid, adulterating, misleading. In essence, Parker turns herself into a skeletal leader of a fatal dance macabre. Her wish for a monolithic "we" rejects the internal divisions and doubleness that she made the technique and subject of her cultural critiques.

This speech was indicative of a cultural sea change. Parker gave this speech in Hollywood, not New York where she had become an icon of sophistication. By 1939, she had had attenuated her connection with the *New Yorker*; editor Harold Ross, wary of her politics, wanted the humorous pieces that Parker was now reluctant to supply. Parker published only six pieces in the *New Yorker* between 1940 and 1960, after publishing at least a hundred items—reviews, poems, and fiction—in that magazine during the 1920s and 1930s. Parker's sense of her own political accountability and the place of earnestness in those politics had changed.

Beyond these biographical details, however, this speech reveals a thread that ran throughout Parker's work. When Parker's speakers swoon, suffer, or bare their scarred flesh to the reader, they inhabit a stereotyped feminine role of passivity. In her *New Yorker* work, Parker's body, suffering or glamorous, cannot be quarantined from the discourses of fashion, sex, and smartness that define women in the magazine and more broadly in modern print and visual culture. Her insistence on the body and its gory details records the violation of the real body by the distorting image, but it also acquiesces to and echoes that violence. It is, for example, chic to admit that dieting is painful, as that cost reinforces the valued attainment of thinness. Could Parker's humor preserve her from the feminine codification she resisted and allow her agency over her imagined body, or did it freeze her into a type and recapitulate the idea that women's bodies were problems to be managed? Arguably, both Long and Loos perpetuated the idea that sexuality was the professional woman's appropriate domain, seductiveness her enduring tactic.

For Parker and other smart magazine celebrities like Long and Loos, literary fame meant slipping on the smooth stockings of the chic feminine masquerade and pointing out where the runs were in the fabric. They turned these performances into self-conscious camp: showing the excessiveness of flapperdom, glamour, sexuality, and celebrity. Their rhetorical gestures remind that femininity is a pose and masculine professionalism another form of receding fantasy, as unattainable and desirable as attractiveness. The fact that Parker ultimately derided her feminine masquerades in literary humor reflects not the flimsiness of such strategies of indirect cultural criticism but rather the power of cultural hierarchies differentiating the marketplace and the literary, the frivolous and the significant, the feminine and the masculine. In her work, Parker bridged these divides and indeed placed their very division in question, but in her life she found it harder to preserve that skepticism. Indeed, in a 1956 interview, Parker deemed smartness the error of her age rather than its opportunity: "Silly of me to blame it on dates, but so it happened to be. Dammit, it *was* the twenties and we had to be smarty."[62] Though it was the 1920s, African-American middlebrow women writers did not have to be "smarty"; in fact, quite the contrary, they were encouraged to embrace earnestness and the kind of political solidarity that Parker espoused in her Writers' Congress speech, an apology for her individualist brand of humor. Novelist Jessie Fauset, however, saw the potential for smartness to serve as more than a form of flapper cuteness, and that vision is the subject of chapter 3.

3 / "First Aid to Laughter": Jessie Fauset and the Racial Politics of Smartness

In Alain Locke's famous 1925 collection, *The New Negro*, Jessie Fauset, the literary editor of the *Crisis* magazine, published an essay on black stereotypes and humor on the American stage called "The Gift of Laughter." Fauset immediately announces the irony of the association: "the plight of the slaves under even the mildest of masters could never have been one to awaken laughter." Given the unlikelihood of the connection, Fauset concludes that the mask of humor is an imposed disguise intended "to camouflage the real feeling and knowledge of his white compatriot." This psychological need to obscure injustices and the lack of remedy for social wrongs can be the only explanation, Fauset speculates, for this insistent translation of suffering into humor, as "no genuinely thinking person, no really astute observer, looking at the Negro in modern American life, could find his condition even now a first aid to laughter. That condition may be variously deemed hopeless, remarkable, admirable, inspiring, depressing; it can never be dubbed merely amusing."[1]

Nor could Fauset's work as a fiction writer be dubbed merely amusing. Her novels and their blend of sentimentalism, domestic fiction, and melodrama would never be classified as humor writing. "The Gift of Laughter" describes the way that social and historical forces shape the form of humor, and the generic and tonal choices in Fauset's novels also reflect cultural pressures. In those novels, Fauset celebrates domesticity and marriage; she frequently employs a didactic tone; and the plot lines feature tragedies and deaths balanced by examples of success and marriage. W.E.B. Du Bois's influential vision of the Talented Tenth uplifting the race contributes to the generic contours of Fauset's class-conscious, moralizing novels. Even as Fauset strikes a didactic, sentimental, and earnest chord throughout her novels, improvised humor serves as a grace note in characters' conversations and attitudes.

According to Fauset in "The Gift of Laughter," humor is "influenced by untoward obstacles," its expression shaped by the experience of inequities both political and artistic. Her novels reflect the historical, social, and literary pressures on a middle-class African American woman writer, and her novels dramatize the premium placed on earnestness, domesticity, and race consciousness for middle-class African American women. In "The Gift of Laughter," Fauset argues that black performers redefine themselves and the American stage through the innovations that they introduce to their narrowly defined humorous roles: "we have used the little which in those early painful days was our only approach."[2] Fauset's thoughts about stereotype and variation shed light upon her own professional role-playing and savvy genre-shaping.

"The Gift of Laughter" theorizes that masquerade permits the rewriting of roles, even within the painful context of uncomfortable stereotypes. In her fiction, Fauset explores the intersection of humor and racial and gender stereotypes. She links her black female characters' evolving understanding of themselves with their increasing access to a sense of humor. In "The Gift of Laughter," Fauset describes the humor of recent black performers as "a state of being purely subjective," being "essentially funny" rather than playing into a prescribed stereotype, and she describes this inhabitation of unabashed individuality as a gain on the earlier "objective" humor of stereotypes.[3] In her novels, Fauset traces her heroines' transformation in these terms of confining adaptation and liberating improvisation; initially, they strain to fit a type, but by the end of the novel, they embrace a multifaceted self, exchanging an adopted role for a more improvisatory and pleasurable sense of identity.

Fauset recognized that the pleasures of wit and banter were prominent features of the cultural fantasy of the modern white woman, while the New Negro woman was imagined as bourgeois, domestic, earnest, and hard-working. Fauset uses the trope of passing to establish the interracial allure of the flapper's flippant voice. For example, in Fauset's 1929 novel *Plum Bun*, Angela, an African American artist, decides to pass in white New York. When she does, she befriends Paulette, an illustrator for fashion magazines. Angela marvels at Paulette's conversational audacity: "As a *raconteuse* she had a faint, delicious malice which usually made any recital of her adventures absolutely irresistible."[4] Angela emulates Paulette's example by "adopt[ing] Paulette's cleverness" (211). This voice is associated with professionalism and modern print culture. Angela begins working for a "well-known journal of fashion," and this job grants her the cultural status that she longed for: "now I'm sophisticated" (235–236). Indeed, Angela banters fluently with the members of the Algonquin Round Table (269).

As is par for the course in novels of passing, Angela's adopted role, however professionally satisfying, generates confusion about her identity and her loyalties. She associates wit with whiteness and longs for a lost cultured past, locating that cultivation in Europe: "Angela half suspected that she was in this company assisting more nearly at the restoration of a lost art than in any other circles in the world save in the corresponding society of London" (269). With the oversight typical of the heroine who strays over the color-line, Angela overlooks the potent roles that humor and irony play in the community she abjured: "coloured Americans . . . [were] whimsical, humorous, bitter, impatiently responsible, yet still responsible" (216). These black urban coteries match a capacity for wit with a commitment to social responsibility that the Algonquin Round Table seems (in this fictionalized form) to ignore.

As Angela realizes the limitations of the seemingly sophisticated white circles she moves in, so too does her understanding of the force and substance of humor become more complex. Unaware that she is black, Angela's white lover Roger spurns her nonetheless—not because of her race but because of her lack of social status and money. In fleeing one instance of her supposed inferiority, Angela is dogged by another. As this irony dawns on her, Angela imagines life as a laughing, bitter New York woman: "it's an idea that has slowly taken possession of me since I've been in New York. The tall woman is Life and the idea is that she laughs at us; laughs at the poor people who fall into the traps which she sets for us" (280). This image personifies humor with a naturalist sensibility. Broader social forces like race and class surround the individual who struggles against an implacable fate.

Rather than embrace Angela's despairing vision of the cosmic joke that victimizes the helpless individual, Fauset demonstrates that ironic sensibilities and humor provide methods of revenge, reveal concealed truths, and motivate and indeed facilitate self-assertion. "Life was bitter," Angela reflects, "but it was amusingly bitter; if she could laugh at it she might be able to outwit it yet" (316). The individual who can laugh at political injustices can also raise a defiant voice. When she wins an art contest because a black painter has been disqualified, Angela mocks the judges when she informs them that she, the runner-up, is also black: "Angela laughed in his face. . . . She could hardly contain herself" (347). This revelation is her joke on them and on the institutional racism they represent. Now more than a status symbol, banter allows her to rebuke reigning powers.

The thematic trajectory of humor in *Plum Bun* matches the narrative unfolding of a novel of passing as a novel of education. In a novel of passing, the biracial protagonist often learns to value African American roots and community after exploring the false promises of passing for white.[5] Fauset employs the structure of her novel to educate Angela and her reader about the benefits of racial community and the potential of humor. In fact, she interweaves these two didactic strands. Humor begins as a symbol of sophistication associated with white culture and then gradually becomes aligned with Angela's increasing consciousness of social ills and her growing bonds with friends within the black community. Irony begins as the passive recognition of racism's contradictions and far-reaching consequences, and by the end of the novel irony helps Angela challenge racial injustices.

Fauset's preoccupation with wit and banter befits her social role within the Harlem Renaissance; Fauset was famous for the literary salons she held in her uptown apartment.[6] Her belletrist reputation diminished her critical legacy. David Leavering Lewis, for example, mocks an early Fauset novel for its snobbery: "*There Is Confusion* . . . [was] a saga of the sophisticated in which French and occasionally German tripped from the protagonists' tongues as readily as precise English; a novel about people with good bloodlines whose presence in the Algonquin Hotel dining room—but for a telltale swarthiness—would have been *tout à fait comme il faut*."[7] In *Plum Bun*, Fauset places her heroine in that very Algonquin dining room that Lewis alludes to, and she questions color as an inevitably "telltale" signifier. In spite of Lewis's impatience with Fauset's class-conscious literary self-positioning, her topical concern with sophistication delineates a fraught area of intersection in interracial New York literary culture. The growth of a bourgeois black professional class supported the flourishing of artistic and literary output in the Harlem Renaissance; as Angela's misapprehensions about wit demonstrate, however, an interracial public still associated sophistication and coterie with European cultivation, which led Zora Neale Hurston, for example, to embrace folk traditions and southern food as tokens of cultural independence.[8]

While Fauset faced criticism from peers and later critical dismissal as a novelist for her sentimental plots and bourgeois sensibilities, feminist critics have since established that conflicts between possible racial and gender roles for women propel her fiction. As Ann duCille puts it, Fauset's "fiction tackles some of the most significant social contradictions of the emerging modern era, including the questions of black female agency, cultural authenticity, and racial and sexual iconography."[9] Similarly, Sandra Gilbert and Susan Gubar argue that Fauset's novels confront the mutually exclusive and race-specific feminine roles of the (white) new woman and the (black) New Negro woman. Drawn to particular aspects of these feminine types but unsatisfied by these roles, Fauset's characters, Gilbert and Gubar explain, "act out the liabilities and the liminality conferred on black women by the social revolutions associated with feminism and the Harlem Renaissance."[10] This sense of conflict, doubleness, and liminality finds expression in Fauset's use of ironies, both structural and local.[11]

One site of liminality that Fauset explores in her novels is the world of modern print culture. African American women consumed magazines produced on both sides of the color-line, and Fauset describes the pleasure that her female characters take in magazines and the careers that some of them find in the magazine industry.[12] Fauset depicts black magazine readers who initially view the glamour of whiteness with desire. They come to recognize that their experience of racial inequality and economic struggle grants them ironic knowledge that renders the hedonistic and self-promoting white magazine producers ridiculous and even infantile by comparison. Fauset treats humor as a valuable element of modern magazine culture, even as she dramatizes the ill effects of buying into the narcissistic fantasies generated by white press magazines.[13] Fauset's conclusion that the combination of humor and self-regard associated with smartness could be leavening rather than deflating is by no means inevitable. In *Quicksand*, for example, a novel by Fauset's contemporary Nella Larsen, the siren song of sophistication associated with white print culture engulfs rather than educates her heroine, as I discuss later in the chapter. Through wry tones and ironic juxtapositions, both writers register the gap between black and white print cultures and the feminine roles that they model and encourage.

Magazines in Black and White

The contrast between the titles of black press magazines from the 1920s and smart magazines from that period indicate their divergent goals for their readers. The black middle class should focus on remedying "*The Crisis*" and seeking "*Opportunity*," the magazine titles suggest. Meanwhile, the white middle class could fritter away its time on the latest "*Vogue*" on display at "*Vanity Fair*." *The Crisis* explicitly criticized the tones and topics of the white press. Reviewing *Quicksand* for the *Crisis*, Du Bois commented: "White folk will not like this book. It is not nearly nasty enough for New York columnists."[14] While *Vanity Fair* and the *New Yorker* popularized African American art forms and sometimes promoted black celebrities, they ignored black readers. The advertising pages either omitted black figures altogether or presented them as servants.[15]

As this allusion to servants might suggest, middlebrow magazines were preoccupied with class and class aspiration. Lewis disparages the class fantasies that black press publications communicated: "Publications overflowed with Horatio Algers successes.... Not only newspapers like *Amsterdam News* and *New York Age* but critical organs like *The Crisis* and *Opportunity* joyously catalogued every known triumph over adversity as particular manifestations of universal Afro-American progress. The supposedly socialist *Messenger* . . . sometimes read more like sleek, snobbish *Vanity Fair* than a protest periodical."[16] This focus on class mobility emphasized African American cultivation and achievement. Much as the smart magazines promised that white middle-class America could belong to the smart set, black press magazines imagined a future with a secure black middle class (a future made much more uncertain by the arrival of the Great Depression).[17] Recognizing the economic challenges and cultural prejudices faced by African Americans, the *Crisis* advocated seriousness and hard work as the corollaries of middle-class attainment. By contrast, the smart magazines, communicating a fantasy of easily traversed class barriers to white professionals, depicted leisure and expenditure as the signs of class ascension.

Consequently, the treatment and use of humor in these magazines were distinct. If we imagine humor as a form of cultural currency in modern print culture, the smart magazines were profligate, while the black press magazines saved their cash for a cause. In his *Crisis* review of Fauset's novel *There Is Confusion*, Alain Locke applauded the author's "Quaker faith," "sober optimism," and "discipline of experience."[18] In spite of such overt espousals of earnestness, the *Crisis* occasionally used humor to underline political goals. A 1924 *Crisis* article about black people internalizing racist standards quipped that "The 'Age of Innocence' is, in the final analysis, just a little white baby girl." Consigning humor to asides, the essay concludes with an earnest aphorism and exhortation: "it is not what other people think that harms . . . but what we think of ourselves . . . we cannot escape the challenge to our teachers, to the writers of advertising copy of our business, to our press, our pulpit, and to all of us as individuals. It must be a conscious and concerted fight against a definite and dangerous menace."[19] This tonal flexibility characterizes Fauset's novels as well, which move from didacticism to a celebration of humor and back again.

The *Crisis* also illustrated the irony of prejudices that constrain worthy individuals. In his article "The Technique of Race Prejudice," Du Bois relates the story of an outstanding black medical student who was denied an internship at a Philadelphia hospital: "Dr. [Lillian Atkins] Moore is one of the best students that the Women's Medical College ever had—which was unfortunate. Colored people ought to be fools and when they are geniuses it makes trouble." The racist administration of public institutions turns genius into a social problem rather than a social benefit. Racist logics and actions reveal the stupidities of racism rather than the limitations of African Americans: "There is no doubt about it, colored Americans have got to quit having brains; it's putting our white friends in all sorts of embarrassing positions."[20] Du Bois uses irony to undercut the authority of prejudice and segregation.

The *Crisis* thus modeled versions of humor and irony that could support racial political goals. This magazine also belittled versions of femininity in white press magazines where advertisements emphasized attaining clear (white) skin and displayed iconic white (and iconically white) women.[21] One short story in the February 1925 *Crisis*, "The Bewitched Sword" by Ola Calhoun Morehead, depicts a black flapper named Mary with "newly shingled hair." She dreams of owning a chic hat that she read about in an advertisement. Anticipating her shopping conquest and the envy it would inspire in her peers, Mary predicts that "she would laugh last and best!" She finds the "hat of her dreams," but her elation in the department store cannot survive the streetcar: "She had scarcely sat down to weave more dreams when suddenly, '*I won't sit by a nigger!*' And Mary felt her knees rudely jostled as a tall blonde woman strode past her into the aisle. Crash! fell Mary's dream towers and instantly, she was swept back into the world of reality."[22] The tall blonde bars the black flapper's entrance into the symbolic world of luxury. The world of reality is one of racism and conflict rather than acquisition and satisfaction.

This story demonstrates the moral message of the *Crisis*: earnest hard work, political activism, and racial community should be the hallmarks of the black middle class. *Vanity Fair, Harper's Bazaar,* and the *New Yorker* did not promote parallel virtues. The *Crisis* advertising pages promoted schools, insurance companies, black dolls, and "race records," in lieu of the ads for clothes and cars that dominated the white magazines' ad pages. Ads for hair straighteners and wigs were heavily featured in the *Crisis,* and one or two advertisements for cosmetics appeared in almost every issue.[23] However, the rhetorical pitch of these make-up ads promised political solidarity rather than simply individual beauty. An advertisement for Madam C. J. Walker Hair and Skin Preparations suggests that the product contributes to both personal beauty and the entrepreneurial successes of the race: "Made and sold by members of our own Race," these preparations allow "you too . . . [to] have long, luxurious hair and a beauty-kissed complexion." This advertisement for Madam C. J. Walker's proclaims that this business and these products are "GLORIFYING OUR WOMANHOOD."[24] By contrast, when a 1928 Coty ad in the *New Yorker* imagines "glorifying" something, it is only the "radiant complexion" of its customers.[25]

The *Crisis* advocated a vision of black femininity that eschewed the hedonism of the modern white flapper. In "Buyers of Dreams," in the December 1921 *Crisis,* Ethel M. Caution offers a fable for the modern girl. In a shop, three young ladies buy dreams for their futures. The first dreamer wants luxury; the second wants a career; and the last wants a family. The third girl chastises the other two for their frivolous dreams. She admonishes the first for materialism and decadence: "It costs a lot, but we can't always measure worth by cost. That dream is for the society butterfly. It means fine clothes, and expensive parties; late hours and breakfasts in bed; yachts and trips; perfume and paint; and in the end, emptiness and dissatisfaction." She dismisses the second for self-centeredness: "the girl who wants a career . . . wants a dream that means bringing the world to her feet for some wonderful bit of work she has cornered. She doesn't realize the emptiness of mere fame and of work done just for personal glory." Worst of all, the wise third girl reminds her foolish peers, a career leads to spinsterhood: "Neither do I want your dream of a career to end my life in loneliness and emptiness and bitterness. This is a dream I shall buy. Love, babies, life!" One can hardly imagine this triad appearing in either *Vanity Fair* or the *New Yorker,* certainly not in the works of the professionally successful and childless Millay and Parker.[26] (Fauset, who married late in life, was also childless.) This parable exemplifies the pressure on black women to be domestic, earnest, and maternal.

The promises of hard work on the one hand (New Negro womanhood) and hedonism and ambition on the other (flapperdom) seem lopsided in their attribution of personal pleasures. It is easy to see how hedonism might seem preferable to self-sacrifice. In the May 1921 *Crisis*, an ad for the National Training School for Women and Girls announced "EVERY GIRL SHOULD LEARN A TRADE." The ad emphasized practicality, thrift, and security: "It is better than a life insurance. It pays while you live. It puts dollars into your pocket. It makes you independent. Give your daughter a trade in a school that has high standards, and you put her on a safe road to success in life."[27] By contrast, an ad for the Condé Nast School Service in the July 1923 *Vanity Fair* promoted "CHARM *in the modern girl*" and assured readers that such schools provided girls with "a good education, social experience, and a knowledge of such things as dancing, music, expression, and the management of a household and servants." White girls could fail socially: "From the very beginning of their social life, they are saved from the embarrassing mistakes of inexperience," but black girls faced the threat of dangerous roads rather than drawing room derision.[28]

This sense of the social and physical threats facing black women resulted in an espousal of attitudinal seriousness. In the March 1923 issue of *Opportunity*, Eva D. Bowles reminded "Educated Colored Women" that "more and more the thoughtful woman is realizing that the business of living is a serious matter."[29] Bowles urged her reader to embrace "courage and strength" and "to take no backward steps, but to go on thru the doors already open . . . [and] press into other realms."[30] In the smart magazines, Dorothy Parker crowed about the joys of laziness, and Robert Benchley catalogued the delights of doing nothing in the office. Black press magazines emphasized the seriousness of the stakes even in consumerism, while white press magazines generally assumed that their audience had the disposable income and social freedoms to please themselves.

One 1929 *New Yorker* cartoon, however, acknowledged the barriers that race and income posed to the fulfillment of the consumer fantasy. In this cartoon, a black child stares into a shop window.[31] The window's contents, a white mannequin and the white fur she sports, stops the child in her tracks, while her mother walks on. The caption in her mother's voice reads: "*Come on—don' stand there gettin' ideas in yo' head.*" The dialect in the caption betrays the potentially condescending and racist dimensions of the cartoon.[32] The two white figures in the cartoon, the mannequin and a female passerby who wears the same fur, both have faces. The two black figures have their backs turned to the viewer. The race of the mother is marked by her speech, and the daughter's race is symbolized by her stand-out curls. In spite of these caricatures, the cartoon alludes critically to the erasure of black femininity in luxury consumer culture. Further, these fantasies of white femininity seem unappealing. The mannequin sticks its nose in the air, while the white passerby flaunts an implacable and unsympathetic Art Deco profile that seems cold in light of the child's vulnerability and awe. The little black girl is both tantalized by and barred from luxury-as-whiteness, hence her mother's admonition "don' stand there gettin' ideas." These ideas can be gotten far more easily than the wealth, the status, or the whiteness they presume.

In *Plum Bun*, Fauset also depicts the consumer scene as the birthplace of the desire for the luxuries associated with whiteness. As a child, Angela accompanies her mother to the department store. Fauset's narrator possesses the knowing perspective that the child lacks: "The daughter could not guess that if the economic status or the racial genius of coloured people had permitted them to run vast and popular department stores her mother would have been there. She drew for herself certain clearly formed conclusions which her subconscious mind thus codified: First, that the great rewards of life—riches, glamour, pleasure—are for white-skinned people only . . . [she felt that] coloured people were to be considered fortunate only in the proportion in which they measured up to the physical standards of white people" (17–18). Angela associates the images of white people with "riches, glamour, and pleasure" and accepts that as her physical standard.[33] Because this operation goes on in the "subconscious mind," there appears to be no corrective opportunity for conscious resistance.

Much like Fauset's department store, the smart magazines helped create a fantasy world in which white people were elegant and black people were either crude or exotic. In the same *New Yorker* issue that featured the cartoon of the black girl at the shop window, an advertisement for the theater shows Al Jolson in blackface.[34] Another cartoon depicts a stereotyped black caddy whose exaggerated and caricatured features throw into relief the Art Deco sophistication of the white golfer he serves.[35] On another page of that same issue, pirate characters of indeterminate ethnicity tantalize the bored middle-class reader to break his humdrum routine and visit Bermuda.[36] These illustrations assume a white viewer oblivious to or amused by (possibly both) racial stereotype on the one hand and racial exoticism on the other. When Fauset's novels place a black reader in this consumer scene, the implicit exaltation of whiteness at the expense of blackness becomes apparent.

However surprising it might seem in light of this problematic use of race in their pages, smart magazines and the subcultures formed by their producers—editors, writers, and illustrators—provided a point of inter-racial literary connection in New York. *Vanity Fair* was the first magazine to purchase poems by Langston Hughes.[37] In his autobiography, Hughes writes about his friend, artist E. Simms Campbell, and his ambition to draw *New Yorker* cartoons (an ambition he realized successfully).[38] In the 1920s, *Vanity Fair* featured articles by Carl Van Vechten and art by Covarrubias that introduced white readers to Harlem Renaissance art and artists. Smart magazine writers also socialized with Harlem writers. NAACP leader Walter White threw cocktail parties for Harlem lumi-naries and members of the Algonquin Round Table, including Dorothy Parker who may have used such gatherings as the basis for her story "Ar-rangement in Black and White."[39]

The accounts of these interracial parties implied that clever conver-sation provided a signal of intellectual attainment and shared sophis-tication. Lewis writes: "Walter [White], a superlative conversational-ist—helped give Harlem cocktail gatherings a brilliant reputation."[40] Wit betokened intellect and cultural conversance; moreover, wit extended the tantalizing possibility that the exile could move into the middle, that the reviled could turn into the envied with a well-chosen word. Suspect-ing that racist prescriptions and institutions could not be ignored or so easily overcome, novelist Larsen traces the potential costs of assimilation into an urbane culture that seems to belong to all New Yorkers but in fact marks out the select few. Her novel *Quicksand* illustrates the pitfalls of smartness for the unwary. Larsen's pessimism about the fantasy of social mobility and self-realization by way of wit provides an important contrast to Fauset's treatment of sophistication and humor as corollaries to achievement and happiness. It was by no means clear that the way out of self-effacement was to enshrine the sophisticated self, for Larsen imagines that shrine could be a tomb.

Quicksand and Quietude: Urbanity as Passivity

In *Quicksand*, Larsen's heroine Helga Crane, a biracial woman, ex-periences a keen "craving for smartness, for enjoyment."[41] In this novel, Helga moves from the South to the North, abroad to Copenhagen, and back again in her search for a coherent identity. Ultimately, she sinks into the morass of marriage to a minister in Alabama, where she bears children and loses her sense of self. In each context that Helga enters, she must repress a part of her identity. She seeks pleasure to fulfill this lack, and, in fact, the pursuit of sexual pleasure leads to her ultimately unsatisfactory marriage. One pleasure that temporarily enchants Helga is the sophistication of salon culture. In New York, Helga discovers a Harlem community united in their espousal of the same delights described in the pages of *Vanity Fair*, the *New Yorker*, and *Vogue*. Larsen read *Vanity Fair*, and her friend Carl Van Vechten wrote for that periodical.[42] Meeting the Harlem elite, Helga delights in "Their sophisticated cynical talk, their elaborate parties, the unobtrusive correctness of their clothes and homes." These Harlem sophisticates scorn southern culture: "Her New York friends looked with contempt and scorn on Naxos [Larsen's fictional version of Tuskegee] and all its works. This gave Helga a pleasant sense of avengement" (46). Sardonic humor allows Helga and her New York peers to hold themselves above Alabama. They choose an "unobtrusive" urbanity over a past of slavery and racial injustice. In the course of its consideration of sophistication and cosmopolitanism, *Quicksand* deals with migration and deracination, interracialism and erasure.

In the modern migration to cities, urban anonymity facilitated metropolitan citizenship and self-reinvention. Larsen, treating this identity amnesia ambivalently, acknowledges the city's generation of new professional opportunities and social circles but also observes that racial codes still determine the reception of the new city dweller.[43] For example, Helga's boss Mrs. Hayes-Rore instructs her amanuensis to hide her biracial background when she moves to New York. Suggestively, the publicity about Larsen from this period also highlights anonymity and adopted city citizenship. A newspaper article on Larsen laboriously avoids revealing her name until the end of the profile: "this person, 5 feet 2 inches in height and weighing 122 pounds, is not a native New Yorker." The article exalts Larsen's flapper-like frame and her adopted urbanity. The article so embraces the conceit that Larsen is both invention and apotheosis of modern New York that it treats her as a type: "'Madame X,' or whatever you want to call her, is a modern woman; for she smokes, wears her dresses short, does not believe in religion, churches and the like."[44]

Like Larsen in this publicity profile, defined by her clothes and her iconoclasm, in *Quicksand* Helga claims citizenship in the city through taste (knowing the right clothes to buy and cars to drive) and cynical humor. She "sneers" at a newcomer to New York: "On Helga's face there had come that pityingly sneering look peculiar to imported New Yorkers when the city of their adoption is attacked by alien Americans. With polite contempt she inquired: 'And is that all you don't like?'" (103). Of course, language like "import" and "adoption" suggests the fluidity of such categorizations. Helga's New York loyalty is precarious, and her desire to define insiders and outsiders is piqued by her anxiety about her own potentially alien status.

Nonetheless, Larsen does associate certain powers of self-expression and rebellion with New York citizenship. The New York emphasis on individuality promised to provide a weapon against the African American humility promoted by Booker T. Washington at Tuskegee, fictionalized here as Naxos. In Larsen's novel, this sense of individuality and resilience and the associated lifestyle of cultural and sexual experimentation (Helga visits a cabaret in Harlem and experiences religious ecstasy at a storefront church) differentiate New York from Chicago, which is represented by the Y.W.C.A. and various programs of genteel racial uplift. Anne Grey, the Harlem salon leader, by contrast "carried herself as queens are reputed to bear themselves, and probably do not" (47). New York for Helga carries the allure of individual, personal power, refinement not self-effacing but self-exalting.

Accordingly, Helga finds herself drawn to other women who are fashionable and smart. Anne Grey in New York is "a tall slim creature beautifully dressed in a cool green tailored frock," and her aunt in Copenhagen is "a smart woman in olive-green" (45). She wears a "carelessly trailing purple scarf and correct black hat," and Helga admires "the perfection of her aunt's costume." This self-presentation, part Isadora Duncan, part Coco Chanel, assuages "all [Helga's] fears and questionings" (67). Clothing provides an attitudinal armor projecting coolness, carelessness, correctness, and perfection. When Helga enters the city for the first time, other people "noticed her, admired her clothes, but that was all, for the self-sufficient uninterested manner adopted instinctively as a protective measure for her acute sensitiveness, in her child days, still clung to her" (37). Larsen indicates that her manner, worn like "clothes," masks Helga's vulnerability.

Larsen implies that Helga's clothes and manner are drawn in part from the magazines that she reads. Larsen depicts Helga tidying and decorating her apartment by "plac[ing] the magazines in ordered carelessness" (59). Helga forswears her interest in white culture in spite of these hints that she bases her image in part upon its fashion precepts: "While the continuously gorgeous panorama of Harlem fascinated her, thrilled her, the sober mad rush of white New York failed entirely to stir her. Like thousands of other Harlem dwellers, she patronized its shops, its theaters, its art galleries, and its restaurants, and read its papers, without considering herself a part of the monster. . . . For her this Harlem was enough. Of that white world, so distant, so near, she asked only indifference." Helga insists that she has not been stirred by white New York and yet she patronizes the venues where it promotes, sells, and mediates its urban middlebrow culture—not only physical locations but also publications, "papers." Although it would be easy to parse "the monster" in this passage as "white New York," one could also read "the monster" as consumer culture and its marketing of the fresh, the smart, the urbane. Helga contributes her disposable income to the monster, just as she bases her ideas of happiness—"the things which she had now come to desire, a home like Anne's, cars of expensive makes such as lined the avenue, clothes and furs from Bendel's and Revillon Frères, servants, and leisure"—on its consumer promises (48).

These consumer promises are entangled with a blasé attitude that Larsen depicts as a form of historical and cultural repression. To claim primary citizenship as an urban sophisticate relies on forswearing the rural past of slavery and continuing racial exploitation. While watching a "picturesque parade" of African American veterans in the Harlem streets, Helga reflects that "when mental doors were deliberately shut on those skeletons that stalked lively and in full health through the consciousness of every person of Negro ancestry in America—conspicuous black, obvious brown, or indistinguishable white—life was intensely amusing, interesting, absorbing, and enjoyable" (98). Humor and amusement became forms of historical, political, and personal amnesia. Larsen used the sophisticated black New Yorker's "contempt and scorn" for the rest of the country—similar to the *New Yorker's* mockery of rural newspapers and H. L. Mencken's famous disparagements of the "booboisie"—to describe a psychological and social effect of the Great Migration. Moving to the North extended the hope of ridding oneself of the painful legacy of the South. Helga's return to the South at the end of the book suggested that such a quick forgetting is impossible.

Anne Grey exemplifies the contradictions of bourgeois identity for African American women. Anne does not listen to "primitive" jazz. The narrator reports that: "She hated white people with a deep and burning hatred. . . . But she aped their clothes, their manners, and their gracious ways of living." Anne's reading practices also betray her cultural confusion. She obsessively reads the black press, "all the complaining magazines, and . . . all the lurid newspapers spewed out by the Negro yellow press." Yet she is also conversant in the celebrity culture of the white mass media: "Like the despised people of the white race, she preferred

Pavlova to Florence Mills, John McCormack to Taylor Gordon, Walter Hampden to Paul Robeson" (51). Anne's attitude combines these two tones, the would-be sophistication of smart New York culture and the didacticism of the New Negro: "And she was interesting, an odd confusion of wit and intense earnestness" (48).

Helga views the contradictions in Anne's character with ironic amusement: "Helga had been entertained by this racial ardor in one so little affected by racial prejudice as Anne, and by her inconsistencies," and she longs to express this irony in a joke: "Sometimes it took all her self-control to keep from tossing sarcastically at Anne Ibsen's remark about there being assuredly something very wrong with the drains, but after all there were other parts of the edifice" (51–52). Helga observes the smart set around her and sees its myopias and hypocrisies. From within the middle class, she mocks the middle ground. In this case, Helga questions Anne's claim to black authenticity when her bourgeois lifestyle is largely defined by mores and tastes advocated by white businesses and publications.

Larsen does not present humor as a utopian, transcendent strategy for self-actualization in this novel. On the contrary, Helga's relationship to humor develops over the course of the novel, shifting with each of her circumstances. She uses sarcasm in Naxos to resist the conformity, drabness, and humility of that lifestyle. When Robert Anderson, the superintendent at Naxos, calls Helga a "lady of good breeding," Helga's instinct to make a joke—"the joke is on you"—breaks out of the refined, class-conscious mold of the lady and also displays the falsity of the gender and racial hierarchies that "good breeding" advocates. At Naxos, Helga uses joking to sabotage her status; in New York, it confirms her status and grants her a sense of superiority. This sense of control is short-lived, however, as Helga's uncontrollable laughter becomes a sign of her increasing hysteria as she surrenders this search for self.

Larsen closed the book by treating smartness as an opiate of the middle class, a class and gender fantasy that facilitates passivity and self-erasure instead of self-assertion: "It was so easy and so pleasant to think about freedom and cities, about clothes and books, about the sweet mingled smell of Houbigant and cigarettes in softly lighted rooms filled with inconsequential chatter and laughter and sophisticated tuneless music. It was so hard to think out a feasible way of retrieving all these agreeable, desired things. . . . So she dozed and dreamed in snatches of sleeping and waking, letting time run on. Away" (136). The dream of "freedom and cities," "clothes and books," the delight in "inconsequential chatter," and the perfume brand "Houbigant," reflect the world imagined and sold by the smart magazines. Helga dreams this dream not in New York but in rural Alabama, which links the dream of sophistication to national circulation and the mass media fantasy of urbanity that is not locatable on the actual isle of Manhattan. Larsen suggested that such pastimes "let time run on" and represent little more than a "dream" of "desired things," things that supplant the self and action. Fauset, however, insisted that a crucial quality of individuality and voice can be gained or restored through the fantasy of smartness—a strength linked to urbanity but not dependent on its rhetoric of narcissism.

"I'll never be a tame cat again": Femininity and Humor in Fauset's Novels

The *Crisis* magazine advertised Jessie Fauset's novels as windows onto a refined urban world, "describing . . . the life among the intellectual circles developing in northern cities among colored people."[45] As Gilbert and Gubar note, Fauset's decorousness and intellectual pedigree (she was the first black female graduate of Cornell University) were fetishized as symbols of Talented Tenth attainment and New Negro womanhood.[46] In his autobiography, Hughes both flatters and undercuts Fauset: "From that moment on I was deceived in writers, because I thought they would all be good-looking and gracious like Miss Fauset—especially those whose books I liked or whose poems were beautiful."[47] In Hughes's description of Fauset, gracious poetry and gracious manners coincide—allowing room to dismiss both because, as he forecasts in the phrase "I was deceived," Hughes must lose his innocence and realize that grace has little to do with modern writing. "Miss Fauset" must be superseded for this male Harlem Renaissance poet to sing his gutsy and bold blues. Hughes was not the only one to see in Fauset the constraining model of an old-fashioned femininity. Larsen, too, though she wrote two articles for Fauset's children's magazine *The Brownies' Book*, spent little time with Fauset and resisted her influence. In his biography of Larsen, George Hutchinson speculates that the all-black tea party that bores Helga in *Quicksand* is Larsen's criticism of Fauset's salons.[48]

While her peers may have found Fauset's literary influence constraining, for the *Crisis*, Fauset served as a sophisticated icon of the professional magazine writer even after she stepped down from her editorship in 1926. The magazine reports her travels to Paris, and she writes of exotic Algiers.[49] Laura Wheeler illustrates Fauset's May 1928 article about Algiers with a drawing of high-heeled Fauset sporting bobbed hair and a suitcase. Her smart appearance counters the typical depictions of black figures in periodicals of the white press.[50] The two white people in the illustration wear heavy coats and scarves. They are shapeless and darker than the trim Fauset whose ensemble is mostly white. Wheeler's visual play with white and black is underscored by Fauset's verbal play with these categories in the title of her article, "Dark Algiers the White." The caption for this illustration, a quotation from Fauset's travel essay, emphasizes her cultural conversance: "Once more we exchange adieux." Her skill in languages and her politesse establish Fauset's superiority next to the white Algerians begging her for money.[51]

In this article, Fauset emphasizes her worldliness through her blasé tone. Even this exotic clime seems old hat to a New Yorker: "So completely had my first glimpse of the city prepared me for a manifestation of life totally different from any which I had known that I was heartbroken to find myself before an array of shops . . . such as one encounters every day in the Boulevard des Italiens or on Forty-second Street. It was unnecessary to close one's eyes to imagine oneself in Paris or New York."[52] Nothing is new to a cosmopolite because major cities like New York form microcosms of the rest of the globe. To Fauset's experienced eye, even the exotic seems tawdry and obvious: "It is too bad that movie-dom has spoiled the integrity of this scene; our sophisticated eyes find in it a touch of artificiality."[53] Thanks to this worldliness and sophistication, the unfamiliar can be colonized. Fauset first describes Arab women as an enigma because of their veils and then later converses with them "after the fashion of ladies calling the world over." Even this conversation seems to bore her, as their topics are merely "polite and amiable banalities."[54]

Private conversation and cultured banter were central to Fauset's projected image of sophistication.[55] She also published light verse about disappointed loves. In "La Vie C'est la Vie," Fauset employs the same theme of cyclical, futile desire that Parker made her poetic trademark:

But he will none of me, Nor I
Of you. Nor you of her. 'Tis said
The world is full of jests like these.—
I wish that I were dead. (lines 17–20)[56]

Fauset's speaker concludes the opposite in her later poem, "Here's April!"

This poem is reminiscent of Millay's carpe diem poems and indeed recalls the title of Millay's volume of poetry, *Second April*:

> For Spring—sweet April's here in tree and grass!
> Oh foolish heart to fret so with your grief!
> This too shall pass! (lines 16–18)[57]

Light verse links Fauset's literary persona with the popular forms of the smart magazines. In a withering diagnosis of "feminine verse," Louis Untermeyer advises in a satirical *Vanity Fair* column called "Versed Aid to the Injured" that female poets should mention April in their poems and then they would sell.[58]

In spite of her emphases on sophistication and individual voice and accomplishment, Fauset as authorial icon was also often subsumed into a racial uplift ideal of the New Negro woman. Gwendolyn Bennett published "To Usward" in the *Crisis*, "*Especially dedicated to Jessie Fauset upon the event of her novel, 'There Is Confusion,'*" and this poem explicitly refuses individualism and finds it "smug": "Not self-contained with smug identity / But conscious of the strength in entity" (lines 8–9).[59] To speak for the race in this context means overcoming the self and finding identity with "upward" (and "usward") mobility. Certainly, Fauset's voice in the *Crisis* frequently communicates a similar tone advocating unity and earnestness. In an October 1922 article in the *Crisis* on "The 13th Biennial Meeting of the N.A.C.W.," Fauset applauds "the sincerity, [and] the forthrightness of womanhood."[60] There seems little room for smartness and irony in this vision of femininity, and the domestic and sentimental plots of Fauset's novels, usually bringing her talented heroines together with an appropriately exceptional black man with a mission, just in time for those heroines to sacrifice their goals to his, might be (and have sometimes been) read as easily consonant with this vision of New Negro womanhood.

In Fauset's short fiction, however, she uses irony to tackle the shortcomings of domesticity and middle-class marriage even within the black community. For example, in Fauset's short story "Mary Elizabeth," which she published in the December 1919 *Crisis*, her self-satisfied first-person narrator is overwhelmed with nerves and headache when her servant Mary Elizabeth does not arrive in time to make breakfast: "I spent most of the day fighting the headache which always comes if I cry. For I cannot get a breakfast."[61] In the course of this story, Fauset reveals the sinister relationship between her speaker and her husband, Roger. In their self-consciously upper-class lifestyle, they embrace the power dynamics of submissive housewife and authoritative husband.

In response to her mistress's panic about the morning, Mary Elizabeth, a character from the South who speaks in dialect, tells the couple a story about her parents, slaves who were separated from each other. The speaker and her husband Roger cannot fathom the trauma of slavery.[62] When the narrator reports that Mary Elizabeth's mother remarried, Roger replies ineffectually ("My hat!"), adding a sexist rhetorical question: "Isn't that just like a woman!'" Roger assures his wife that if she slept with another man, as did Mary Elizabeth's mother, "I'd have killed you, killed you." When the narrator points out that Mary Elizabeth's father remarried, too, Roger reiterates his double standard, insisting that a man who marries "'fifty times'" could not compare to the betrayal of a woman marrying twice and not remaining loyal to her first husband (314). The story ends, ironically, with the narrator assuring the reader that the threat of hypothetical murder "healed the breach" between the married couple. This forced language of reconciliation reveals that the psychological breach between the Talented Tenth and the legacy of slavery has not been healed.

"Mary Elizabeth" examines the fracture lines in the class and gender ideals of the Talented Tenth. Fauset's novel *There Is Confusion* features the tension between black feminine domestic roles and modern women's professional ambitions. This novel follows two black women who pursue prominent careers. In childhood, working-class Maggie encounters the respectable and wealthy Marshall family and falls in love with their eldest son Philip. His sister Joanna Marshall possesses bold professional ambitions, and she disapproves of Maggie's social climbing. Joanna intervenes to break off the relationship, and a devastated Maggie embarks on ill-advised romantic entanglements before becoming a nurse and reuniting with her ailing love Philip in Europe during World War I. After pursuing a successful acting career, Joanna comes to regret her prideful ways, resigns her career ambitions, and marries her childhood friend Peter. Philip and Maggie also marry, but Philip dies so Maggie founds her own cosmetics company.

The do-se-do that Joanna and Maggie enact centers on their respective relationships to humor and magazine culture.[63] Ensconced in black culture, Joanna is earnest, serious, and, as her peers put it, "'high-brow,'" but, upon entering interracial magazine culture, she finds herself in on jokes and ironies that the white community does not recognize.[64] Joanna sees a friend passing for white and pretends to appeal to the altruism of this "white woman." She addresses her friend in front of an unsuspecting group of white auditors: "'When I think of the illimitable power for good which your people possess—.'" This punch line promises that black people possess illimitable power for good and punctures white people's condescending self-conception as the Great White Hope. This exchange brings pleasure and renewed energy: "the two girls went off into gusts of inextinguishable laughter" (233).

While this subversive humor enlivens Joanna, the superficial sparkle associated with the vogues (and *Vogue*?) of white mass media culture alienates her: "For in spite of her vogue, her unbelievably decided successes, Joanna frequently tasted the depths of ennui. She saw life as a ghastly skeleton and herself feverishly trying to cover up its bare bones with the garish trappings of her art . . . her press clippings" (233). The celebrity offered by the white press is "garish," and, by focusing on her own ambitions, Joanna has become "singularly narrow . . . and egocentric" (234). The self-centered pursuit of celebrity and wealth ignores the political realities of racial injustice and economic disparity. Joanna is unable to lose herself in this fantasy as can the white participants in this periodical culture. She realizes that these "[white] girls who had already arrived in their chosen profession" do not realize their luck. Their "successful, chattering, happy" attitudes blithely ignore the advantages that black women did not share. Joanna felt "like a battle-scarred veteran" among them. She is wounded, experienced, while these white women are unscathed, inexperienced, and unaware. Joanna cracks jokes at her newfound peers' expense: "One woman, it is true, told Joanna that she had always liked colored people. 'My father would insist on having colored servants. He preferred them.' Joanna made an impish reply: 'My father employs both white and colored servants. But he prefers the colored ones'" (235). Joanna and her white peers share class positioning and professional ambitions, but Joanna, poised for success in a white world, discovers that her white peers are laughable rather than enviable.

Working-class Maggie aspires to a higher social class. Her smartness is a sign of her social mobility, just as it promises to be for smart magazine readers who wish to circulate in the elite urban sphere. Maggie tries to be "markedly clever," and the wealthy Marshalls recognize her "quick wit" (63, 65). Maggie's fear of failure in her social ambitions renders her humor sardonic; Maggie is subject to "merciless self-attack," "horrible amusement," and "a bitterness that was worse than tears" (88, 89, 92). Smartness threatens to offer Maggie the same solipsism it presented to Joanna. Much like Helga Crane, however, Maggie learns a protective cynicism. Maggie's experience suggests that a sense of humor can be adaptive and self-affirming. Further, Maggie, like Joanna, learns this ironic perspective *because* of, not in spite of, her racial positioning.

Maggie travels to Europe as a nurse and finds inspiration in the black soldiers' perspective on the hardships that they face: "The determinedly cheerful though somewhat cynical attitude of 'the boys' in such conditions seemed to her one of the most wonderful things she had ever witnessed. It was as though they said to hostile forces: 'Oh, yes, we know you'll do for us in every possible way, slight us, cheat us, betray us, but you can't kill the real life in us, the essential us. You may make us distrustful, incredulous, disillusioned, but you can't make us despair or corrode us with bitterness'" (259–260). Fauset exploits the ambiguity of the phrase "hostile forces" to evoke the irony that prejudice in the American military was as much a "hostile force" as the German enemy.[65] Cynicism defends "the boys" from vulnerability, and ironic knowledge strengthens their hope rather than eroding it. Fauset literalizes the metaphor she used earlier to describe Joanna's position as black woman (battle-scarred). Furthermore, this identification of cynicism with "the boys" suggests that Maggie rejects constraining forms of femininity when she cultivates this stance, much as Parker aligned her persona with the modern men of the *New Yorker*. The modern woman gains in power and independence when she takes on a humorous toughness associated with masculinity. Maggie becomes an entrepreneur, a figure of middle-class ambition and commercial smarts.

Though both women end in appropriate domestic destinies, Fauset introduces an ironic note into Maggie's happy ending that suggests the frustrations Fauset may have encountered working for W.E.B. Du Bois on the *Crisis* magazine. The novel initially raises the promise of the black press magazine, hinting at a utopian professional future where black women can work alongside black men. Maggie tends to the ailing Philip, and they concoct a plan to start a magazine. Philip conceives of this magazine as a corollary to an organization serving "the interests of coloured people," like the NAACP, which sponsored Du Bois's publication. Maggie promises Philip domestic and professional bliss: "you'll take up your magazine again. I'll be your secretary, your assistant, your whole force" (266). This girl Friday sublimates her individual ambitions to bolstering Philip's "force." But Fauset mocks the illusion of such harmonious cooperation just when Maggie proclaims her happy conversion: "I have never spent five minutes in trying to help our cause . . . I have been a selfish, selfish woman always—looking out for my own personal advantage. . . . But now we've found ourselves, Philip. You have learned ordinary personal consideration and I have learned unselfishness—to a degree" (267). Courtship plots frequently highlight such mutual moral edification; he has abandoned pride, while she decides to fight prejudice. However, Maggie's last statement ironically twists what otherwise seems to be an earnest embrace of reform. Informing her lover that he has finally "learned ordinary personal consideration," Maggie tweaks his pomposity. The tag "to a degree" adds reserve and even reversibility to her espoused embrace of "unselfishness." These rhetorical checks placed on the utopian vision of this harmonious pair are mirrored in the structure of the novel. This imagined future of magazine collaboration never comes to pass. While the magazine seems an opportunity for the sexes to cooperate for the good of the race, the only figure who steps confidently into the "new" future—whether that of the New Woman, the New Negro, both or neither—is thoroughly modern Maggie.

In Maggie, we see one of Fauset's few references to what she was able to accomplish for the *Crisis*. Maggie and Philip's symbolic but unfulfilled marriage offers an analogy to Fauset's relationship with W.E.B. Du Bois.[66] Like Maggie, who promises to be both secretary and assistant for Philip, Fauset also executed the bulk of the work in the *Crisis* office on Du Bois's behalf.[67] While Fauset certainly admired Du Bois, perhaps in the spunky Maggie tending the sickly Philip we can see an authorial acknowledgment of her own accomplishment as indispensable amanuensis, organizer, and editor.[68] Perhaps in Philip's death Fauset took minor revenge on Du Bois who faced his own deficits in "ordinary personal consideration," to borrow Maggie's phrase.[69]

Maggie's discovery of her voice is only one example in Fauset's oeuvre when humor challenges the reign of New Negro feminine modesty. For example, Laurentine in *The Chinaberry Tree* embodies this self-effacing domestic ideal; she is both a modest woman and an excellent housekeeper. Her cousin Melissa, by contrast, embraces vanity and narcissism, which she learns in part through her passion for white magazines and fashion. These cousins embody the two extremes of the modern woman type: the New Negro feminine role, limiting because it allows for little sense of self, and the white magazine model, damaging because it insists on self-obsession. The narrator reports that Melissa is "the embodiment" of "liveliness, gayety, and laughter," and these qualities sustain her obliviousness to real life and its trials (108). Her story warns of the costs of narcissism through the figure of incest. Melissa does not know when she comes to live with her aunt and cousin that her mother had an affair with a married man in their town. In wishing to find a mate as refined and stylish as she, Melissa finds a mate who is too close to herself—her unknown brother Malory.[70]

Throughout the novel, Melissa is preoccupied by her own appearance; her "spirits ris[e]" when she views her own "thin, supple figure" in the mirror.[71] Malory mirrors Melissa. Fauset describes him as "feminine, womanish," and Malory claims that "'you are me—I'm you'" (171). While this detail foreshadows the revelation of Melissa's paternity, it also indicates Melissa's self-obsession, which is linked to her love of magazines. Malory also loves magazines, which offer him an escape from disappointing realities: "Fortified with magazines . . . Malory felt he could endure the dank, gloomy house" (217). The white press magazines also distort Melissa's vision of marriage and domestic bliss. When Melissa describes her dreams for her future with Malory, her fantasy of domestic happiness is defined by "the advertisements of all the magazines. The wife is hustling her husband off to work . . . and in a moment the whole house is transformed. That day of all days her husband comes home to lunch . . . 'What a wife' he cries! Oh Malory, that's the way it will be with us, won't it?" (271–272). White press magazines turn house cleaning into magic; they erase labor. Melissa accepts that message unquestioningly: "Housekeeping is lots of fun nowadays if you just know how to go about it," she assures Malory (272). Melissa parrots ad copy, and her delusions are laughable, as she leaves the actual housework, even dressmaking, to Laurentine.

These magazines encourage girlish delusion and distraction from the more important and adult focuses in life. For example, when her respectable, hard-working suitor Asshur proposes, Melissa brings a "picture magazine" on their outing (89). Melissa rejects Asshur and embraces the superficial appeal of Malory. Her union with Malory, compared by Fauset to a magazine illustration, threatens to turn them into caricatures and consumers, creatures rather than subjects: "the leaves swirl[ed] about them making a magazine picture cover as they stood almost touching each other, absorbed in feeding two very tame, very greedy squirrels" (171). In setting this scene, Fauset casts Melissa and Malory as characters in a Depression-era animal parable about what happens to the "very greedy." Their discovery that they are brother and sister appears to be their punishment for imagining that life is going to be as easy as an advertisement.

Fauset's treatment of Laurentine complicates this didactic message about print culture and frivolity. The self-sacrificing Laurentine discovers both cosmetics and the comic over the course of the novel. These discoveries facilitate her access to smart culture in Harlem, gain her a professional, established husband, and prompt her to take pleasure in the inconsequential details of daily life. While Helga's "craving for smartness" in *Quicksand* reveals the tragic incompatibility of New Negro womanhood with a sexual self, Laurentine's discovery of smartness allows her to experience the "spontaneity and fresh enjoyment" that characterizes Melissa (127). Even though Melissa is chastened, Laurentine's transformation suggests that there might be something more to humor and self-regard than the benighted banalities of the white press.

The romance plot places a high premium on humor, as banter strengthens the bond between Laurentine and Denleigh, the doctor she marries. At first, Laurentine's modesty stands in the way of her full participation in irreverent conversations. Fauset explicitly blames this rigidity on her attempt to embody a mistaken ideal: "she was the epitome of all those virtues and restraints which colored men so arrogantly demand in the women they make their wives" (124). Denleigh's approach to love chooses flirtation over admonition. At first, Laurentine is unnerved by his sense of humor: "She thought [her lover] was jesting and threw him a dubious glance," and then she is both embarrassed and excited by his sally: "[her] face grew slowly crimson." Finally, she haltingly finds her voice to respond to his flirtation: "'I suppose,' she told him slowly, 'if I were really bright I'd be able to say something clever, just like that.' She snapped her fingers" (102). Denleigh is teaching her to joke, trying to change her slow, deliberate speech into the snap of a "really bright" impromptu remark. Ultimately, his model of humor teaches her to make a joke herself: "'I've found my line now,' she laughed down at him, liking but not esteeming his frankness" (103). This frankness and facility that one can enjoy but not esteem correspond with the naughty appeals of seduction. Her lover is impressed with her (forgettable) punch line, and the love affair begins.

Fauset implies that this model of the heterosexual romance can provide the first step to a community, even an intellectual subculture that flourishes through conversation. Laurentine progresses from banter with Denleigh to a visit to the metropolis, where she discovers that other black people possess such charm and acuity: "In Harlem too she met charming and amazing people of wealth and culture and ambition, which they were satisfying according to their ability to present themselves as being just a little more advanced than anybody else; New York not caring greatly who serves it as long as it is served" (308). Laurentine's fledgling sense of humor grows with her exposure to elite urban lifestyles. Her engagement in "gay badinage" with Denleigh sparks a new sense of sensuality, self-worth, and playful defiance (305). Laurentine recognizes that she "'can never be that wretched, diffident, submissive girl again . . . I'll never be a tame cat again'" (204). Clearly, Melissa's penchant for the "flippant phrase," though curtailed by the novel's plot, has imparted something valuable to her country cousin (212). By the end of the novel, Laurentine has become "a pretty chic young woman," and she embodies smartness: "Laurentine came in at her handsomest, her beautiful head in its smart little hat nestling on the folds of her snug collar, her eyes sparkling, her cheeks glowing, her whole body radiating happiness" (162). Laurentine's posture implies sensual pleasure and self-regard, and these delights do not mislead her but help direct her to her happy ending.

Fauset's introduction makes it clear that she intended the interracial allure of the sophisticated ideal to serve as a major theme of her novel. She counsels her reader that the "sons and daughters" of the "coloured American . . . respond as completely as do the sons and daughters of European settlers to modern American sophistication" (xxxii). Fauset's verb is ambiguous. A response need not be positive, merely reactive. Melissa "responds" to sophistication by losing her sense of perspective, duty, and priority, while Laurentine adopts sophistication as a method of self-preservation and a source of romantic connection and social pleasure. Through these two examples, Fauset suggests that the modern culture of urbanity must be evaluated with skepticism and experience rather than naïveté and immersion.

Fauset nonetheless treats the ideal of the witty woman as an emblem of modernity's possibilities and also as an exemplar of survival. Melissa, recalling her mother, says that "'she was stylish—and—and modern'" and "'always gay.'" This combination of smart qualities, her attitude that was "'jolly and funny'" was also "'very courageous.'" Malory replies that to be "'*Toujours gai, toujours riant,*'" is a gift that Melissa's mother passed on to her, "'a gift, my dear, worth more than money'" (112). As Melissa learns that she has overvalued money and appearance, Laurentine learns how to inhabit a new feminine type (stylish, modern, and gay) and preserve the moral courage she manifested from the beginning. In Fauset's novel of passing, *Plum Bun*, she suggests that modern white women may be forgetting the importance of courage and political commitment in their adopted roles as flappers, professionals, and sexual free agents.

Plum Bun, Dorothy Parker, and Dis-arranging Black and White

No aspect of Fauset's work indicates the power of the flippant phrase more forcefully than its role in her novels as the marker of destructive temptation. The seemingly moralizing plot of Fauset's novel of passing, *Plum Bun*, turns Paulette, the cynical white magazine illustrator, into the voice of temptation. Much like Helga who craves smartness, the protagonist of *Plum Bun*, Angela, wishes for cleverness: "Why should I shut myself off from all the things I want most,—clever people, people who do things" (78). Angela ignores the possibility that African Americans could be "clever people . . . who do things" and passes for white to attend art school in New York. As I recounted at the beginning of the chapter, Paulette introduces Angela to a wealthy white man who makes Angela his mistress and then refuses to marry her because she is not wealthy and has no familial connections. When the art school refuses a scholarship to a deserving black student and awards Angela the prize, Angela dramatically admits that she too is black. At the end of the novel, she marries a black man who had also been passing for white, and they decide to return together to the black community. The moral seems (deceptively) clear: return to the community, remember the values of home over the corruption of the city, and reject the false promises of flapperdom.

Other black female characters in the novel demonstrate frugality, conversational caution, and racial allegiance, choices that call attention to Angela's failure to appreciate or emulate these ideals of black womanhood. Angela impulsively rejects the legacy of her parents' home in favor of three thousand dollars from their estate so that she can move to New York. Her responsible sister Virginia keeps the house, which had "increased in value" and was a "'fair enough investment'" (81). No wise-cracking flapper, Virginia "preserved a discreet silence" and "was certainly able to keep her own counsel" (210). Similarly, Miss Powell, the student who justly earns the art prize, "preserved her attitude of dignified reserve," and, instead of admiring her poise, Angela finds this responsibility and restraint dull: "Either Miss Powell was actually dull, or she had decided never to let herself go in the presence of white people" (108–109). The flapper was renowned for frankness, not discretion, and profligacy, not frugality. While passing for white, Angela embraces a "curious mixture of materialism and hedonism," which the narrator associates with "a curious detachment toward life tempered by a faint cynicism,—a detachment which enabled her to say to herself: 'Rules are for ordinary people but not for me'" (207). She has learned the heedless individualism that Paulette modeled: "[She] lived in a state of constant defiance. 'I don't care what people think,' was her slogan" (112). Over the course of the novel, Angela learns that a sense of duty or responsibility to others is not the same thing as humorlessness, and she also learns that iconoclasm can mean solipsism rather than independence. She learns that real defiance can come from caring a great deal about other people's experiences and actions. In short, Fauset revises the model of wit embodied by the white smart magazine writer in order to support the model of irony and activism that I traced in *Crisis* articles from the 1920s. In so doing, she also comments on the limited forms of irony that pass for worldliness in sophisticated white circles.

Fauset's revelation of Paulette's flaws implies a diagnosis of smart magazine culture's flaws, not only because Paulette works for magazines, but also because the segregation of magazine production exposes that modern white literary circles are not as worldly as they pretend. One white bohemian Angela meets has "the *Nation*, the *Mercury*, and the *Crisis, a magazine of the darker races*, left on the broad arm of an easy chair" (113), but Angela must pass for white to work for fashion magazines. Magazines are a locus of racial exclusion in the novel. During Angela's school days, her white best friend Mary becomes the editor of the school magazine. Mary, unaware that Angela is black, enlists Angela to help run the magazine, but their peers complain that they will not "trust my subscription money to a coloured girl" (43). The discovery of Angela's race alienates Mary, and Angela may not participate in the magazine project. As is typical in the novel of passing, Angela then questions the practicality of admitting to her race: "she began to wonder which was more important, a patent insistence on the fact of colour or an acceptance of the good things of life which could come to you in America if either you were not coloured or the fact of your race were not made known." The magazine represents not only the vocational and symbolic embodiment of the American "good things of life" but also an opportunity for interracial conversation and banter; Mary, however, will not engage in this conversation. Once she learns that Angela is black, Mary "was less frank, at times even restrained," and their conversations lack "spontaneity" (46). Verbal improvisation is a province of trust and community, and the color-line impedes that connection between the two girls. Because of Mary's prejudice and guilt and Angela's mistrust and disappointment, the genuine exchange of interracial banter seems impossible.

In a parallel to this school-age scenario, Paulette, a white magazine

illustrator, does not know Angela's racial identity. This friendship introduces Angela to banter connected with both professionalism and promiscuity, and it quickly becomes clear that Paulette relies on the latter
for economic security when she finds the fruits of the former insufficient
for her luxurious appetites. Paulette self-confessedly "use[s] her wiles as
a woman" to get what she wants and "employ[s] the qualities of men,
tenacity and ruthlessness to keep it" (105). Fauset's narration heightens
the eerie infantilization that accompanies and inoculates the audacity of
the flapper's frankness and ambition. Paulette's lofty, intellectual "talk
of . . . her books and of her pictures, of her work" is couched in a pose
of childishness: "with her babyish face and her sweet, high voice she was
like a child babling [sic] precociously" (107). Paulette's pose of immaturity feigns "the bright shamelessness of a child" rather than offering
subversive sexual daring (126).

Fauset's morality tale thus reflects critically on the role that Paulette
adopts rather than simply chastising Angela's choice to cross over the
color-line. Paulette is playing a role that combines immaturity and vulnerability with a veneer of intellectualism and sophistication. This role
fails the ideals of worldliness even as it embraces cynicism and iconoclasm, and such failure bears consequences for racial relationships as
well as modern feminine roles. Paulette sees herself as an enlightened
modern woman, appreciative of black artists and even black bodies. Fauset's narration and Angela's perspective on Paulette's attitudes expose
her iteration of racism under the guise of patronage. Parker, who willed
her property and copyrights to Martin Luther King Jr. and the NAACP,
also wrote about the hypocrisies of white patrons of black performers.
Appearing in the New Yorker in October 1927, Parker's critically ac-
claimed story, "An Arrangement in Black and White," features a southern woman fawning over a black musician. Fauset may deliberately al-
lude to "An Arrangement in Black and White" in Plum Bun; in any case,
a comparison of these two texts throws Fauset's narrative ironies into
relief, as she mocks sophisticated white New Yorkers who congratulate
themselves on interacting with black people. When Angela recognizes
the embarrassing racial condescension that Paulette deems an amusing
manifestation of her superiority and modernity, Angela is finally able to
break out of the enchantment cast by this bewitching figure.

In Parker's story, a white woman begs to meet a black singer. Her
stumbling and repetitious monologue betrays her condescension: "'Well,'
I said to Burton, 'It's a good thing for you Walter Williams is colored,'
I said, 'or you'd have lots of reason to be jealous.' . . . 'I don't see why

on earth it isn't perfectly all right to meet colored people. I haven't any feeling at all about it—not one single bit.'"[72] Her words expose her obvious and unconscious racist "feeling." Parker's narration emphasizes this character's snobbish pride in being introduced: "The woman with the pink velvet poppies extended her hand at the length of her arm and held it so for all the world to see, until the Negro took it, shook it, and gave it back to her."[73] The black celebrity dispatches the offering of her approval and her hand as dismissively as possible.

Fauset dramatizes a similar scene in her novel, but she substitutes chic New Yorker Paulette for Parker's ignorant southern high-society dame. Paulette laughs with her friends about her performance when she meets a famous black writer: "'I gave him my prettiest smile, grand white lady making up to an 'exceptional Negro' and he simply didn't see me; took my hand,—I did my best to make my grasp a clinging one—and he passed me right along disengaging himself as cool as a cucumber and making room for a lady of colour.' She finished reflectively, 'I wonder what he would be like alone'" (220). The first line of this anecdote recapitulates the terms of Parker's satirical short story, but Paulette's ironic knowingness about her play-acting and condescension fails to exonerate her from the offenses she describes. Paulette's clinging handshake is an explicitly erotic gesture, and her final remark suggests a sexual fantasy about the black intellectual. Parker's story mocks the southern matron who would find such an assignation unthinkable. Fauset, in contrast, skewers the New York flapper who flirted with Harlem culture in an effort to experience the exotic. Thus, she hits closer to home, addressing urbanity and smartness rather than assigning racism to the comfortingly distant and backward South. Paulette's self-mockery in recounting the tale fails to counteract her condescension and fetishization of blackness.

Like Parker's character in "Arrangement in Black and White," Paulette views the encounter between a black man and a white woman as a grand joke. She credits herself with orchestrating and arranging this comedy; she is "consumed with laughter" and announces "'I've just played the biggest joke on myself'" (221). Paulette recognizes the potential ridiculousness of her excitement about meeting black man, and she thinks this ironic awareness distinguishes her from the benighted bigot. In Parker's story, the implied author offers up the inconsistencies in the character's dialogue for readerly scorn, and the few descriptions supplied by the narrator reinforce a tone of skeptical superiority. However, Parker also treats the encounter between a white woman and a black man as a joke; her story relies on the comic possibilities of this situation. Obviously, Parker's point is to expose the bigotry of supposedly elevated social groups, but Fauset's revision of this scene suggests that even self-consciously modern women like Paulette/Parker are implicated in racism by treating black people's entrance into sophisticated culture as a comic performance.

To counter Paulette's arrogant self-congratulation and amusement, Fauset allows Angela to retell the scene. Paulette shares her anecdote with her friends, including Angela, though she does not realize that Angela is black. Paulette tries to beat denigrators to the punch by insisting that the joke is "on her." Angela takes private pleasure in the black writer's dismissal of the unctuous Pauline. Her "reading" of this story translates it into an entertaining tale for a black audience: "Angela conscious of a swelling pride, stowed the incident away as a tit-bit for [her sister] Virginia" (222). Fauset thus advances a version of wit authored by black people. She further hints that such humor may already exist, even if Angela has overlooked its presence. When Angela returns across the color-line, she envies the camaraderie, conversation, and humor enjoyed by her sister's black peers, their "badinage . . . [and] laughter bubbling from some secret spring" (254–255). Later she realizes that a "high degree of humor" unites the community in Harlem that champions "racial pride" (326).

When Angela recognizes the wit in her own community, she begins to direct her ironic sensibility toward the pursuit of political goals by using her sense of humor to prompt the public acknowledgment of injustice. When she rejects the art prize that the judges had refused to an openly black artist, she feels empowered by humor: "Certainly [Angela] herself was bubbling over with mirth or what served for that quality" (359). Through this qualifying aside, Fauset carefully avoids celebrating the web of historical ironies and social injustices that excludes Angela and her peer from receiving the award. In granting Angela the ability to speak ironically and to reveal unspoken social ironies, Fauset accords her heroine confidence and independence, informed by participation in a black community. Angela turns the tables on the white audience, the panel of judges, and thus finds an assertive voice. Her technique of humorous criticism recalls the rhetoric of the *Crisis* and *Opportunity* writers who mock the experts and authorities that espouse racism as truth. Humor provides a strategy for opposing that authority and questioning the legitimacy of its power.

In "The Gift of Laughter," Fauset wrote that "an oppressed and too hard driven people breaks over into compensating laughter and merriment. It is our emotional salvation."[74] She might have said the same about her female characters faced with the constraints of domesticity but resisting the indignities of domestication. The humor of the white flapper connotes expenditure, the wastefulness of excessive drink, profligacy, and sexual promiscuity. For Fauset's women, however, humor compensates for a lifetime of self-denial and hardship. Fauset's novels offer irony as a corrective for social injustice and wit as a verbal corollary for self-regard. Irony and wit become powerful tools when wielded by black women who appreciate their cost.

4 / The Indestructible Glamour Girl: Dawn Powell, Celebrity, and Counterpublics

Dawn Powell is the only writer featured prominently in this book who did not occupy a heralded position in the firmament of interwar literary New York. She remained largely unknown outside literary circles in spite of her impressive productivity as a novelist (publishing fifteen novels, the first in 1925 and the last in 1962), her steady work as a book reviewer for the *New York Evening Post* and later (briefly) for *Mademoiselle*, and her prolific freelance writing in magazines such as *Snappy Stories, College Humor,* and the *New Yorker.* In 1962, her friend Edmund Wilson honored her with a *New Yorker* profile. He blamed her relative obscurity on her failure to play a feminine role for publicity: "no effort has been made to glamorize her, and it would be hopeless to try to glamorize her novels."[1] Appropriately, then, Powell's satires criticize the collusion of feminine roles, glamour, and celebrity in the modern mass media.

In *Plum Bun*, Jessie Fauset uses magazine illustrator Paulette as a representative of white magazine culture's shortcomings and an object of satire; she seems at first to be an enviable modern professional and ultimately proves to be a laughable fraud. In her novels, Powell employs a similar strategy, featuring female celebrities whose position in the spotlight proves problematic at best, destructive at worst. In Powell's novels, magazines divert audiences from recognizing the operation of money, politics, and corporate control that guides their messages, and these publications encourage their readers instead to focus on glamorous surfaces, feminine poses, and celebrity gossip. In her novels, Powell renders female celebrities ambiguous figures indeed, both in terms of their individual agency and their cultural significance.

In *Turn, Magic Wheel*, *The Happy Island*, and *A Time to Be Born*, Powell depicts three female celebrities: an author's wife, a cabaret performer, and a magazine writer. In each novel, Powell emphasizes the pervasive influence of periodicals, sometimes ventriloquizing the press in snippets of her chapters. Powell uses three representational strategies to puncture the media bubble she describes. First, she tallies the cost of the schizophrenic conception of self that results from publicity and personae in her characterization of female celebrities and their discontents. Second, her plots reveal that male artists who purport to hold themselves above the mass media fray are in fact in the thick of it. No one is truly outside the market, and hence all should be equally concerned about its effects. Finally and most crucially, Powell advocates humor as a corrective tool that can challenge consumer, gender normative, or propagandistic messages. Through her characters' relationships and small acts of defiance, Powell substantiates the belief shared by Fauset that humor can provide the basis for the formation of counterpublics. These counterpublics can elevate intimacy and irony over estrangement and the status quo by allowing potent revisions and refusals of mass media messages and cultural ideals.

In depicting the tug of war between the potential counterpublic and the omnipresent mass media, Powell targets a growing literary preoccupation of the thirties and early forties, evident also in the work of Fauset and Mary McCarthy. The friction between subculture and national culture became a prevalent theme for both political and aesthetic reasons. The rise of fascism in Europe demonstrated that broad information dissemination could be a tool with dangerous consequences. Also, anxieties about the 1920s explosion in print culture left many critics and intellectuals with the desire to monitor the boundary between so-called imitation and actual art, a desire that I discuss further in chapter 5.[2] The interrelationship and asymmetry of mass media culture and counterpublic in Powell's work also reflects the duality that she felt in her life and career.

On the one hand, Powell defined herself as a bohemian Greenwich Villager. Powell moved to the Village in 1924 and stayed there for the rest of her life. According to an anecdote in a 1954 letter, a niece once refused Powell's invitation to visit, claiming that she needed time to visit the Village, and Powell contemplated the reply "but dearie, your Auntie Dawn IS Greenwich Village!"[3] In her favorite café at the Hotel Lafayette, Powell liked to sit in the corner where she could spot new arrivals and wave them to her table should she wish to chat.[4] Less than six degrees of separation from literary high modernism, Powell was close friends with John Dos Passos and Edmund Wilson. She spent evenings with Genevieve Taggard, Maxwell Bodenheim, Floyd Dell, E. E. Cummings, and Ernest Hemingway.[5] There were even promising (if ultimately unfulfilled) signs that her work might share the heady literary perch that such literary luminaries occupied. Hemingway once called her his "favorite living novelist," and, like Fitzgerald and Hemingway, Powell published with Scribner's. The famous Max Perkins served as her editor. (As a result, Powell dubbed her cat "Perkins.")

On the other hand, when not reading Gogol or writing satiric novels, Powell published in numerous middlebrow magazines. Her publishing connections, businessman husband, and literary rivals brought the Village-loyal Powell into the commercial orbit of midtown. Powell socialized with the Algonquin Round Table, though she deemed them eternal adolescents "in a permanent prep school where they perpetually haze each other."[6] Much to her chagrin, Powell was frequently confused with the other D.P. whose success Powell attributed to modern celebrity culture. In a diary entry from 1940, Powell dismissively deemed Dorothy Parker a perfect example of "the famous writer who is touted to fame by journalists, whose actual work is of no importance but rides on personal notoriety."[7] In spite of her irritation with the Algonquinites and their queen bee, Powell buzzed in the hive of midtown sophistication. She counted *New Yorker* movie reviewer John Mosher among her close friends, and she wrote stories for the cabaret singer and performer Dwight Fiske. Powell lived uncomfortably between two literary, cultural, and even geographical worlds and was thus well-situated to document the symbolic friction of novel and magazine, highbrow and middlebrow, downtown and midtown, and to expose their actual interdependence. In so doing, Powell anticipated the dismantling of the Great Divide undertaken in much recent critical work of the new modernist studies.

In defining the Great Divide between modernism and mass culture, Andreas Huyssen framed the broadly accepted modernist fallacy that man was to high modernism (good, authentic, virile) as woman was to mass culture (bad, ersatz, promiscuous).[8] This symbolic dichotomy complicated artistic production and authorial personae for modern women writers. In 1934, assessing the poetry and fiction of Louise Bogan and Kay Boyle, Powell wrote: "women now [make] their art serve their female purpose whereas once it warred with their femininity. Each page is squirming with sensitivity, every line—no matter how well disguised the heroine is—coyly reveals her exquisite taste, her delicate charm, her never-at-a-disadvantage body." In this feminine ideal, admirable qualities boil down to taste, charm, and sexual attractiveness, and Powell questions this candied version of womanliness, especially because of the brittle snobbery it betrays: "what *aristocrats* these women writers are."[9]

It might appear that Powell is simply echoing the misogyny that Ann Douglas identifies as the battle cry of modernity in New York literary culture.[10] Powell's remarks could be slotted easily into a familiar framework of modern complaint about women writers and popular fiction. She aligns women's supposedly intellectual and artistic efforts (novels) with their excessive embodiment in their literary works and in the public mind. Targeting her combination of snobbery and sex appeal, Powell puns that the woman writer is she "whose pen advertises the superiority of [her] organs." But Powell continues her analysis to make the more piquant and less customary point that literary men also play a gendered masquerade in their fiction. Powell cites the "he-man writers—Hemingway, [Murray] Burnett, [James] Cain—imitation he-manners whose words tersely proclaim their masculinity, every tight-lipped phrase shows the author's guts, his decency, his ability to handle any situation." Powell's witty neologism creates a compelling double meaning: "he-manners" suggests both the practitioners of macho and the etiquette of masculinity. Powell describes masculine literary display as a fantasy of physical display: "Through the words shot out of the type-writer clip-clip one watches the play of his muscles; one sighs to lay one's head upon that hairy shoulder."[11] Men bear the weight of the literary marketplace and the gender roles it promotes on their hairy shoulders, too.

Powell's ambivalence about and even antipathy to magazine writing as a career—she complained in another diary entry that magazine writers "dignify a suspect profession by the solidity of their finances"—does reflect some regrettable attitudes about femininity that accompanied the imaginary Great Divide. All the more passionate in her judgments, given her own career and sex, Powell belittled women writers for "writ[ing] magazine trash" and called women "the most unscrupulous artists in the world—they turn any genius they have into money without a pang—whereas the man artist, supporting his family by distortions of his genius, never ceases to bemoan his lost ideal."[12] This statement articulates standard sexist appraisals of women, especially women artists, deeming them unscrupulous, commercial, amoral, and promiscuous.

Powell's view of magazine writing was rather complicated in spite of her artistic squeamishness, however, as she experienced firsthand the benefits of a steady income. In her diary, she confessed that magazine writing gave her a feeling of security and autonomy: "I want the dignity of my own work, my own earnings and control of my own life."[13] The literary shame that riddles her diaries when she talks about magazine writing belies this arguably feminist sentiment about maintaining an independent career. Her novels reflect a similarly ambivalent response to the magazine industry and women's autonomy. In her novels, the press objectifies women, turns their life stories into advertising blurbs or punchlines, and manipulates their images and reputation for profit. Powell describes feelings of helplessness and even voicelessness that accompany this public role. At the same time, publicity and profit offer her female characters a sense of professional and personal autonomy akin to Powell's experience. In *Turn, Magic Wheel*, Powell depicts fame as both relentless exposure and self-making opportunity. This novel also allows Powell to criticize the Great Divide through three exaggeratedly gendered figures: the manly modernist, the feminine celebrity, and the epicene male magazine writer. In so doing, she debunks the purported independence of manly modernism from the mass media world where it makes its home.

Effigy and Exposure: The Magic Wheel of Mechanical Reproduction

In the same year that Powell published *Turn, Magic Wheel* (1936), Walter Benjamin published "The Work of Art in the Age of Mechanical Reproduction," perhaps his most famous essay, in which he observed that the aura of authenticity surrounding an original artwork was "depreciated" when mechanically reproduced copies eroded "the authority of the artwork." He associated this depreciation primarily with film but also with magazines and popular literature. Thanks to "the increasing extension of the press," anyone could become a writer, and thus the author was no longer a heroic and distant figure: "the distinction between author and public is about to lose its basic character." Benjamin was hopeful about the political ramifications of this expanded mass culture; he associated an artistic tradition with class stratification, political hierarchy, and even fascism. But Benjamin also recognized that the aura, removed from the realm of tradition and artistry, did not evaporate but rather migrated to the cult of celebrity: "the shriveling of the aura [corresponds] with an artificial build up of the 'personality.'" This effect, what

Benjamin called "'the spell of the personality,'" he decried as "the phony spell of a commodity."[14]

As even this all-too-brief summary should suggest, Benjamin's account relies on the pairing of enchantment and disenchantment, mystification and exposure. At first, he implies a historical progression from past magic to present rationality, from past deception to present awareness. As Benjamin's essay continues, however, the aura reveals its polymorphous nature. If the personality still enchants, then perhaps the audiences of Charlie Chaplin movies whom Benjamin imagines participating in a politically progressive collective experience might instead divert their emotions and attention into a new form of hero worship. Furthermore, the opposed categories of enchantment and disenchantment are by no means ethically or psychologically transparent. For Benjamin in this essay, disenchantment illuminated the artificiality of authority and allowed for new collective pleasures of close examination, productive distraction, and unlimited access (instead of the distant worship, absorbing attention, and staged unveilings that Benjamin associates with art's aura). Equally convinced that mechanical reproduction and media duplicability defined a crucial shift in the modern era, Powell depicts the force of disenchantment as both a source of profound loss and a salutary reminder of self-worth.

In *Turn, Magic Wheel*, Powell makes disenchantment her theme in interlocking plots about publicity, publication, and betrayal. Effie Callingham is the former wife of author and celebrity Andy Callingham, known for his big-game hunting, his womanizing, and his spare prose. (Three guesses as to which literary celebrity of Powell's acquaintance she alludes to in this character.) Effie discovers that her best friend, magazine writer and dandy Dennis Orphen, is publishing a roman à clef that mocks her quixotic dream that Andy will return to her. To her dismay Effie further learns that Callingham's new wife has returned from Europe to New York and is in a hospital dying of cancer. An unlikely advocate for her former rival, Effie pleads with Andy to visit his new wife on her deathbed. When she finally garners an appointment with the Great Author whose myth she spent so much time defending and adoring, Effie pretends that she had not been pining for Andy and that Dennis is her new, younger lover.

In *Turn, Magic Wheel*, Effie's psychic need for enchantment produces real distress when the object of these cultural mystifications (Andrew Callingham) proves a fake. The plot debunks the aura of authenticity that surrounded masculinity and modernist literary production. Powell reveals that mass media publicity sustains this myth of masculine roles and sacrosanct highbrow literature, hence crossing and indeed constituting the Great Divide. But she also recognizes a cost of the diminution of the aura: psychic fragmentation can result from the abandonment of ritual and the collapse of belief. Enchantment, after all, has undeniable emotional and cultural appeal and offers succor not extended by the cold comfort of ironic skepticism. While the title of the novel alludes to the wheel of fortune, the magic wheel of mass media circulation also effects influential and distressing transformations in this novel by turning friendship into a bestseller and romance into a gossip column.

This publicity cycle may seem like Effie's enemy, but Effie takes pleasure in the public presence and social value she gains by playing the role of author's wife. Dennis finds her act as wife of the Great Author absurd: "Dennis's lips slipped into a sardonic smile. Effie courting a new audience for the Callingham connection," but she makes friends and influences people through her masquerade of warmth and wistfulness as Callingham's faithful wife. Intrigued by her presentation of the Callingham connection, Dennis's publisher deems her "'an amazingly compelling personality.'"[15] It is a historical commonplace that the allure of personality overtook the value of character in the early twentieth century, and personality encompassed the ability to manipulate external appearances, to make an impression on others, and to constitute an identity through a combination of products and attitude. Warren Susman influentially argued that this shift to a celebration of personality enabled the growth of "a new profession," that of celebrity.[16] Effie's self-presentation is her living in both senses of the word.

Appropriately, her name, Effie, sounds like the word "effigy." This submerged pun connects Effie with duplication and persona; she translates her life story into a celebrity narrative.[17] From her real role of abandoned wife, she extracts the phantasmal role of faithful wife, a Penelope to Andy's Odysseus. Disguising her private loneliness, Effie courts an admiring public with her performance as a literary celebrity. These translations imbue Effie with a sense of self, albeit a borrowed one. Dennis observes that "her brief connection with Callingham" influenced her self-presentation: "a confident way of holding her head, a consciousness of her public, so to speak, and this sweet arrogance affected people, even crowds" (21). Effie is thus the author of enchantments, rather than simply the enchanted. Effie has embraced the normative role of "the wise gentle wife" coping with "his long absence" (12).[18] She seems traditionally domestic and devoted and can use those very qualities to augment her celebrity appeal. Indeed, Dennis, associating her with the nineteenth-century sentimental tradition, imagines her "float[ing] gently and sadly up to heaven like Little Eva" from *Uncle Tom's Cabin* (21).

But Powell recognizes that this presumption of intimacy between celebrity and public can result in risky vulnerability. Inviting the public into the private life relinquishes power about how that private life will be read, interpreted, or spun. When Effie learns the plot of Dennis's satirical novel, she realizes that his version of her will both intensify the public scrutiny she undergoes and deplete her aura of elegance and dignity. The narrator reports that Effie's use of Callingham's name heightens its value because of her personality: "when the illustrious name was not recognized . . . it was thereafter remembered because it must be fine indeed to bestow such dignity on the wearer" (22). Effie designs the costume of her celebrity rather than vice versa. But Dennis burlesques this costume and views it as an exaggerated fake. He writes in his book that her myth "has the shabby sheen that comes from long usage" (12). Effie fears that her public will accordingly shift their opinion of what has previously appeared like dignity and devotion. Effie tells Dennis: "'I wouldn't dare go anywhere with you if it was already published. Everyone would know then that it really was about me—everyone would laugh'" (15). Dennis has now changed from the caring friend into the dangerous press.

Where once she found intimacy with this young writer, Effie now finds cruelty: "even now his wicked lenses might be directed at her, cynically analyzing her reflections. There were no longer private shutters against the world, the dearest friend, spying, becomes a foe" (53). Effie's criticism targets Dennis's opportunism but also metonymically suggests the fickleness of media culture. The periodicals that first seem friends to the celebrity quickly become prying enemies. Powell plays on the words "lenses" and "shutters" in this description to suggest the perspective of the camera. Magazines in the 1920s generally prioritized illustration over photography, but by the 1930s photographs dominated the magazine form.[19] Benjamin considers the camera a critical tool that grants power to the audience. The object of the photograph can control neither the angle of the camera nor the extent of the exposure. Benjamin celebrates this function of the camera, which he claims dispels the cult of the art object. Powell, by contrast, imputes blame to this relentless gaze. This exposure is not the salutary disenchantment of cult status; it is the willy-nilly disparagement of human emotion and behavior that discounts consequence to the individual whose life story is thus judged.

Benjamin associates the photograph with the power of the audience to "take the position of a critic, without experiencing any personal contact with the actor."[20] Powell criticizes the marriage of the audience's detached judgment with its ravenous consumption of celebrity narratives through Effie's grief. Effie has no recourse from the merciless lens. She cannot close the shutters in a world characterized by mass media exposure. She can control only the exterior that she presents to this invasive camera gaze, and she adopts "A front for Everybody, the enemy. A special public face decorated with a smile, a special manner" (70). In this passage, the strain of modernist alienation in city life—the defensive need "to prepare a face to meet the faces that you meet" as T. S. Eliot famously writes in "The Love Song of J. Alfred Prufrock"—conspires with the mass media's relentless gaze to render the public sphere antagonistic.

As a result of this shift, Effie experiences city spaces as intensely transparent.[21] She attempts to regulate her exterior expressions of internal emotion. But Dennis's invasion and betrayal have left her feeling constantly watched. While she stands in a phone booth on a city street, Effie's emotions revolt against her body's attempts at restraint: "Without warning, tears streamed down her face, she leaned her face against the telephone." Effie's face exposes the emotional devastation that she wants to keep hidden, and Powell's slightly awkward repetition of the phrase "her face" makes it seem like an object with an independent life, a mask that Effie wishes she could put down, a symbol of her celebrity.[22] Effie does not want to perform and tries to extinguish the spotlight and shroud her emotion: "[she] mechanically pulled the booth door slightly open so the light would go off and hide her," but she soon realizes that she has drawn attention anyway: "The soda fountain boy was looking at her. The marcelled blonde at the Helena Rubenstein counter was looking at her. The customer was looking at her. They could see through both glass doors, dark or light." In the phone booth, Effie is like a black-and-white photograph under glass. Powell also equates Effie's body with the phone booth. The phone "receiver [is] dangling from the hook," and "her body [is] shaking"; both machine and self send uncontrolled messages. Like the phone booth, Effie is transparent and public. The strangers in the city who are watching her become like the readers who will pour through copies of Dennis's novel: "They could see through everything but she could not stop crying. She picked up her pocketbook, left the receiver still hanging with I'm-fine-I'm-fine-I'm fine and ran outdoors into the brilliant sun" (116). Even Effie's escape into natural light leaves her exposed.

This poignant scene reveals Powell's compelling concern that publicity and surveillance exact psychological costs. In the system of celebrity where Effie once found self-expression and a safe haven, she now lives in fearful anticipation of exposure. Effie also fears losing her sense of an authentic, interior self as her actions become more and more alienated from her emotions, more implicated in masquerade and redirection: "how did people live to be old, each year betraying themselves more, crippling themselves with lies until the person herself is lost" (216). When each seemingly private conversation becomes a press release—like Effie lying to her former husband and telling him she has a new lover—intimacy becomes impossible. She has increasing trouble reading her own emotions: "My brain has broken up . . . into a thousand bits, I can put together only a few of them to spell out the anagram of my own misery" (62). She feels alienated from her voice and her body: "hear, hear, this is the real me, don't listen to what I say and don't look at what I do, this is the real me beneath all that changed into nothing but a little unheard voice, and if this wicked witch's body flays you don't be hurt for it isn't really I" (216). These negations suggest the self-division and fragmentation created by serving as a public effigy. The facsimile of the body and the manufactured personality displace a transcendent experience of self, whatever could be imagined as "really I." Effie's romantic betrayals and personal losses have become part of her celebrity narrative, and, once Dennis alters the reception of that narrative from heroic to farcical, Effie feels alienated from that enshrined identity.

If Effie embodies celebrity's liminal status between private and public, traditional femininity and modern womanhood, acceptance and alienation, Dennis exemplifies the male magazine writer's ambivalence about both his gender role and his commercial craft. He questions the source of his own commercial successes: "Clever, clever Mr. Orphen with his nice little knack of thumbnailing his dearest friends" (15). Dennis's caricatures seem opportunistic, infantile, and disposable. The trademark cynicism of the magazine humor writer thinly disguises his envy of Callingham's literary reputation for genius and greatness: "Easy enough now to make fun of people's wide-eyed reverence for that name, no doubt about it, he had been as impressed as anyone else" (18). By making Effie the subject of his book, Dennis attempts to profit from the reverence attached to great literature and the aura of the author. This profit motive bars him from any hope of such literary grandeur. Dennis imagines himself as a sort of pimp, selling Effie's literary celebrity: "This was a living woman he was putting on the market, the living Effie" (13).

Dennis manages his own anxiety about his commercial role and its estrangement from literary greatness by attempting to masculinize his authorial talents. Dennis claims that he can "see so savagely into people's bones and guts" (13). Dennis casts himself as a scientist and a savage—two wielders of potentially (and potently) masculine control. Even Dennis's own language undermines that hypothetical force, as he concludes his description of his satirical art with a prim assessment of the literary product that results from his examination of bones and guts, a "nice analysis" (13). Unsatisfied with these two figures for his authority, Dennis tries out a third masculine role to describe his merciless vision: newspaper man.[23] He criticizes Effie's expectations of etiquette when he embodies the aggressive objectivity of the (masculine) reporter: "You've been around, you know there's no Emily Post rule as to what's legitimate copy and what isn't" (14). By mentioning Emily Post in the same breath with legitimacy, Dennis again draws attention to his fraught professional role. Like Emily Post the etiquette columnist, Dennis creates an image of upper-class life and mores for a mass audience. He does not seem as much the *Kansas City Star* newsman as he does the *Vanity Fair* columnist, and the distance between the two is marked by gendered styles of prose and persona.

Dennis is, after all, a dandy who prides himself on his sophistication, charm, and swank clothes: "As a matter of fact he was a mighty personable figure of a man, a fine commanding physique (if he just remembered to stay away from tall women), a rather nonchalantly Prince of Wales way of wearing his clothes (if he just stayed on Fourteenth Street or Second Avenue), and a manner all his own that he got by combining Clark Gable and Wallace Beery" (8). These parenthetical narratorial asides imply that Dennis employs self-deprecating wit to try to maintain a dividing line between fashion and vanity, sophistication and foppishness. These asides also introduce a narrator willing to betray the protagonist and his self-assessment, an implied author who records Dennis's narcissism and opportunism. Finally, the flurry of celebrity references—the Prince of Wales, Clark Gable, and Wallace Beery—casts Dennis's poses and postures as imitative. The male magazine writer is susceptible to the lures of mass cultural masculine ideals. There is no "manner all his own."

Thus, while Dennis views Effie as part of that "rich, fat enemy world . . . of New York through Park Avenue curtains," he reveals his own hypocrisy as he writes about this society world for magazines and in his book (9). The more vehemently Dennis criticizes Effie, the clearer it is that he feels implicated in the cultural crimes that he describes. He imagines Effie borrowing "all the little words of the rich" with "little baby fingers": "How charmingly Effie wore her little rich words thefted from the Glaenzer fatness, weaving a spell about her present despair, throwing out a splendid marquee and rug to lead to her bare closet" (10). Dennis depicts Effie as a parvenu and enchantress. But Dennis's excitement about his book release betrays that he shares these aspirations to wealth and sophistication: "I must be happy because I am young, beautiful, and rich, because I am the darling of New York, the toast of Paris, because at any moment in a million and two homes all over the world fascinated readers will be opening up their copies of *The Hunter's Wife*—" (91). The more Dennis denigrates Effie, the more he reveals his own likeness to her. The female celebrity and the male magazine writer have a lot in common.

Dennis fears the deleterious effects of this desire for celebrity on his literary aspirations. In this fear, he acknowledges the permeability of the Great Divide between high culture and low culture, or, perhaps even more threatening, the collapse of high culture into middlebrow culture.[24] In an anxious moment, Dennis imagines "that his so-called creative process was sheer Pelmanism" (72), a training course in concentration imagined as a self-help method for professional success and mental advancement. Its popularity was intimately related to the growth of middlebrow culture.[25] In the November 1922 issue of *McClure's*, for example, the ad pages promote various methods of intellectual improvement for the middle class: learning etiquette, reading the twenty-five most important books, and indeed parsing advertisements.[26] The advertisement for the Pelman Institute of America promises: "New Minds For Old in 12 Weeks!"[27] The Pelman system promised that mind and memory training would produce financial success; it represented "modern psychology distilled for mass consumption and use," as Mathew Thomson describes it in his history of modern psychological discourse.[28] Alluding to Pelmanism, Dennis worries that his mind has become smart rather than profound, that he is a hack rather than a genius.

Powell maps Dennis's anxieties about literary uniqueness eroded by mass media duplication and degradation onto his fraught relationship with his body. He decorates his "figure" and his "physique" (8); he inhabits the role of modern dandy and appreciates his body with narcissistic gusto: "Dennis blew a happy little ring of smoke into the happy air. He stretched out his bare feet—beautiful arches, he observed with pleasure, and hooked the exquisitely matched toes of the bottom rung of the chair" (91). But Dennis fears that he will be exposed for his pleasure in the body, in fashion, in luxury: "Dennis uneasily saw them whispering, exchanging

their unfavorable thoughts about him, the snob, the pansy, the phony"
(165). Dennis's anxieties about middlebrow literary production, his quest
for fame, and his pleasure in materialism are mirrored and enlarged by
his fears about sexuality and masculinity.

Dennis projects these anxieties about properly performing his gender
onto Effie, whom he accuses of overplaying the role of grande dame: "He
wished . . . that some day he could persuade her to a definitely stylish
outfit so that she would look less a personage and more a person" (22).
Dennis complains about the excessiveness of her attire and pseudo-
bohemianism: "But no, she must wear capes and flowing sleeves, Russian jewelry, Cossack belts on velvet smocks."[29] He tries to imagine how
her adopted role would translate to the screen and thus connects her
feminine masquerade with debased mass culture: "Come to think of it,
Alfonso of Spain was the man for her, he thought, like a producer doing type-casting. Wonder if we could get hold of old Alfonso? Call up
Packards, Browns, all the agents—what?—in Hollywood? Take a wire to
M.G.M. Studios." At first, it seems as though he wants to cast Effie with
the king of Spain as her romantic lead, but then he delivers his punch
line at her expense: "Dear Alfonso, would you consider a return to the
stage in role particularly adapted— " (22). In Dennis's derisive view, Effie
is a woman best played by a man in drag.

Dennis accuses Effie of a femininity that rings false, of gestures and
costumes that verge on the parodic in their grandiosity. His derogation
of her outré performance of femininity cloaks his literary fascination
with playing a female role: "Spread out in type, detail added to detail,
invention added to fact, the figure whole emerges invisibly you creep
inside, you are at last the Stranger." The Stranger that Dennis refers to
in this passage is Effie, and he uneasily asks himself: "Why *she*, why not
some one else?" Dennis's fascination with Effie is only one example of
his pleasure in imaginatively occupying a woman's point of view. In one
scene, he follows a blonde down the city street, and he window shops,
speculating about "which hat delighted her, the red feather toque or the
black taffeta" (5). Dennis observes that "she paused before a gown shop
and saw herself in the blue velvet evening dress she would wear." Imagining the thoughts of this mysterious stranger allows Dennis to dream of
flamboyant costumes and their public display. To his chagrin, the blonde
spots his gaze: "Dennis's inquiring eyes [were] reflected in her pocket
mirror" (6).

The significance of Dennis's interrupted flânerie is twofold. First, the
blonde looks back, interrupting his gaze and its accompanying fantasy

that he can dictate her subjectivity. Second, Dennis becomes the blonde's mirror image for a moment. This fleeting image of himself in her mirror consummates his fantasy of cross-gender identification. This street scene generates such a compelling association of Dennis with femininity that he reacts with immediate and forceful refusal. Once the blonde sees him and exposes his fantasy, he belittles her artificiality: "Dennis found now a conscious coquetry in the rhythmic swirl of her skirt," and he was "disillusioned" (6). This rational (masculine) superiority to feminine illusion and artifice implies the desire and pleasure it denies. Indeed, Powell associates this motive with his cutting ironies: "[Dennis] must justify himself by looking on his friend Effie cynically, reluctantly worshiping he must make his sardonic asides, must in fact make her an amusing character in his book" (11). The enchantment of femininity is so potent that it calls for cynicism and sardony to exorcise it. Dennis's posture of sophistication abjures the femininity with which he toys.[30]

Sexual politics affect the literary marketplace as much as they do Dennis's authorial self-conception. Dennis's liminal position between newsman and celebrity hound, satirist and susceptible fan—articulated in his fears about eroded masculinity—situates him squarely within publicity culture. Dennis laments his own embeddedness and longs for an ideal of literature untarnished by the market. Dennis imagines this ideal personified by great male authors who possess the artistic purity he cannot achieve: "not even if he were Proust, Homer, or Hemingway himself . . . could there be . . . [an] excuse for telling the world about Effie" (14). Dennis views himself as an invasive gossip columnist and imagines true authors as defenders of privacy and literary ideals: "He had no business following his heroine through her own secret story. Wells wouldn't do such a thing. Proust wouldn't have" (74). While Dennis exalts this masculine authenticity and embraces the impersonal promise of style as an escape hatch, his publisher, that purveyor of literary style and authorial persona, recognizes that style itself is a gendered category, one that does not correlate directly with bodies or sex. "It was an age of the present tense," the publisher Johnson reflects, "the stevedore style" (102). Pared-down rhetoric corresponds with a popular fantasy of a muscled male body and heteronormativity. The writers whom Dennis admires, "Pater, Proust, and Flaubert," by contrast, stand for style, aestheticism, decadence, homosexuality, and even femininity ("Madame Bovary—c'est moi!"). Johnson concludes wryly that this proto-modernist trio "had betrayed" modern writers who "would have learned better modern prose by economizing on Western Union messages." Dennis is, according to

Johnson, "a coddler of fine phrases, a figure-of-speech user, a master of synecdoche," and this very stylishness is sexually and commercially suspect for its artificiality and refinement. Most damning of all, it renders Dennis beloved by female middlebrow readers, as his work is greeted with accolades by "the women of England in *Time and Tide*" and "the women of America in *Books*" (103).

This treatment of Dennis as an epicene sophisticate who achieves popularity in lieu of greatness might seem to confirm the gendered Great Divide between mass culture and literature. Powell recognizes what Dennis cannot, however: "the great man" role personified by Callingham, a big game hunter and womanizer, is a masculine masquerade (9). The sales of Callingham's new novel will be buoyed by the celebrity scandal generated by Dennis's novel: "what a break for sales!" (104). The feigned purity of modernist achievement disguises its basis in the same celebrity system that Dennis thinks is degraded.[31] Loren Glass argues persuasively that "Hemingway's characteristic hypermasculinity emerg[ed] explicitly in response to the fission of his marketplace" and "Hemingway's struggles with gender identity were tightly stitched into his struggles with celebrity."[32] Powell comes to a similar conclusion in her comic depiction of Callingham/Hemingway. She establishes both the mythos and the bathos of Callingham, who, like Hemingway, is an icon as well as author. The press fetishizes Callingham's appearance, and Powell quotes a fictional newspaper: "'Callingham appeared to be a tall, bronzed, healthy specimen in the prime of life, gray mustache and sparse gray hair, keen dark eyes under unrimmed spectacles, speaking with the unmistakable twang of the Yankee'" (208–209). He is practically a trophy or statue already and embodies both masculine and all-American authenticity. In accordance with his legend of literary greatness, Callingham feigns indifference to press attention: "'He waved his hands disparagingly at photographers and the autograph hunters outside the hotel'" (209).

The stripped-down modernist literary aesthetic does not reflect the lifestyle of the author, however. Powell hints through the "chintz counterpane" and his "English tweed dressing gown" that Callingham lives a cozy, even effete existence as a wealthy, pampered author (210). Effie perceives a pervasive unreality in her former husband, deeming him an "Andy-façade" (211). While Effie at first blames the comic exaggeration of Andy's bluster and self-regard on age—"Andy [was] caricatured by that unkind cartoonist Time"—she subsequently realizes that fame itself has colonized Andy: "there was no Andy left, he had been wiped out by Callingham the Success as men before him had been wiped out by the thing they represented" (211–212). Even Callingham can now only conceive of himself through a photographer's lens; he brings out his "snapshots" to share with Effie (211).

This scene of confrontation with Callingham arrives at the conclusion of the novel after much hubbub about the author's reputation, and Powell reveals through Callingham's absurd arrogance that it is a small man indeed who stands behind the curtain and manipulates the imposing aura of the Great and Powerful Callingham. This disenchantment is even more distressing for Dennis, the middlebrow author and magazine writer, than it is for Effie, Callingham's former wife. Dennis has imagined his own role as subsidiary to real literary genius, and when Callingham seems to exemplify just another facet of publicity culture, Dennis is shaken in his fantasy that masculine superiority exists somewhere. He vows that "No matter what happens I will never let it take me this way. . . . I'll be damned if I'll have a bedful of literary agents, movie magnates, lawyers, brokers, Spanish and Russian translators, editors, gossip columnists, and old college roommates." Dennis depicts Callingham's complicity with the culture of publicity as a sexual infraction (he is "in bed" with them). In a revealing association of celebrity and femininity, Dennis decries Callingham's "prima donna act" (204). Callingham has lost his masculine and high cultural aura.

The divide that Dennis maintains in his mind between masculine modernist authenticity and feminine celebrity collapses, and Powell implies that this divide never existed in practice. Effie realizes celebrity Callingham is a copy with no discernible original: "So, this big gray man had once been her husband, the pattern from which she had cut her real lover, the dream Andy" (211). This realization liberates Effie from her mourning and devotion; she can invent herself again. For Dennis, however, the revelation of Callingham's artificiality makes it difficult to read the world through the hierarchal divisions of true and false, male and female that he relied upon. The Great Divide gave him an interpretive schema, and its dismantling produces a muddle. Dennis hears street noises and imagines "quaver[ing] and blurr[ing] like ink on wet paper" (224), and he no longer knows how to talk to Effie; instead, he seeks shelter from interaction behind the enchanting sounds of the radio.

Dennis does not want the aura of literary authenticity to be dispelled; he does not want the female celebrity to talk back or to alter the narrative course of her role. Dennis's Pygmalion longs for a new, more pliant Galatea to serve as his subject: "'I'll have to get to work on my new book. . . . The story of a woman with the soul of a statue, animated only by rum'" (228). Dennis regrets the shift that the disenchantment of Andy's aura produced in his own relationship with Effie, "a perturbing modulation from author and heroine to man and woman that made their conversation now strained on his part but far more confident on hers" (225). By contrast, Effie has found a new voice and "a quiet air of consummation" that Dennis "could not understand" (226).

Powell reveals that personality—mythologized in modernist literary production, middlebrow magazines and popular novels, and even in the amorphous text of celebrity—is a mask that enables performance rather than a metonym for encompassing, authentic identity. While Dennis fears that masquerade because of its destabilization of masculinity, Effie embraces masquerade because it allows her to rewrite her context and her role. In the plot's denouement, she induces Andy to visit his new wife on her deathbed and thus sustains his heroic reputation, the role for him that she prefers. Further, Effie pretends to possess a younger lover, casting herself as the desirable older woman instead of the abandoned wife. Dennis realizes uncomfortably that there is "a new Effie being born" with this shift to self-authorship (228). Ironically, in the novel's final scene, when Effie asks him to play along with her lie that he is her lover, Dennis acquiesces to the very action that he fears vitiates masculine authority and authenticity: "'Oh, I'll act the part,' promised Dennis" (227).

The Smart Woman and Her Counterpublic

Thus far, I have primarily focused my critical attention on Powell's citation and ridicule of the gendered Great Divide and the turn of the magic cultural wheel from enchantment to disillusionment. Through her characters' anxieties, Powell explores the psychological consequences of Benjamin's insight that modern mass culture has diminished and displaced (onto celebrity) aura and reverence. Powell also implies that, no longer awed by illusory greatness, female celebrities could control their self-presentation, stop fretting about the supposed lowness of manipulating publicity, and bob more or less happily on the cultural tide of proliferating print culture that carried all literary types—no matter their high-brow affectations—in its wake.

What I have not discussed explicitly is Powell's thematic attention to humor. Irony and cynicism represent Dennis's flailing attempts to duck vulnerability and identification. His literary tools of humor and satire fit with his publication venues (magazines, popular novels) and middle-brow popularity. But when Dennis's satiric perspective fails him, Powell reveals the flimsiness of irony-as-control. Dennis's pretenses to distance and detachment reveal his intense feelings of uncontrollable proximity to Effie. For her part, Effie is not a primarily witty or ironic character, in spite of one fleeting quip; when Dennis fails to bring her a corsage for her birthday, she comments that she "wear[s] a Martini beautifully" (17). Effie's escape into self-invention involves contented silence rather than banter. In both cases, the ironic voice of the individual fails in *Turn, Magic Wheel*, which seems to limit its psychological or social usefulness. At the same time, Powell employs irony in her content and technique, illuminating cultural ironies through caricature (Callingham's arrogance, self-obsession, and stylized macho speech) and deflated narrative expectations. The transition from enchantment to disenchantment that the novel represents is a shift from absorption in the hype to ironic detachment about both high modernism and the media circus. Powell points out the unexpected similarities between these supposedly unlike things. She thus ironizes the Great Divide and reveals that it is a handy fiction obscuring the origins of modernist reputation.[33] Although the ironic voice may fail the individuals in this novel, ironic juxtaposition as a narrative strategy provides a necessary lens for viewing cultural contradictions clearly.

Powell's later novels about celebrity, *The Happy Island* (1938) and *A Time to Be Born* (1942), deal more directly with the theme of humor and its social importance. They test humor's potential to foster self-expression, cultural criticism, ironic awareness, friendship, and community. In each novel, Powell recognizes warily that humor can collude with feminine stereotypes and the commercial goals of modern print culture. When personality trumps all and modern tempos rely on zinging headlines rather than slow explanation, humor provides shorthand for belonging and popularity. *The Happy Island*, for example, follows a New York cabaret singer, Prudence, famous for her scathing wit. A would-be proletarian playwright, Jefferson Abbott, comes to New York from Prudence's hometown in Ohio, and when he and Prudence become romantically involved, he chastises her for the insincerity and elitism he sees in her group of sophisticated friends. Smitten, Prudence follows Jefferson back to Ohio, only to discover that Jefferson's earnestness allows him to take patriarchy perfectly seriously. At the end of the novel, she returns to her beloved New York.

Powell introduces Prudence through her quips, thus establishing the importance of her sense of humor to her public persona. In the first chapter, Prudence phones her former lover to inform him that she is having lunch and several cocktails with his new mistress. Her side of the conversation sounds like a Dorothy Parker short story: "'I'm *not* maudlin, darling, I'm only mad as hell!'"[34] Prudence wears a "smart crazy hat set jauntily over one eye" (11), and this accessory reflects her chic, devil-may-care persona: she is "petite, jaunty, blond, and hard as nails to the casual eye" (21). Of course, Prudence the celebrity seldom deals with the casual eye; instead, she faces the relentless gaze of an admiring public, prying gossip columnists, and her own self-scrutiny. Privately, Prudence worries about her "queer moments between personalities, moments such as the hermit crab must have scuttling from one stolen shell to the next one." Prudence inhabits the shell of the funny, tough, urbane modern woman. While this persona enables an outrageous voice and facade, it also threatens alienation and self-estrangement: "In those nightmare seconds Prudence wondered if one could permanently become the third person singular, lose oneself, be nothing but one's name in a society column, one's photograph in *Vogue*." The "nightmare" of celebrity is the prospect of "los[ing] oneself" and "be[ing] nothing." Iconicity easily overtakes the "I" at the very moment that the "I" seems to become something grander than itself. Humor's enhancement of the voice is parallel. When humor's brassiness turns the vulnerable individual into the powerful joker, its reliance on verbal and attitudinal convention transforms the idiosyncratic person into a familiar comic type. Prudence's tone facilitates her absorption into clichéd feminine roles: "Prudence-Against-the-World" and "Small-Town-Girl-Makes-Good-in-Metrop" (44–45).

The public nature of these roles, the connection of humor with celebrity, expands their potential significance. Because the pose of ironic detachment and aggressive humor is conventional, it invites audience identification. This identification, as P. David Marshall notes in his work on the celebrity sign, occurs precisely because the celebrity cites conventional personality types; the power of celebrity relies upon heightened familiarity rather than uniqueness. Once the identification occurs, however, it permits the channeling of both hegemonic and countercultural impulses. In *The Happy Island*, Prudence's cynical, witty aggression provides a voice for other women: "Women often truly liked her, for she was as brutal as they longed to be" (44–45). It also inspires her urban coterie of sophisticated gay men: "In her they dimly felt they had a valuable machine gun, a weapon against society" (44). Just as the gangster narratives of the 1930s act out the fantasy of the disempowered grabbing hold of fame, fortune, and power, Prudence grants her circle an aggressive voice in the world.[35]

Powell treats Prudence as both a product of publicity culture in which her witty voice is the preferred tone of periodicals and an author of countercultural critique, where her humor becomes the mouthpiece for modern women and gay men.[36] In this double role, Prudence anticipates the work of contemporary cultural and queer theorists who propose a flexible interchange between identification and normativity in mass media culture, rather than viewing the force of publicity, iconicity, and celebrity as purely prescriptive or unidirectional. There is a helpful conceptual rhyme, for example, between Marshall's treatment of celebrity and Michael Warner's theory of counterpublics that thrive within a mass media–dominated public sphere.[37] Marshall similarly imagines celebrity as a cultural text through which subcultural fantasies can play in the very backyard of normative regulation.[38] Powell establishes a symbiotic relationship between Prudence's professional life as a celebrity and her participation in an urban subculture. Much of *The Happy Island* depicts the parties and liaisons of Prudence's friends, the circle of gay artists who support her work and applaud her attitude. Prudence is, in a very real sense, *their* celebrity; one of her friends rhapsodizes that there is "'no one like her! No one!" (66). Viewed as a symbol, Prudence allows her circle to valorize the self-display and sophistication often used to demonize their sexuality.[39]

In spite of her crucial role in this group of friends, Prudence considers abandoning her sense of humor and indeed her urban milieu. Powell makes her most prominent argument for the power of ironic awareness in this section of the novel when Prudence strays from her circle. Inspired by Marxist Jefferson's moralizing zeal, Prudence tries to erase her "wisdom" and "experience": "She tried to disown it, practiced privately wiping her mind clean of all asides but simplicity only confounded her." Jefferson's vision of simplicity presumes a gendered hierarchy of masculine authenticity and feminine artifice, manly honesty and feminine bitchiness. Prudence's verbal power offends Jefferson; he complains about her letters: "your remarks on paper, without the benefit of your personal attractions, are frightening and make me suspect I fell in love with a witch." To convince him of her blameless and innocent femininity, Prudence censors her prose, a rhetorical masquerade: "At least if there was no cure for doubt, there were disguises for it so Prudence took to laboring over her letters, going over each one to cross out anything that sounded worldly wise, naughtily oversexed or cynical." When Prudence excises the ironic sensibility from her identity, "a letter would emerge that pictured a Prudence dewey-eyed [sic] and filled with naïve joy . . . rapt in baby adoration rather than horrid lust for the big strong mannykins." Earnestness and infantilization are quite literally on the same page: "Sounds as if I had my finger in my mouth. It positively lisps, thought Prudence in disgust, reading over her final drafts. One more revision would have me playing with my toes." Being "worldly-wise, naughtily oversexed, and cynical" allows Prudence to express her views, catch the attention of the public, and seduce "strong mannykins" (not to mention other women, as she shares an apartment with a lesbian lover in an earlier section of the novel). When Prudence censors her ironic asides, she muffles her voice; she has a "finger in [her] mouth" and her prose "lisps" (230–231).

Powell thus indicates that knowing humor, though it corresponds with a stereotype of the modern woman, also represents a crucial feminist strategy. Prudence's wit is not just a decorative addition to conversation; it is a defense of her personal and social freedoms, which are curtailed when she sets up housekeeping with Jefferson in small-town Ohio. Witnessing his assertions of authority, Prudence realizes that his tactics of control, although comically outdated and stereotypical, bear serious consequences. Jefferson silences her speech: "It was funny at first to have him turn into such an old-fashioned man, rejecting the female overtures in conversation." He also depends on her domestic exertions; Prudence could "laugh a little to herself until it got too serious that her labor should be no surprise but an expected service." This skewed power relationship and these constricting gender roles necessitate blatant refusal and active resistance. A crucial medium of this defiance is the feisty voice. When Prudence leaves Jefferson, she celebrates the value of banter and humor: "'What do you want to do?' he said. 'Talk,' she said. 'I want to talk about something that doesn't matter with people who don't mean what they say. I want to rest my kind heart for a thousand years while I play with loaded words and see who gets hit. I want to put my real soul back in the Safe Deposit forever before it cracks. I can have ten times more fun with the paste one. I want to have no feelings and to be cheap and superficial and pit my wits with a few pit-wits.'" By comparing her persona to costume jewelry, Prudence claims the agency of performance. The glitter of wit is preferable to the dull trappings of a housewife's pseudosimplicity. Further, Prudence acknowledges the importance of her counterpublic when she longs to talk to "people who don't mean what they say" and to "pit my wits with a few pit-wits" (265). Instead of consigning herself to a life amid nit-wits who treat any woman as the "Little Woman," Prudence decides to consort with others who challenge dominant value systems by privileging surface, performance, and verbal invention (261). This vision of community and banter as a source of strength and independence recalls Fauset's depiction of Harlem Renaissance coteries and their transformative influence on Laurentine in *The Chinaberry Tree*.

From the local pleasures of banter, Powell draws the broader philosophical and political conclusion that an ironic perspective facilitates cultural evaluation. Jefferson objects to Prudence and her social circle being "damnably wise." Parker considers this wiseacre sensibility "a language everyone spoke, X-ray lenses they all used for detecting motives in each other, a panning for sham as if it were gold nuggets to be triumphantly declared when found" (230). This image of the group "panning for sham" suggests self-reflection and canniness about the pervasiveness of performance and the circulation of language. Jefferson's objection to this tone and its accompanying universal skepticism fits Warner's argument that a counterpublic offends: "The discourse that constitutes it is not merely a different or alternative idiom but one that in other contexts would be regarded with hostility or with a sense of indecorousness."[40] Prudence's return to New York, her embrace of indecorousness, is not just a matter of taste but of survival: "New York was my instrument, or I was its. A fish out of water is a dead fish, not a neurotic or discontented or irritable fish, but a dead fish" (261).

The Happy Island defends the political importance of humor for women and for gay men in creating and sustaining counterpublics. Powell also implies that the link between smartness and the publicity machine can be educative rather than corrupting. Prudence and her friends, accustomed to angling for their own places in the public eye, have "thoughts so trained to seeing money or publicity prizes for every unexpected heroic deed" that they are not affected by the "infantile acceptance of surface nobility, the feeble-minded faith in leaders" (231). This knowingness is expressed through snobbery; Prudence and her peers see the susceptible masses as infantile and feeble-minded. Nonetheless, the recalcitrance of this doubting posture in the face of ideological persuasion serves as a valuable model, in spite of its tendency to self-exaltation. Powell published this novel in 1938 when the rise of fascism demonstrated both the ease and the danger of accepting surfaces and sacrificing individual judgment to faith in leaders.

A "Beautiful Blonde Figurehead" for Every Cause: The Mass Media and Propaganda

The cult of personality that supported the persuasive power of fascism rendered the megaphonic influence of the mass media deeply threatening, as evidenced by the Frankfurt School's pessimism about mass culture. In *A Time to Be Born* (1942), Powell poses the political and ethical problems of the (pseudo) smart woman as a mouthpiece for powers both corporate and political. She creates a monstrous character in the glamorous Amanda Keeler Evans, a magazine celebrity, plagiarist cum editorial writer, and the wife of a media magnate. Powell depicts her as a ruthless opportunist: "At thirty Amanda . . . knew exactly what she wanted from life, which was, in a word, everything."[41] Amanda is a sinister incarnation of the female celebrity.

A Time to Be Born satirizes Henry and Clare Boothe Luce and their publishing empire. Millionaire Luce owned *Fortune*, *Time*, and *Life*, and he strongly directed the content, style, and political positions of his publications during the 1940s.[42] His second wife, Clare Boothe Luce, a glamorous blonde, was a former smart magazine writer and editor of *Vanity Fair* magazine.[43] In a 1943 diary entry, Powell spoke of the dangers posed when the veneer of style collaborated with wealth and political influence: "There is almost no fighting the success of combined wealth, looks, chic, and aggressiveness." She went on to condemn Luce's new political career as a Republican congresswoman: "After Clare Luce made such evil use of her new Congressional power I was glad I had slashed her in my last book and realized that my immediate weapons are most necessary and can help. The lashing of such evil can only be done by satire."[44] This last observation suggests the political potency Powell attributed to humor—it allows a fight from those who seem powerless, and it does not require wealth, looks, or chic, though it partakes in a healthy share of aggressiveness.[45]

In Powell's novel, Amanda's husband Julian Evans owns *Peabody's,* a smart magazine that he uses to manipulate public spirit during wartime. Amanda writes political columns whose substance she steals from other thinkers employed by her husband. The narrator wryly observes this ventriloquist's act: "Amanda's very lips seemed to move simultaneously with the lofty statements of her experts; she signed the words the second they left the other speaker's lips" (836). Amanda is dangerously pseudosmart. The narrator reports that "Amanda had all the beauty, fame, and wit that money could buy." Wit, like fame and beauty, is a commodity and an illusion. Smartness is an acquisition rather than a native faculty: "Presented with a mind the very moment her annual income hit a hundred thousand dollars, the pretty creature was urged to pass her counterfeit perceptions at full face value, and being as grimly ambitious as the age was gullible, she made a heyday of the world's confusion" (772). Amoral transactions and economic success parlay into political influence. Powell reports that "fabulous profits . . . piled up for the pretty author" that made "her random thoughts on economic and military strategy . . . automatically incontrovertible." Amanda substantiates her cleverness through her costume, not her conversation: "Ladies' clubs saw the label on her coat and the quality of her bracelet and at once begged her to instruct them in politics." Powell's narrator suggests that Amanda is just one instantiation of a broader cultural phenomenon: distraction by the glamour girl. The narrator reports, "This was an age for Amanda Keelers to spring up by the dozen, level-eyed handsome young women with nothing to lose, least of all a heart, so they were holding it aloft with spotlights playing on it from all corners of the world" (771). The narrator calls this "unbridled female exploitation," but the phrase remains ambiguous. Is Amanda exploiting the public with feminine wiles; has a female public longing for style and luxury been exploited; or are corporate and political powers exploiting these celebrity mouthpieces? Perhaps all three effects conspire. In politics, the narrator reminds the reader, "every cause had its own beautiful blonde figurehead" (772).

Powell seems to blame women for their facilitative role within the manipulative mass media. Powell depicts glamorous urban women as sirens: "their happy voices sang of destruction to come" (769). Women are the monstrous, well-dressed harbingers of doom, and they are dupes as well—happy to be bribed by "the loving-hearted gentlemen who make both women and wars possible" (770). Not only are such glamorous women willing to sell their copyright for a mess of publicity, but they don't even perform sophistication well: "Amanda's gayety consisted in laughing a great deal whether the conversation merited it or not" (793). Dressing up replaces verbal acuity: "Amanda had only to exploit her blonde good looks with an arresting costume to make his blood turn to water" (788). In fact, Amanda fears diminishing her seductiveness with her journalistic achievements: "Is it that I'm losing my looks or that intellectual success scares men and freezes your magnetism?" (795). In Amanda, Powell creates a humorless Lorelei Lee to bear the brunt of the mass media's political, financial, and cultural infractions.

But Powell complicates her vision of feminine smartness by introducing a rival to challenge Amanda, just as Millay introduces the "Woman Without Jewels" in "Knock Wood" to undermine the "Very Clever Woman." Mousy single girl Vicky Haven comes to New York from Amanda's home town, and Amanda sets her up with a job and an apartment. Amanda has selfish motives for this act of charity; she wants to disguise her adultery with smart magazine writer Ken Saunders by having a pied-à-terre where she can host him during the day. In bringing Vicky close, however, Amanda inadvertently undermines her love affair when Vicky and Ken begin an unexpected romance.

Vicky represents a version of smartness stripped of glamour. The narrator calls her "plain" and emphasizes her intellect: "Victoria Haven, at twenty-six, was considered one of Lakeville's brighter young women" (772, 801). Instead of pretending that she is conversant with all topics, as Amanda does at her parties, Vicky admits both her intellectual aptitude and her areas of ignorance: "Vicky, like everybody, was sure she was far smarter than the average and it sometimes surprised her that she was so dumb about the simplest things, such as understanding politics, treaties, who was who, the use of oyster forks, service plates, back garters on girdles, the difference between Republicans and Democrats, and the management of a lover" (801). This hodge-podge of troublesome topics from politics to fame, etiquette, romance, and lingerie reflects the subjects tackled by a smart magazine. While Amanda feigns universal expertise, Vicky hesitates before claiming understanding. She may be a middlebrow reader—"like everybody . . . sure she was far smarter than the average"—but she is skeptical of easy mastery.

Powell advocates this skepticism as a tool for opposing the magazine's messages. Vicky's native wit resists the platitudes of magazine "experts": "All Vicky could do was to read the women's magazines and discover how other heroines had solved this problem. The favorite solution, according to these experts, was to take your little savings out of the bank, buy a bathing-suit, some smart luggage, put on a little lipstick, throw away your ugly glasses and go to Palm Beach or Miami for two weeks." These commercial sops for emotional hurts bolster body image; according to the magazine's promises, a "smart but inexpensive bathing-suit bring[s] out . . . highlights in your figure." Consumerism and narcissism make way for materialism of a grander kind—the promise of a good match: "On the fourteenth day, if not before, a tall bronzed Texas oil man would appear and be bowled over by your unaffected passion for peppermint sticks, unlike the snobbish society women he knew." Vicky wryly reimagines the conclusion of this modern fairy tale: "if you turned to page 114 you would find yourself as heroine, bumbling down the church aisles without your glasses led by the Texas oil king and possibly a Seeing Eye dog." Powell implies that magazines advocate blindness to the mechanisms of commerce and glamour. To comfort vulnerable women, magazines offer fantasies that encourage further purchases and bodily improvements in search of unattainable romance. Vicky resists this fantasy through mockery: "Vicky was not convinced by this remedy, nor even certain she wanted to live in Texas, or that the sight of her rather thin figure in a smart but inexpensive bathing-suit would knock a millionaire off his feet" (803).

This passage teases out the dimensions of the word "smart," from intelligence and education to sexiness and fashion. In fact, tonal smartness helps Vicky regain her poise. At the beginning of this passage, Vicky is desperate, which prompts her to consult the sentimental narratives of women's magazines. Vicky's cynical view of this material, however, generates feelings of detachment and a practical resolution for the future. With her powers of critical reading, Vicky recognizes the subtext of these stories—money and materialism bring success and happiness: "The lesson of all these stories boiled down to saving your money, since all the secret solutions devolved on dipping into this ever-present savings account" (804). Her realization that the "ever-present savings account" allows mobility for these heroines inspires her own practical resolution to move to New York and get a job. When Vicky mocked her own hopes, she realized more literal ambitions. By parodying magazine romances in her mind, Vicky finds motivation and means for self-assertion. She can take dominant discourses and transform them to permit other interpretations and tones.[46]

Amanda dislikes other people's humor because it can transform the messages that she wishes to convey and control. The narrator reports that Amanda "was most enraged when important guests turned from her earnestly informed conversation to exchange nonsense with each other, nonsense which she was unable as she was unwilling to follow" (787). Irrelevancies reject the coercive nature of platitudes and pieties. Nonsense offers interpretations that stray from the party line and indeed from commonly accepted logic, and, because of this improvisation and revision, humorous non-sequitur allows genuine exchange between individuals rather than planned press releases. Amanda refuses to participate; this kind of free exchange reveals that her ideas are derivative and her ideologies inflexible. Suggestively, when Vicky meets Ken Saunders, Amanda's lover, they establish a bond based on their sense of humor.

Vicky and Ken both work for the smart magazine that is owned and controlled by Amanda and her husband. They connect through their unspoken cynical instincts about this profession: "What specialist in mediocrity determined the prize-winners and ruled what measure of banality was required for success?" They react to these insecurities, "the thoughts that brightened Ken's nights" and "the dark queries that clustered around Vicky Haven's pillow" with banter and lunches. They form their own Algonquin Round Table for two: "it was the most natural thing in the world for them, these two frightened people, to have the merriest lunches together in the Peabody Building. Since neither Ken nor Vicky was the sort to reveal private problems, each found the other most comforting, and almost disgustingly carefree" (875).

The banter between Ken and Vicky reveals the silliness of feminine brainlessness and glamour, the distortion of women's lives and bodies by media ideals, and the political inconsistencies of the consumer public. Ken jokes that Vicky is all seduction and no substance: "'I try to talk to you about life in the large and all you do is waggle your little peepers and look seductive,'" while she pretends vapidity: "'I wasn't trying to look seductive . . . I was only trying to look interested. I'm the type of girl that tries to give everything to what the gentleman is saying. Later I mull it over in my mind and can't make head nor tail of it'" (876). Vicky talks like Lorelei Lee who frequently alludes to the inscrutability of her "gentlemen" and would indeed waggle her "little peepers" at them for distraction, but the connection between Vicky and Ken relies on mutually recognizing this feminine brainlessness as an act that parodies Amanda's approach to journalism—mouthing what a gentleman expert says without being able to "make head nor tail of it." Vicky and Ken also mock the fashion industry and its connection to consumerism: "'Now I spend every cent on my back,'" Vicky says as she confesses to buying new outfits to wear to work at *Peabody's*. Her quip calls upon Ken to play the straight man: "'A fine thing in times like these,' rebuked Ken." Vicky answers with a joke about the supposed patriotism of consumerism: "'It gives me all the more to donate to Bundles for Britain'" (876). Like Parker in her Common Reader persona, Vicky confesses her unattractiveness to Ken and invokes several taboos of feminine appearance: "'I wasn't always the girl that I am now . . . I was fat and freckled and bald. Typhoid'" (877).

This newfound ability to speak freely in both senses of the word—both without hesitation and with liberty—imparts to Vicky the ability to confront power in social situations. Julian and Amanda Evans throw a dinner party where Vicky meets a college president, Dr. Swick. The narrator observes his vicious gaze: "The outside world was protected from these dangerous rays by unrimmed bifocal glasses, doubtless crash-proof, since he leveled his glance straight at people as if he neither knew nor cared that it was loaded" (937). Dr. Swick's intellect is his weapon, and Vicky seems vulnerable by comparison: "Doctor Swick machine-gunned the circle with his glittering eyes, his final ocular bullet piercing Vicky's quivering form." This doctor of philosophy deploys his intellectualism as a form of phallic dominance, and he uses his cynical perspective on politics to excuse his lack of ideals. While he takes pleasure in the spectacle of Amanda's body, as he leans forward to bring "the curve of her slim breasts into focus," Dr. Swick sees the political agenda for which she provides the figurehead as a smokescreen (938). Swick the intellectual laughs that only the "'moron public'" would believe in the ideals that World War II was supposedly being fought for and that the "'anti-fascist flavor'" of current discourse is "all a matter of who's in fashion" (940).

Powell hints that Swick has hit upon a pertinent insight about Amanda's flexible iconicity; she could just as easily play fascist as patriot. Swick's description of women magazine writers who "write or talk . . . with an anti-fascist flavor" but "could make a graceful pirouette backwards if the ball goes their way" fits Amanda. He derides women's magazine writing directly: "They [the Nazis] don't care about your little pieces. . . . You ladies weren't radical until it was chic" (940). The specter of fascism exposes the will-to-power displayed by American corporate imperialists, cloaked by nationalist messages and consumer dreams. The Luce periodicals shifted in political content and tone from the end of the 1930s into the 1940s. During the late 1930s, the foreign editorial section flirted with fascism while other writers aired liberal and radical views. By the 1940s, Luce feared that the Nazis could threaten America's dominance as a world power, and historian James Baughman observes: "No other publisher of his rank had offered, in his own words, such resolute calls for American hegemony." Luce was so influential in this posture that "rival mass communicators had come to accept the fundamental premises of the American Century" as Luce defined it.[47]

Vicky enjoys that Swick has exposed the propagandistic power of the Evans media empire. She muses that Ken "would have reveled in this catastrophic attack on the castle" (940). However, the professor's accuracy does not diminish his accountability. His posture of cynicism and intellectualism constitutes passivity and disengagement. The humble but plucky Vicky, by contrast, speaks out against him: "She wanted to make him squirm, too, and so she said, courageously, 'Doctor Swick finds much to admire in Hitler, don't you, Doctor Swick?'" Her punch-line lands: "Vicky was pleased to see that the doctor grew red, and flustered. 'I may have made some remark in a satirical sense,' he said stiffly. 'Naturally I have no respect for the Nazi régime.'" Swick's discomfiture is not Vicky's only triumph. A wealthy woman at the party calls Hitler an upstart who "used to sit around in cafés with other hoodlums" (976). Vicky marvels at the dangerous snobbery of this circle that derides Hitler for his bohemianism, not his Nazism. The wealthy, Vicky concludes, manipulate the public's patriotic fervor in order to maintain their power, privilege, and caste: "Making a country club of a great cause, joining it only because its membership was above reproach, its parties and privileges the most superior, its officers all the best people." This elitism and hierarchy disgusts Vicky. She exposes their transgressions and hypocrisies with a quip: "'You don't object to cannibalism, then,' she said. 'It's the table manners they use, isn't it, Mrs. Elroy?'" (977).

Vicky's sense of humor allows her to talk back to the powerful and the complacent. Meanwhile, the glamorous Amanda, is slowly losing her panache: "The war was getting too big for Amanda, it was no longer her private property, it was beyond one person's signature" (980). Because she does not invent her own voice, Amanda relies on external forces to support and sustain her popularity and celebrity. As her relationship with her husband the media mogul begins to fray, it dawns on Amanda that she is but a mass media puppet, dependent on the publicity that he controls: "'I'm a dummy. They've made a dummy of me,' she thought. 'They own me'" (986). In this insight, Amanda connects the voice of the ventriloquist's dummy and the money sponsoring her media prominence. The latter buys the former. Indeed, when the marriage collapses and Amanda resolves to reinvent herself for her public, even Andrew Callingham, the Hemingway character from *Turn, Magic Wheel* who reappears in *A Time to Be Born*, doubts that she could accomplish this without her husband's money and power: "'Has it occurred to you that you may find it harder 'fixing' everything once you break with Julian? I don't think you know yet what you're up against, my dear girl'" (1035). Amanda has fallen in love with her own reputation, but in her narcissistic absorption in her own charms she has failed to realize that their enchantment relies on the power and influence of men like Julian.

Depicting Amanda's exile from her former fame, Powell again suggests the self-estrangement entailed by celebrity. Amanda is a media monument, and, when she falls out of the spotlight, she no longer possesses a coherent identity: "Amanda, broken with her little misfortune, was no Amanda to Vicky but the curious awful spectacle of a statue in fragments" (1003). The statue in fragments image suggests not only personal ruination but also a political monument that has been superseded, forgotten. Amanda, like a statue of a dictator or a religious idol, faces defacement and blasphemy when she loses her aura. She craves the recovery of this exalted cultural status. When Andrew Callingham calls, Amanda ignores her own physical suffering and goes to meet the celebrity author. The narrator reports: "the pale, wan creature of a moment before suddenly transformed into the brittle, competent woman she was supposed to be." The adjective brittle suggests that in spite of Amanda's attempts to fit an ideal, her persona might still break. Vicky views her recovery with rueful wonder: "The woman was indestructible." Amanda may prove indestructible after all—her final scene in the novel, trying to seduce Callingham, makes her fate unclear—but this language objectifies Amanda and implies her solipsistic rigidity. She lacks the warmth and flexibility of humor that might allow her to be skeptical about her own legend. Indeed, Powell emphasizes Amanda's lack of humor as she "laughed mirthlessly" (1012).

Threatened by public extinction, Amanda would rather become a media-produced machine than admit her frailty. She pulls back from disaster by sacrificing her humanity to her celebrity: "it took as much human energy, blood, and tears to produce an Amanda as it did to produce any other successful institution" (1012–1013). She likes serving as a symbol of something larger than herself and does not know how to be a mere subject. Productive laughter pokes fun at institutions on behalf of the individual, as Vicky's experience demonstrates. The anthropologist Mary Douglas argues that if the joke "devalues social structure, perhaps it celebrates something else instead. It could be saying something about the values of individuals as against the value of the social relations in which they are organized."[48] Registering the contrast between the individual and organized social relations is crucial for more than individual reasons of emotional survival, as the international political context of the rise of fascism and the cultural context of mass media expansion that Powell stresses in this novel demonstrates.

Because Amanda can't acknowledge let alone embrace the value of the individual, her laughter is mirthless and hollow. Tyrus Miller deems the motif of mirthless laughter a defining convention of late modernist texts of the 1930s and 1940s. He contends that humorless laughter marks "the voice of 'damaged life' persisting at the threshold of disappearance as a self," and he describes this version of the comic as an attempt to establish "a new sort of minimal self, as much corporeal as psychic, as much technical as organic, and held together by the stiffening bonds of a laughter without an exterior object."[49] Amanda attempts to survive by clinging to the objectifying process of publicity and the corporeal and technical role of celebrity. As Miller argues, "'mirthless laughter'" administers "a mortifying jolt that may yet work to stiffen and preserve."[50] Amanda recomposes herself, but that gesture may mark the decomposition of the human subject. Like a statue, Amanda relies on other people to endow her with meaning and force. Vicky's less prominent, more autonomous, and more flexible social persona seems more resistant, more conducive to survival and self-sufficiency. She lives in Greenwich Village and consciously defines herself and her environs against Amanda's midtown media empire. In a minor act of revenge on her romantic and professional rival Vicky dubs her cat Amanda, but the original misses the joke: "'How funny for you to call your cat Amanda,' said Amanda" (1009). Unlike the monumental Amanda frozen in her perception of her own grandeur, Vicky is able to tease, grow, and change, small but vital gifts.

The book ends with the union of Ken and Vicky, an ending that drew Diana Trilling's scorn, for it smacked of a happily-ever-after: "At any rate, the wee note of cynicism she introduces into her love idyll doesn't save it."[51] I argue that this "wee note of cynicism" demonstrates the philosophy underpinning the novel and Powell's vision of how individuals can preserve meaningful voices in a mass-media-dominated world. Powell closes her novel with these words: "Ken kissed her. 'You're the one for me, darling. There couldn't ever be any Amanda in my life, now that I know about you. Never, never again.' Vicky stroked his hair. 'Thank you for that, darling,' she said gratefully. But she was not at all sure whether he was speaking the truth or what he hoped was the truth. For that matter, neither was Ken" (1041). The lovers' combination of hope and uncertainty puts in quotation marks the clichéd sentiment "'You're the one for me, darling.'" Ken and Vicky banish Amanda's jingoism while acknowledging her power, and this refusal represents a small but significant step toward liberty. The gap between "the truth" and "what he hoped was the truth" allows space for experience and muddled choices. The couple quotes the language of sentiment, but they reserve, smartly, the right to doubt.

5 / "Scratch a Socialist and You Find a Snob": Mary McCarthy, Irony, and Politics

For a female magazine writer raised on *Vogue* and educated at Vassar to join a Marxist intellectual elite would seem unlikely if not actively quixotic. Perhaps best known as the author of *The Group* (1963), a novel about a circle of Vassar graduates and their experiences in New York, Mary McCarthy addressed quite a different group in her first novel, *The Company She Keeps* (1942): leftist thinkers, liberal magazine writers, and New York intellectuals. In this work, McCarthy's ironic sensibility amplifies the dissonance between her fashionable feminine authorial persona and the milieu of the leftist magazine the *Partisan Review*. McCarthy heightens this contrast to explore the age-old tensions between leftist politics, consumer desire, and the class identity of intellectuals. McCarthy also mocks the strenuously defended yet easily undermined position of masculinity coded as intellectualism.[1] She uses smartness, in other words, to unsettle the authority that the very phrase "New York intellectual" imparted to her circle.

McCarthy's wit was a controversial element of her persona and her work. Indeed, Philip Rahv, cofounder of *The Partisan Review* and McCarthy's lover during her early involvement with the magazine, was so hurt by her satirical depiction of him in *The Oasis* (1949) that he began a lawsuit, which he later dropped, "alleging 132 violations of his rights," according to McCarthy's biographer Carol Brightman.[2] A wit capable of violating 132 rights in a single publication carried not inconsiderable clout. William Barrett described McCarthy as an "attractive and engaging woman, all smiles" from whom "[men] recoil[ed] . . . as if an ogress, booted and spurred, had entered the room brandishing her whips. In fact, from the point of view of the possible victims, she did carry a stinging whip—that impeccable syntax with which she might lash out in print at any time."[3] Barrett attributes to McCarthy both the indirection of feminine deception and immediate violence of verbal castration. McCarthy is a gracious hostess, terrifying monster, and relentless dominatrix all at once. This extended metaphor is so absurdly intense that it helps to suggest the overdetermination of McCarthy's vilification within her circle and beyond. The smart woman at the center of the ideological fray was frequently imagined as the source of that fray, as McCarthy was well aware; she explored this theme in *The Company She Keeps*.

Smart magazine culture informed McCarthy's literary sensibilities and cultural development. Born in 1912, McCarthy grew up with the popular periodicals of the 1920s and thus experienced as a given, not as an experiment, the advertising culture that publicized feminine types across the nation and created an enviable, elite, imaginary New York. In *How I Grew*, McCarthy describes the magazines that inspired her desire for urban sophistication and social distinction: "All those mornings spent poring over *Vogue* opposite my grandmother with her mending in the upstairs bay window had left their mark. I still yearned for admission into the New York society I read about but which was forever barred to me by our position on the map—there was never a word in *Vogue* about what happened socially in Seattle." The smart magazines helped to shape McCarthy's sense of humor as well: "I was soon reading *The American Mercury* and had induced my grandmother to subscribe to *Vanity Fair*, a Condé Nast publication that I could look at the day of its arrival in the sewing-room, along with her *Vogue*."[4]

In spite of this early affection for Condé Nast publications, as a professional writer and a well-known public intellectual, McCarthy strove to differentiate herself from predecessors like Edna St. Vincent Millay and Dorothy Parker. Though Millay and Parker both marched in protest of the Sacco and Vanzetti conviction in 1927, radical politics shaped McCarthy's career more decisively because of her formative professional years in the 1930s. The perceived apoliticism and sentimentality of Millay and Parker provide fodder for McCarthy's scorn in her autobiographical writings. One night at boarding school, an adolescent McCarthy recited Millay's verse while "sitting in an open casement window with my legs hanging out while I consider[ed] throwing myself down."[5] (She did not.) In her memoir *How I Grew*, McCarthy dismisses her Millay admiration as a childish, sentimental taste, implying that she can't even be bothered to remember how or when she abandoned her former literary idol: "And Edna Millay? . . . Did Anna Kitchel [a Vassar professor] 'kill' her for me with a jovial dart of satire?"[6] In her posthumously published *Intellectual Memoirs: New York, 1936–1938*, McCarthy recalls her disappointment at meeting the famous Dorothy Parker at a protest: "It was the only time I saw Dorothy Parker close up, and I was disappointed by her dumpy appearance."[7] Millay and Parker might have been famous for their iconoclasm, public prominence, and 1920s chic, McCarthy implies in her memoirs, but McCarthy trumped them (at least in her own version of her life) with her intellectualism and political voice while maintaining an even higher standard of fashion and grace. In the smart Olympics, Millay and Parker could only lag behind McCarthy's gold with silver and bronze.

By mocking Millay and Parker in her memoirs, McCarthy reinforces a literary divide between profitable humor for *Vanity Fair* or the *New Yorker* and serious essays for the *Partisan Review*. But her explicit rejection of Millay and Parker betrays how formative they were for her self-conception and her enduring literary priorities. Later in life when McCarthy diagnosed the limitations of her style as a theatre reviewer for the *Partisan Review*, she lamented her humorlessness: "it is not usually the opinions I aired . . . that give me such pain to hear again. It is the tone of voice in which they are pronounced." McCarthy further associates that "pedantic" tone with the decade and literary circle: "The period was 1937—the time of the Spanish Civil War and the Moscow Trials. The place was Union Square, New York."[8] In this reminiscence, McCarthy allies her voice with the earnestness and pedantry of radical ideologues, but in *The Company She Keeps* McCarthy grants a sense of humor and a critical, skeptical sensibility to her protagonist Margaret Sargent, who writes for liberal weeklies and espouses leftist politics. Margaret's smart attitudes and self-presentation alarm the male politicos who surround her, the "company she keeps."

By depicting her heroine Margaret as a variously admired and reviled wit, McCarthy addresses the vexed symbolic roles played by women in intellectual and print cultures. At one point, Margaret describes herself as "a princess among the trolls."[9] Even as she invokes the allure of imitating a feminine ideal, McCarthy also criticizes the elitism, xenophobia, and narcissism that can hide under the pretty face of feminine iconography. Margaret fears that the so-called trolls of her intellectual circle might tarnish her: "the clever ones were alcoholic or slightly homosexual, the serious ones were foreigners or else wore beards or black shirts or were desperately poor and had no table manners. Somehow each of them was handicapped for American life and therefore humble in love. And was she too disqualified, did she really belong to this fraternity of cripples, or was she not a sound and normal woman who had been spending her life in self-imposed exile" (112). In her catalogue of "cripples," Margaret disparages subcultures (homosexual, immigrant, bohemian) associated with intellectualism and sophistication, and she imagines their alterity as a threat.[10] McCarthy establishes Margaret's anxiety about sexuality, class, and ethnicity early in the novel in order to set up her satire of the "sound and normal" version of "American life" associated with hetero-normativity, plain speaking, nationalism, narcissism, whiteness, WASP-iness, and materialism. Over the course of the six stories in the book, McCarthy reveals that each of these supposed values are limitations.

Margaret's exceptional position as the fashionable, attractive, witty woman in her social and professional circle reflects McCarthy's own position amid the New York intellectuals. In 1937, McCarthy was conscripted by Rahv to become the only female founding editor of the *Partisan Review*. As a publication of the John Reed Club and an alternative to the *New Masses*, the *Partisan Review* had begun in 1934. It closed briefly, before resuming publication under the editorship of Rahv and William Phillips as a Trotskyite vehicle actively critical of the Stalinist line of the Communist Party.[11] The *Partisan Review* soon became a symbol of iconoclastic leftist intellectualism. McCarthy's name appeared in the list of editors, but her assigned task, reviewing theatre, was considered peripheral to the magazine's main aesthetic and political missions. Dawn Powell, who knew McCarthy, observed acidly in her diary that condescension greeted women's participation in such intellectual circles: "The intensely political woman—'We intellectuals'—although her legal friends and intellectuals treat her like a fondly regarded idiot child—yes, yes, throwing 'how right you are' etc., to her as you would quiet a noisy puppy with tidbits to keep him from interrupting your preoccupations."[12]

While not as vehement or negative as Powell in her assessment, McCarthy did joke later in life that her *Partisan Review* compatriots saw her as feminine, decorative, and out of touch: "I remained, as the *Partisan Review* boys said, absolutely bourgeois throughout. They always said to me very sternly, 'You're really a throwback. You're really a twenties figure.' I was sort of a gay, good-time girl from their point of view. And they were men of the thirties. Very serious."[13] Much as Jessie Fauset responded to the masculinist dimensions of the New Negro movement by celebrating women's humor, McCarthy responds to the masculinist pretensions of the New York intellectuals by championing the political value of wit and irony. Margaret embodies an urbane, chic, and witty modern feminine stereotype. In his introduction to McCarthy's collected essays, *New York Times* writer A. O. Scott compared Margaret Sargent to Carrie Bradshaw: "[McCarthy's] devotees may infer traces of her influence everywhere they look . . . even in *Sex and the City*, the popular HBO series about a smart, sexually adventurous New York writer and the company she keeps."[14] In addition, humor is a unifying theme and technique in the six stories of *The Company She Keeps*. In these stories, Margaret warms to characters with a sense of humor, faces professional criticism because of her sarcasm, and acknowledges her use of humor as a defense mechanism. Margaret's wry demeanor allows her to deflect the criticism she faces as a woman in a male-dominated professional context.

Significantly, this tone also reflects the intellectual vivacity of her ideologically serious peers. Terry Cooney explains in *The Rise of the New York Intellectuals* that "A number of the New York Intellectuals were so exuberant in their exercise of mind, so in love with the evidences of wit, that they seemed unable to resist the clever retort, the colorful remark, the apt phrase."[15] Banter provides a forum for intellectual and political exchange that escapes the rigidity of organized debate or theorized dialectics. McCarthy defends this political role of humor in the face of the ideologically defensive in *The Company She Keeps*. She also recognizes, however, that humor can confirm snobbery instead of unsettling hierarchies and that an ironic stance can excuse intellectual superiority and detachment rather than foster egalitarian engagement. McCarthy reveals that this dilemma about the role of humor and irony in an intellectually and politically engaged life is not simply the burden of the smart woman but also of the New York intellectual.

"The Airs of a Marquis": Intellectualism, Elitism, and the Middlebrow

The Company She Keeps was McCarthy's first major publication outside of magazines. In spite of its episodic nature, this collection was marketed as a novel, in part because of Margaret's increasing self-awareness over the course of the six short stories. McCarthy published this novel before she divided her literary output into two major modes: that of witty memoirist and that of intellectual and political satirist. (*The Group*, like *The Company She Keeps*, falls somewhere in the middle of these two poles.) In *Memories of a Catholic Girlhood* (1957) and *How I Grew* (1987), McCarthy plays with narrative voice and irony to explore the development of a personality through friction with authority and fleeting yet indelible impressions of human foibles and internal moral directives. In satirical novels like *The Oasis* (1949), *Groves of Academe* (1952), and *A Charmed Life* (1955), McCarthy sets the action in symbolic locales that bring together intellectuals: a utopian settlement, a university, and a bohemian village, respectively. In these novels, McCarthy, caricaturing her characters' appearance and tastes, suggests their predictability and mechanicalism in spite of their self-conception as originals and iconoclasts. In each plot, characters who see themselves as intellectuals and moral crusaders overreact to minor conflicts, absurdly debating the inconsequential with high seriousness; McCarthy, however, also uses them as mouthpieces for legitimate cultural, political, and philosophical debate. *The Company She Keeps* unites McCarthy's approach to memoir with the thematic thrust of her later intellectual satires. It focuses on the development of a personality and a narrative style even as it interrogates the cultural complications and pragmatic failings of self-conscious intellectualism.

One problem of intellectual identity is its aptitude to collapse into posturing or pretense, even when grounded in political ideals. Political affiliations can seem much like brand names in the social performance of taste and judgment. In *The Company She Keeps*, political convictions often amount to simplistic sentimentalism or social performance. In "The Genial Host," for example, the wealthy host of a dinner party prompts Margaret to play the role of outraged Trotskyite. Heartfelt ideology metamorphoses into cocktail hour humor and cynical resignation:

> "Meg is a violent Trotskyist," he said tenderly. "She thinks the rest of us are all GPU agents." . . . Martin Erdman was watching you, too. He clapped his hands twice in pantomime and gave you a long, ironic smile. You bent your head and blushed, and, though you were excited, your heart sank. You knew that you were not a violent Trotskyist, and Erdman must know it too. . . . You admired this romantic trait in yourself and you would confess humorously: "All I have to do is be for somebody and he loses." Now it comes to you that perhaps this was just another way of showing off, of setting yourself apart from the run of people. (140)

Elitism and wit modulate political conviction until it is reduced to powerless pantomime. Like magazine wit—or, indeed, *Partisan Review* political editorials—ideological poses can produce many issues, in both senses of the word, without resolving or confronting them in the real world. Humor about these political convictions reveals the elitism in the adopted role; Margaret likes always losing because it renders her distinct. This detached attitude is not quite the fervor of the committed revolutionary.

The *Partisan Review* circle was a boys' club focused on political theories, and the members thrived on debate and discussion. Reflecting on "the sectarian thirties," McCarthy quipped that "the only pleasures that were considered 'serious' were sex and arguing."[16] Cooney observes: "An air of masculine clubbiness hangs around the early years of the New York Intellectuals. Young women were sometimes present, sometimes mentioned, but seldom treated as equals."[17] Far from the man about town, the New York intellectual was deliberately out of step with the mainstream and the more heroic for it.[18] This figure was exemplified for some by the formidable Rahv, remembered by McCarthy as "grumblingly out of sorts with fashion, except where he felt it belonged, on the backs of good-looking women and girls."[19]

The members of the *Partisan Review* editorial board were invested in one kind of fashion: they prided themselves on being the intellectual vanguard. Not afraid to get their hands dirty in modern literary and political debates, these Marxist thinkers staked their intellectual tents in muddy ideological territory; they opposed proletariat literature and social realism and promoted instead the ambiguity and complexity of high modernism. They wanted to wed the values of the revolution with the values of New Criticism.[20] They accomplished this in part by insistently differentiating their highbrow tastes from the middlebrow kitsch of popular humor magazines like the *New Yorker*.[21] By disparaging the middlebrow, they could defend authentic art and authentic politics, and they could claim intellectual grounds for both. If they could convey the idea that commercial kitsch wallowed in the swamp waters of modern print culture, then they could claim that their radical politics were safely on the high ground.

The chic urban woman was a central emblem of the objectionable elitism, imitation, and mass appeal of middlebrow culture. This symbolic association proved problematic for McCarthy as a public figure and productive for her as a satirist as she makes it the subject of *The Company She Keeps*. Alfred Kazin linked McCarthy's critical faculties with the bourgeois mass media: "she despised the world in which she moved; her judgment represented that insignificant display of cleverness which a cynical society photographer might use in emphasizing a double chin and the dribble from an open mouth."[22] Kazin lambasts McCarthy for her snobbery and shallowness, and he associates her with the regrettable forces of mass culture and the public's attention to the body rather than the mind. All of these traits align McCarthy (and implicitly her feminine persona) with the worst infractions of middlebrow culture.

In *The Company She Keeps*, McCarthy also alludes to the smart woman as a symbol of bad faith, but she unpacks this all-too-easy misogyny. Margaret admits that she cherishes her Marxism as an elite status symbol: "The truth was that she hated [the middle class] shakily from above, not solidly from below, and her proletarian sympathies constituted a sort of snub that she administered to the middle class, just as a really smart woman will outdress her friends by relentlessly underdressing them. Scratch a socialist and you find a snob" (260). At first this analogy between Marxists and fashionable women competing with their friends seems to bolster a feminine stereotype: women are susceptible to trends, ideologically frivolous, and consumed with appearances. Also, it seems a literal and critical description of Margaret, a fashionable woman who tries to outdress and outthink her peers. The moral might seem misogynistic (i.e., "Smart women make bad socialists"), but McCarthy uses this figure to represent the movement's endemic flaws.

The narrator's cynical aphorism ("Scratch a socialist and you find a snob") makes this judgment universal, not aimed exclusively at women. The narrator continues seamlessly from the appraisal of Margaret's bad faith to a critique of Marxist rhetoric: "In the Marxist language, your opponent was always a *parvenu*, an *upstart*, an *adventurer* . . . the proletariat did not talk in such terms; this was the tone of the F.F.V. What the socialist movement did for a man was to allow him to give himself the airs of a marquis without having either his title or his sanity questioned" (260–261). McCarthy uses four male pronouns in that final sentence, not to mention the male form *marquis*, to connect socialism with masculinity. She then deflates the intellectual's aspiration to virility with her mocking allusion to the socialist's unquestioned sanity. The emperor has no clothes. By the end of this passage, the burden of snobbery has traveled from the single "smart woman" to the whole "socialist movement," even to the socialist man.

McCarthy explores the problem of snobbery for the politically committed intellectual in her most famous story from *The Company She Keeps*, "Man in the Brooks Brothers Shirt." Notorious when it first appeared in the *Partisan Review* in 1941 because of its sexual frankness, the story details Margaret's liaison on a train with a steel man named Breen. This man exemplifies the characteristics that leftist, bohemian Margaret opposes: midwestern values, earnestness, big business, simplicity rather than sophistication. Indeed, Breen's qualities reflect the attitudes and allegiances that editor Harold Ross eschewed in his 1924 prospectus for the proposed *New Yorker*. Rejecting middle America and "the old lady in Dubuque," Ross insisted that his magazine would "be what is commonly called sophisticated" and would be "published for a metropolitan audience" rather than for middle America. Equally distressing to Ross, however, was the implication that his publication might be "highbrow or radical"—he reassures his readers it will not be.[23] Margaret Sargent, by contrast, proudly claims radical status, though she shares with the *New Yorker*—as did the *Partisan Review*—contempt for middle America. The symbolic terrain of the Midwest, as Susan Hegeman notes, "became synonymous with the middle (bourgeois) stratum of cultural taste" in the 1930s, and cultural discomfort with middlebrow cultural production and middle-class status played out in assessments of the region.[24]

The pertinent difference between the *Partisan Review* attitude of urban superiority and that of the *New Yorker* rested in their divergent judgments of the middle class. The *New Yorker* projected a vision of an urban professional middle class that could be more with-it than the supposedly out-of-touch denizens of middle America. The magazine embraced a class fantasy that included both the aspiration to cultural capital and the more or less untroubled pursuit of material goals. *Partisan Review* writer Clement Greenberg, however, denigrated what he saw as the false consciousness of this bourgeois class in his famous 1939 essay "The Avant-Garde and Kitsch." He condemns the middle-class desire to purchase intellectual and cultural status symbols, maligning their consumption of devalued culture. We can see both attitudes in Margaret's character: her desire for comfort, social status, and material rewards on the one hand and her pride in iconoclasm, intellectual status, and insider knowledge of the avant-garde on the other. Viewed in this light, "Man in the Brooks Brothers Shirt" could be subtitled "The Battle of the Avant-Garde and Kitsch." The *Partisan Review* used its negative judgment of middlebrow culture to justify hostility to midwesterners who might otherwise have seemed like members of the proletariat whom intellectuals were meant to defend. "These Midwestern 'people,'" Hegeman explains, "belonged not to an organic 'culture' but to a liminal—middle—space in transition to full modernity, too replete with the goodies of a massified consumer culture."[25] McCarthy's story covers this symbolic middle ground as Margaret leaves New York and crosses the country on a train.

McCarthy's descriptions of the midwestern landscape reflect Margaret's vacillating ability to insulate herself from middle America as a sophisticated urbanite. At first, she imagines Oklahoma as an artistic backdrop for her private party with Breen: "Outside the flat yellow farm land went by, comfortably dotted with haystacks; the drought and the cow bones strewn over the Dust Bowl seemed remote as a surrealist painting" (97). This "remote" description of the Dust Bowl is a far cry from the pathos of John Steinbeck's *The Grapes of Wrath* (1939). Through this simile that turns the landscape of poverty and want into art for intellectual consumption, McCarthy tweaks Margaret's self-absorption and easy aestheticization of the world around her. Margaret abstracts the aesthetic details of the landscape from the painful social realities, an ironic move for a proclaimed radical. Later Margaret decries the dreariness and desolation of the landscape, the bleakness of which escalates based on her physical proximity to midwesterner Breen. After they have sex, Margaret observes: "They had been going over it [the Great Salt Lake] for hours, that immense, gray-brown blighting Dead Sea, which looked, not like an actual lake, but like a mirage seen in the desert. She had watched it for a long time . . . an interminable reminder of sterility, polygamy, and waste" (115). Margaret only notices the Great Salt Lake because it reminds her of her own sexual disgust. McCarthy thus comments on the potential solipsism of the modernist thinker, viewing the modern wasteland and exalting the individual's perspective over the masses.

Margaret's expressions of regional and cultural snobbery betray the avant-garde's perpetual vulnerability, its aptitude to collapse into the middlebrow. McCarthy dramatizes the permeability of this would-be intractable divide when Margaret meets Breen. Margaret holds an advance copy of a politically radical book on the train, and she imagines bragging to a stranger, "'Why, you probably haven't heard of it. It's not out yet.'" Margaret hesitates, realizing that this use of the book could be construed as pretension, and she raises the question of her own authenticity: "really, she could not be accused of insincerity. Unless it could be that her whole way of life had been assumed for the purposes of ostentation" (84). Margaret seeks cultural tokens of her own superiority, and she is horrified when she realizes that Breen has read works by this author: "It was incredible that this well-barbered citizen should not only be familiar with but have a taste for the work of an obscure revolutionary novelist" (85). One effect of the modern expansion of middlebrow culture, however, was the quick dissemination of previously high cultural artifacts, preparing the ground for both cursory familiarity and taste formation.[26]

In his influential analysis of class identification and the pursuit of cultural distinction, the sociologist Pierre Bourdieu argues that intellectuals scorn artifacts that wend their way to a broader middle-class audience. Once a broad base embraces these tastes, intellectuals seek newer, more abstruse artifacts with which to defend their cultural positioning. McCarthy's depiction of Margaret's pretension and disgust anticipates Bourdieu's analysis and the "deep ambivalence" about the middlebrow that he attributes to intellectual culture.[27] Intellectualism and ostentation are on the same plane in McCarthy's characterization of Margaret and her motives.

Margaret's boundary monitoring reflects the cultural gate-keeping undertaken by the *Partisan Review* circle. In "The Avant-Garde and Kitsch," Greenberg described the middlebrow reader as "insensible to the values of genuine culture" and "hungry nevertheless for the diversions that only culture of some sort can provide."[28] Margaret also employs an appetitive metaphor for cultural consumption, depicting the middlebrow reader as a bookworm who reads and excretes knowledge with misplaced complacency:

> Two alternatives presented themselves: either the man belonged to that extraordinary class of readers who have perfect literary digestions, who can devour anything printed, retaining what suits them, eliminating what does not, and liking all impartially, because, since they take what they want from each, they are always actually reading the same book (she had had a cousin who was like that about the theater, and she remembered how her aunt used to complain, saying "It's no use asking Cousin Florence whether the show at the stock company is any good this week; Cousin Florence has never seen a bad play")—either that, or else the man had got the name confused and was really thinking of some popular writer all the time. (86)

Margaret's complicated comfort to herself—that Breen might have read something by the author but he could not have understood—displays two strategies of differentiation from the middlebrow: individual discernment and participation in the avant-garde. Either Breen lacks the taste to assess what he reads, hence Margaret's witty literalization of the function of the *Reader's Digest*, a magazine founded in 1922, or he has not actually read it. Between these two rationalizations comes a revelation: the middlebrow is very close to home for Margaret, only a cousin away. We learn later in the story that Margaret is not from New York and used to envy "the world that had looked magic from Portland, Oregon" (89). As the popularity of New York-themed magazines in the 1920s and 1930s attests, Margaret is participating in a masquerade of the metropolitan (and indeed the cosmopolitan) that is part and parcel of, not opposed to, middlebrow culture.

As her scornful allusion to cousin Florence implies, Margaret finds the specter of the middlebrow most threatening in the form of other women. She protests too much that they are ersatz while she fancies herself the real thing. Through Margaret's anxiety about womanliness and the middlebrow, McCarthy tackles both the pervasive misogynist discourse used to define literary and cultural hierarchies, as Andreas Huyssen's *After the Great Divide* attests, and the self-lacerating combination of anxiety and discipline that characterizes class aspiration and cultural snobbery. Margaret scorns Breen's wife Leonie who "was interested in culture, too, particularly the theater." Leonie perhaps most disturbs Margaret because she reads the liberal magazine that Margaret writes for: "Leonie was a Book-of-the-Month club member and she also subscribed to the two liberal weeklies." While Breen shares his wife's omnivorous middlebrow reading habits, Leonie earns Margaret's automatic animosity: "nothing on earth would have induced her to talk to Leonie" (90–91).

McCarthy implicates Margaret in the forms of femininity and cultural status-seeking that she derides, however. Listing Breen's other lovers, Margaret imagines herself as the third in a series of bourgeois women: "She could see Eleanor, now an executive in her forties, good-looking, well-turned out, the kind of woman that eats at Longchamps or the Algonquin; and then Leonie, finer-drawn, younger, with a certain Marie Laurencin look that pale, pretty, neutral colored rich women get; then herself, still younger, still more highly organized" (122). Margaret reduces both of these women to social types. Leonie even seems as though she has been photocopied a few too many times, a process that has washed out her colors. From Margaret's point of view, Leonie is "drawn," a sketch of a woman. The ambiguous narration, however, turns on Margaret as she envisions herself as the third in this trio. Is Margaret more "highly organized" in her cultural interests than the indiscriminate middlebrow women she targets? Or is she more "highly organized" into a type, the way that caricature eliminates the messy details of personality that do not fit in its frame?

Indeed, Margaret wishes she could live up to a fantasy of polished exteriors: "She had a sudden vision of herself in a black dress, her face scrubbed and powdered, her hair neatly combed, sitting standoffishly in her seat, watching Utah and Nevada go by and reading her publisher's copy of a new *avant-garde* novel" (107). Unsatisfied by her behavior and thwarted by her embodiment, Margaret envies the physical standards of femininity that she cannot reach: "in a bathing suit at Southampton she would never have passed muster, and though she never submitted herself to this cruel test, it lived in her mind as a threat to her. A copy of *Vogue* picked up at the beauty parlor, a lunch at a restaurant that was beyond her means, would suffice to remind her of her peril" (112). To "pass muster" in a military sense is to "present oneself for inspection."[29] Like the middlebrow women she scorns, Margaret wishes she could marshal herself into a recognizable and enviable type.

This wish reflects class anxiety as much as insecurity about the unruly female body. In a 1950 essay, McCarthy characterizes *Vogue* in the 1930s as "an almost forbidding monitor enforcing the discipline of Paris." This discipline rested on the importance of class: "the woman of fashion, by definition, was a woman of a certain income whose clothes spoke the idiom of luxury and bon ton."[30] Margaret's clothes do not speak the idiom of luxury; she wears "a pair of white crepe-de-chine pants, many times mended, with a button off and a little brass pin in its place" (107). In her essay on *Vogue*, McCarthy makes no bones about the implacable barrier between the upper class and the aspiring middle class: "taste without money had a starved and middle-class pathos." She revels in the sadism of the magazine's imperious rhetoric: "*Vogue* of that epoch was cruel, rather in the manner of an upper servant."[31] In "The Man in the Brooks Brothers Shirt," the psychological upper servant of self-assessment hands Margaret her hat. In spite of her ideological allegiances, Margaret experiences intense shame about physicality and fashion. By connecting Margaret's desire for cultural status with her quest to fit a feminine physical ideal, McCarthy demonstrates that women's bodies serve as a symbolic focal point for anxiety about class.

Suggestively, the parvenu Breen complains about Margaret's dishevelment and cheap attire. He later buys her "several pieces of glamour-girl underwear and a topaz broach" to replace the pinned panties—perhaps not a sign of his fluency in the idiom of bon ton but certainly an assertion of cultural authority (131). Breen also deems her bohemian lifestyle gauche: "It was as if he had made a point of telling her that her gayest, wickedest, most extravagant hat was ugly and out of fashion" (127). Margaret initially pitied Breen for his middle-class pathos, "ensconce[d] in the dignity of sadness." She both condescended to and sympathized with what she understood to be his inevitable aspirations to cosmopolitan grandeur, a quality of all "small-town men newly admitted into world-citizenship" (97). Now the tables are turned, and Breen is the monitor enforcing the discipline of class, informing Margaret that her desire to play "the Bohemian Girl" betrays that she is not "the great lady" but instead a middle-class aspirant longing for "that sense of ritualistic 'rightness' that the Best People are supposed to bask in" (88).

In the sexual encounter between Breen and Margaret, McCarthy suggests the costs of this longing for status. After Margaret exposes her naked body to Breen and has sex with him, she imagines her body as the victim of a machine: "it was as if, carelessly, inadvertently, almost, she had pulled a switch that had set a whole strange factory going, and now, too late, she discovered that she did not know how to turn it off . . . some sense of guilt . . . kept her glued to the spot, watching and listening, waiting to be ground to bits" (119). In this metaphor, McCarthy treats her body as a passive recipient of external direction and discipline. In an anecdote that recalls the dragon-like hair dryer in Millay's story "*Madame a tort*," Margaret compares her sexual passivity to an occasion when self-improvement regimens went awry: "Once, in a beauty parlor, she had been put under a defective dryer that remained on high no matter where she turned the regulator; her neck seemed to be burning up, and she could, at any time, have freed herself by simply getting out of the chair; yet she had stayed there the full half-hour, until the operator came to release her. 'I think,' she had said then, lightly, 'there is something wrong with the machine.' And when the operator had examined it, all the women had gathered round, clucking, 'How did you ever stand it?'" (120). The sheer force of individual will, inspired by the ideal of self-discipline and bodily improvement, strains through pain toward impossible physical ideals. Consumer products promise to regulate the uncontrolled female body. Thus, paradoxically, a culture of narcissism (grooming, fashion, self-presentation) also advocates the ethos of feminine self-abnegation, the value of "stand[ing] it," whether in the beauty parlor or the bedroom.[32]

McCarthy makes it clear that Margaret's self-image and desires are filtered through discourses she borrows from magazines, advertisements, and popular fiction.[33] Margaret envies Breen's "highballs, gold in the glasses, [that] tasted, as her own never did, the way they looked in the White Rock advertisements" (88). Her confessions of her sexual past "with thumbnail descriptions" Margaret cannot help but pattern "like a drugstore novel" (100). Influenced by mass media prescriptions, Margaret longs for a total vision of herself that would turn her internal self into a legible exterior. She longs for someone to "show her her own lineaments." This caricature could instruct her on appropriate gesture: "If she once knew, she had no doubt that she could behave perfectly." Margaret's search for an interior leads only to further exteriors: "For a while she had believed that it was a matter of waiting until you grew older and your character was formed; then you would be able to recognize it as easily as a photograph" (101). Like Effie in Powell's *A Time to Be Born*, Margaret is uncertain that she can recognize herself without the sharpening lenses of publicity and mechanical reproduction. Even in her private exchanges with Breen, Margaret imagines viewing herself from the outside: "It was exactly as if they were drinking in a show window, for nobody went by who did not peer in, and she felt that she could discern envy, admiration, and censure in the quick looks that were shot at her. The man sat at ease, unconscious of these attentions, but she kept her back straight, her shoulders high with decorum, and let her bare arms rise and fall now and then in short parabolas of gesture" (88). She wants to be watched and admired for her behavioral and postural precision.

Even as she mimes upper-class decorousness, however, Margaret also plays the devil-may-care modern woman: "There was an air of professional rowdyism about their drinking neat whisky early in the morning in a disheveled compartment, that took her fancy" (110). She plays a hard-drinking literary type, indicating her detachment from the rendezvous at hand and straining for cultural superiority. Alone with Breen, Margaret admits to drunkenness, quotes poetry, and bargains with God, three features of Parker's monologues "A Telephone Call," "But the One on the Right," and "The Little Hours": "She must be getting drunk, she knew, or she would not have said this, and a certain cool part of her personality protested. I must not quote poetry, she thought. I must stop it; God help us, if I'm not careful, we'll be singing Yale songs next. But her voice had broken away from her; she could only follow it, satirically, from a great distance. 'It's from Chaucer,' she went on, when she saw that she had his attention. 'Criseyde says it, 'I am myn owene woman, wel at ese.' . . . Oh my God, she said, get me out of this and I will do anything you want" (105–106). It is trebly ironic that Margaret has to borrow from Chaucer to proclaim her self-possession, that she invokes this quotation at just the crisis moment in her encounter with Breen (right before they have sex) when she feels the least at ease, and that her implicit Parker imitation suggests that Margaret's idea of her "owene woman" is derivative and stylized. The title of McCarthy's story also ironizes Margaret's drunken declaration of autonomy. The story is, after all, "The Man in the

Brooks Brothers Shirt," not "The Young Woman in the Crepe-de-Chine Underwear."

In spite of her wish to highlight "a cool part of her personality" and to watch this scene "from a great distance," Margaret's desire for detachment falters when she seeks to confirm her worth in Breen's eyes. This desire for cultural and gendered affirmation reflects a similar thematic strain in Parker's work. At the end of Parker's "The Garter," discussed in chapter 3, a man "who looks a little too Brooks Brothers to be really understanding" approaches the woebegone narrator with her broken garter, presumably offering conversation, rescue, or both.[34] She depends on his intervention for her redemption. After having sex with her Man in the Brooks Brothers Shirt, Margaret is also left garterless: "She saw herself locked in an intolerable but ludicrous dilemma: it was impossible to face the rest of the train with one stocking hanging down; but it was also impossible to wait for the man to wake up and enlist him in retrieving the garter" (108). Both Parker and Margaret are left vulnerable in their need for the Brooks Brothers man—Parker because only he can pull her out of the corner and Margaret because she has come to realize that he is as fallen as she is. The brand name Brooks Brothers promises status, superiority, and masculinity, but, in Margaret's case, it has left her with a mere mortal, even a buffoon.

The absurdity of this situation unexpectedly brings Margaret to a renewed state of clarity: "as the comic nature of the problem grew plain to her, her head cleared" (108). Throughout the story, Margaret is overwhelmed by the desire to be better—the desire to sound more intellectual, to bandy more obscure cultural references, to dress more fashionably, to behave more aloofly, to outshine competitors in both sex and work; the list goes on. Humor promises to lower the stakes: "If the seduction (or whatever it was) could be reduced to its lowest common denominator, could be seen in farcical terms, she could accept and even, wryly, enjoy it. The world of farce was a sort of moral underworld, a cheerful, well-lit hell where a Fall was only a prat-fall after all" (111). The vertical fall— from status, from morality, from discipline—is replaced by the bounce of comic survival. Humor levels Margaret's internalized hierarchies.

At the same time that humor facilitates resilience, this genre of monologue risks the perpetuation of ethical shrugging and political detachment. If it is comical for Margaret to sleep with Breen, then she does not have to investigate her motives for doing so, her class aspirations and prejudices, her ideological inconsistencies and her snobbery. Ironic amusement provides a blank check of permission that shortchanges real self-examination. The gesture of self-examination purports to prove that the speaker is higher than the "lowest common denominator." Hegeman complains that this ineffectual and exculpatory self-examination characterizes New York intellectuals and their literary output more generally. She criticizes their exaltation of "their own—infinitely complex, fascinatingly ambiguous—position of self-imposed marginality in relation to the political and ethical questions of their day." Hegeman fears that in this work, "the self is recentered as the object of interest, the reason for writing."[35]

McCarthy dramatizes this narcissistic dimension of self-deprecating humor in Margaret's performances for Breen. Turning her confessions into flirtations with her audience, Margaret plays up her contradictory qualities: "she knew for sure in this compartment that she was beautiful and gay and clever, and worldly and innocent, serious and frivolous, capricious and trustworthy, witty and sad, bad and really good, all mixed up together, all at the same time." Ironic inconsistency allows personal caprice to overtake ideological commitment: "She could feel the power running in her, like a medium on a particularly good night" (89). Margaret's excitement about "power running in her" suggests complicity with institutions of power in channeling this persona. Margaret later tells Breen "Money is your medium," as she accepts the promise of gifts from him (129). The repetition of the word "medium" leaves readers with the question: Is Margaret's witty persona her self-invented medium, or is money talking through her as it does through Amanda Keeler in Powell's *A Time to Be Born?* Bourdieu argues that even intellectuals and artists rely upon "the field of production of cultural goods, itself governed by the dialectic of pretension and distinction" that "endlessly suppl[ies] new goods or new ways of using the same goods."[36] Is Margaret repackaging market complicity as ironic self-awareness to minimize the impression of political bad faith?[37]

To further complicate the promise of ironic distance, McCarthy reveals that Margaret's persona disguises her intense insecurity. McCarthy thus renders the performance of sophistication another incarnation of social conformity rather than critical distance. Margaret remembers her adolescence, trying "to show that she was sophisticated and grown-up," and this masquerade leads to sexual encounters: "what she was really asking all along was not that the male should assault her, but that he should believe her a woman" (103). This anecdote throws light on the persona Margaret adopts in her professional circle, a group of "sophisticated and grown-up" intellectuals who withhold belief, not in Margaret's femininity or sexuality, both of which are taken as insurmountable givens, but rather in her intellectual and political legitimacy. Even Breen assures Margaret that she is just a beautiful girl, not the committed leftist and bohemian she would like to be: "'underneath all that you're just a sweet girl'" (127). The surface of appealing femininity eclipses her interior substance, a self-defeating strategy of legitimation.

McCarthy uses the strain to embody the myth of femininity as an illustrative example of individual identity's distortion in the social masquerade. Wishing to be appropriately womanly, Margaret feels divorced from her exterior: "hers was a kind of masquerade of sexuality, like the rubber breasts that homosexuals put on for drags, but, like the dummy breasts, its brazenness betrayed it: it was a poor copy and a hostile travesty all at once" (104). McCarthy puns on "travesty," alluding to both transvestitism and parody.[38] Margaret attempts to copy modern feminine ideals and, while doing so, covertly expresses her hostility to those traits through humor. This hostility, however, does not lead to her refusal of the feminine type, only to her frustration at her own failures in embodying it: "All her gestures grew over-feminine and demonstrative; the lift of her eyebrows was a shade too arch: like a *passée* belle, she was overplaying herself" (133). In these descriptions of Margaret playing a woman, McCarthy dramatizes the psychological stakes of playing a social role. The figure of the passée belle explicitly alludes to a failed performance of femininity and further connotes an archaic aristocracy, a past social order of pedigree and ceremony. Margaret longs for class security as well as feminine appeal.

McCarthy depicts Margaret's self-assessment as a form of capitalist logic. Margaret hopes that Breen will literally buy her act: "That was what had been missing in the men she had known in New York—the shrewd buyer's eye, the swift, brutal appraisal" (111). Because he has so much money, Margaret imagines Breen as the ultimate arbiter of her worth in a paradise of conspicuous consumption: "This man now—surely he came from that heavenly world, that divine position at the center of things where choice is unlimited. And he had chosen *her*" (113). McCarthy undercuts this attitude even as she articulates it. Margaret's momentary testimony to the divinity of his wealth notwithstanding, Breen is a mere bureaucrat and salesman, "a Chief Purchasing Agent and Fourth Vice President" (123–125). Margaret has been taken in (at least temporarily) by the wealthy middle class that Greenberg disparages in "The Avant-Garde and Kitsch." If Margaret the self-aware intellectual lapses into consumerist approaches to self-assessment and exults in the material allure of Breen's money, then the political prospects for widespread radical departure from capitalist ideology seem bleak. Breen observes bluntly: "'You're never going to get anywhere in America with that proletariat stuff. Every workingman wants to live the way I do. He doesn't want me to live the way he does'" (93). McCarthy's satirical perspective echoes Breen's sense that the battle for socialist revolution has already been lost in the sphere of desires before it gets hammered out in the arena of political debate.

Margaret embodies the contradictions of consumer longings and revolutionary resentments. Following Breen's orders, Margaret goes to get a bath on the train, and she sulks while she is there: "She lay in the bath a long time, gathering her forces. In the tepid water, she felt for the first time a genuine socialist ardor. For the first time in her life, she truly hated luxury, hated Brooks Brothers and Bergdorf Goodman and Chanel and furs and good food." McCarthy's humor skewers Margaret's self-righteous position. The "forces" of Margaret's personal socialist revolution are simply thoughts marshaled in the bath. The "tepid water" puts a damper on this so-called "genuine socialist ardor," and Margaret's catalogue of luxury goods undermines her new hatred of luxury. She associates the status symbols of fashion and consumerism with her own body and condemns both: "All the pretty things she had seen in shops and coveted appeared to her suddenly gross, superfatted, fleshly, even, strangely, unclean." This fixation on the grossness of the body and its "superfatted" nature corresponds with the bodily discipline that Margaret embraced in the name of *Vogue*. Finally, her attempt to allegorically reread her situation as one of ideological victimhood collapses into a feminine stereotype of sexual passivity: "she saw herself as a citadel of socialist virginity, that could be taken and taken again, but never truly subdued. The man's whole assault on her now seemed to have had a political character; it was an incidental atrocity in the long class war." To call consensual if unpleasant sex on a train with a businessman an "atrocity" and "assault" smacks at least of self-importance and at most of political bad faith. Margaret's superior perspective reveals her self-deception: "She smiled again, thinking that she had come out of it untouched, while he had been reduced to a jelly" (117). The third-person narrative places a skeptical check on Margaret's own conclusion about the situation ("*thinking* that she had come out of it untouched," emphasis mine). Furthermore, the metaphor that Margaret selects for Breen's vulnerability ("he had been reduced to a jelly") draws uncomfortable attention to Margaret's own situation; she is suspended in the bath. Is this attempt to join Diogenes the cynic in his tub an inevitable gesture of passivity rather than countercultural critique? Through this story, McCarthy suggests that intellectual status and political commitment can collude with rather than correct snobbery and narcissism.

"Preserve Me in Disunity": The Value of Irony

McCarthy does not end her analysis of ideological inconsistency with Margaret's confessions of class-based anxiety. In the penultimate story of the six-story collection, "Portrait of the Intellectual as a Yale Man," McCarthy reveals that Margaret's male colleagues also cannot square their political commitment with their elitism. Their desire to proclaim authenticity results in an exaggerated performance of ideological virility. From their point of view, the female magazine writer is an outsider in a political and intellectual sphere for men. In this story, the reader views Margaret only from the vantage of her colleague Jim Barnett, the Yale Man and Intellectual of the title. From his perspective, Margaret seems to dodge every pitfall of urbane intellectualism with agility and humor. Worse still, she points out the male intellectual's every misstep.

The narrator colludes with Margaret in this exposure of masculinist intellectualism. In overstated figurative language, the narrator characterizes Marxism as a titillating "actress" and a "scarlet woman of the steppes" (172). Barnett, a writer for a magazine called *The Liberal*, compares his translation of Marxist ideas into popular language to undressing a woman: "The ideas he put forward, familiar enough when clothed in their usual phraseology, emerged in his writing in a state of undress that made them look exciting and almost new, just as a woman whom one has known for years is always something of a surprise without her clothes on. And, in the end, it was not the ideas that counted so much, as the fact that Jim Barnett held them" (169). The free indirect discourse indicates Jim's arrogance, knavishness, and self-congratulation. He is like an adolescent boy, wishing to see familiar women naked; now the titillating object is not a woman but an idea. Though Jim does not extend the metaphor in his own mind, McCarthy uses the logical conclusion of the analogy—that women do not count so much as the fact that Jim Barnett held them—to indicate his benightedness. Jim is obtuse about the full personhood of women, just as he misses the nuance of ideas.

Margaret turns this objectification of women on its head in her bantering dialogue when she compares Jim and the other editors—all male—to prostitutes. She says: "'You keep patting yourself on the back because you're not working for Hearst. It's like a lot of kept women feeling virtuous because they're not streetwalkers. Oh yes, you're being true to your ideals; and the kept women are being true to Daddy. But what if Daddy went broke, or the ideals ceased to pay a hundred and a quarter a week?'" (192). In this comparison of magazine editors to kept women, Margaret perpetuates the conventional modernist association of popular writing with prostitution and mass media with degraded femininity. In this view, to be paid by a periodical, however liberal the magazine, is emasculating. At the same time, Margaret implicitly claims the worldly power of femininity for herself. She characterizes these men as kept women who require masculine protection and delude themselves; they are an infantile version of the sexualized woman, while Margaret is a sexy, worldly cynic. In the largely Stalinist office of *The Liberal*, she makes a joke in defense of Trotsky: "'What would you have [Trotsky] do? Hold up his hands like a girl, and say, 'Oh, no! think of my reputation! I can't accept presents from strange gentlemen!'" (193). Margaret's parodic ventriloquization of shrinking-violet femininity draws attention to her implicit appropriation of masculine prerogative in her professional ambition.[39] A well-dressed woman in a male-dominated office, Margaret imitates the "Old Man," Trotsky, and she imitates him imitating a girl. Her joke suggests that it is absurd for Trotsky to behave like a girl and in turn that it would be absurd for a woman of her intellect to behave "like a girl" and back down from her forceful political opinions.[40]

With Margaret's comment, McCarthy alludes to a gendered swipe that Trotsky made at the *Partisan Review* editorial board for their ideological wishy-washiness. Trotsky contacted the editors after their early issues to criticize their concern with intellectual respectability. He wrote: "You defend yourselves from the Stalinists like well-behaved young ladies whom street rowdies insult."[41] Margaret similarly remarks: "You people worry all the time about your integrity, like a debutante worrying about her virginity. Just how far can she go and still be a good girl?" (192). Thus, Margaret becomes the mouthpiece for Trotsky. The smart woman, not the intellectual man, speaks for a major scholar and politician through the very wit that makes her attitudes problematic from Jim's point of view.

While Margaret performs womanliness in order to talk like a man, her performance throws into relief the fact that Jim is merely feigning a coherent identity. The fear of femininity haunts Jim's certainty about his literary and political identity: "he was now confronted with what he imagined to be a general, undiscriminating hostility, a spirit of criticism embodied in the girl that was capricious, feminine, and absolutely inscrutable, so that he went about feeling continually guilty without knowing just what it was he had done. It haunted him that, if he could anticipate every objection, he would be safe, but there was no telling *what* this strange girl might find fault with" (227). On one hand, this "undiscriminating hostility" and its association with a "capricious, feminine" type reflect Jim's sexism; he thinks that Margaret is a bitch. On the other hand, a critical principle that "objects" and "finds fault" also motivates the story and the narrative perspective. The narrator highlights Jim's perpetual rationalizations and accommodations, thus revealing his moral compromises much as Margaret insists on doing. These two "strange girl[s]," Margaret Sargent and the implied author, look askance at the all-American masculine Marxist (and indicate what an odd marriage of roles this hodge-podge represents).

The narrator's dry asides undermine Jim's accomplishments from the beginning. The narration introduces Jim's adoption of Marxist ideology with incongruous metaphors: "In much the same tone (that of a man in an advertisement letting another man in on a new high-test gasoline) Jim began to write about his convictions in articles and book reviews for the liberal magazines ... if Jim had committed an unpardonable breach of manners in interesting himself in Marxism, his rough-and-tumble vocabulary was a sort of apology for this, a placatory offering to the gods of decorum, who must have appeared to him in the guise of football players" (169). Jim's bluff masculine pretensions and his consumerist approach to ideas render his political affiliations suspect. If Margaret Sargent did not point out his hypocrisies, the narrator would have already made them obvious.

In the context of this story, then, femininity becomes an advantage for critical distance in the face of a corrupting establishment that remains predominantly male. To be an outsider allows intellectual integrity at a time when insiders will just be absorbed into the system and its attendant rationalizations.[42] Though Jim strives to espouse Marxism with earnestness and good faith, the contradictions of his role implicate him: "The inconsistencies he found whenever he examined his own thoughts troubled him a good deal. He found, for example, that he liked to drink and dance and go to medium-smart night clubs with medium-pretty girls. Yet he believed with Veblen that there was no greater folly than conspicuous consumption. . . . This was a problem all well-to-do radicals had to face" (175). Jim is seduced by the promise of smartness, allied with newness and urbanity (night clubs and pretty girls) as well as a comforting averageness, a middle-class medium. Both comforts—being on the cutting edge and resting in the middle—represent the allure of bourgeois lifestyles and material gains.

The story's satire is aimed directly at liberal thinkers working for magazines more mainstream than the *Partisan Review*. Jim Barnett was based at least in part on *New Republic* writer and *New York Times* book reviewer John Chamberlain who moved steadily rightward in political and professional affiliations, until he ultimately worked for the Luce publication *Fortune*. So too does Jim start out writing for the *Liberal*; he became disillusioned with Stalinism thanks to the Trotskyite influence of Margaret and ultimately resigned his post. By the end of the story, Barnett is employed by *Destiny* magazine and enjoys the perquisites that a popular, conservative magazine offers. Jim's drift to the political right offers an implicit authorial investigation of the status and effectiveness of irony.

Though Margaret's "ironical smile" explodes Jim's vaunted composure, the other references to irony in the story make this attitude problematically passive (191). Jim has trouble engaging Stalinists, for example, in debates about the Moscow Trials because the accusations against Trotsky seem so absurd: "it was all like a bad spy picture that you hissed and booed and applauded (ironically) from the gallery of the Hype in New Haven" (213). The ironic perspective provides a safe position of literal and figurative height and a safely passive role of spectator. This passivity infects the other Trotskyites as well, at least in Jim's assessment: "It seemed to him that every committee member wore an expression of injury, of self-justification, a funny, feminine, 'put-upon' look . . . ironical smiles of vindication kept flitting from face to face." Jim projects his own feelings of guilt and abjection onto his Trotskyite peers. He wants to separate himself from them as a single, heroic male champion of the cause: "Watching them all, Jim would wish that he was the only guy in the world who took Trotsky's side" (218). Of course, Jim ignores what the reader recognizes: over the course of the story, Jim has felt injured, attempted to self-justify, and claimed to be put upon. If these are the terms of femininity, then Jim is also feminine, not the masculine champion he covets.

The threat posed by this form of ironic detachment is not just that of feminine passivity but indeed of total solipsism. Jim observes "the dean of American philosophy," John Dewey, as he attends the meetings of the Trotskyites: "Dewey truly appeared to have no reservations; you could not call that mild irony a reservation, for it was a mere habit, like his

Yankee drawl, that was so ingrained, so natural, that it seemed to have no specific relation to the outside world, but only to his own, interior life" (221). McCarthy aligns irony in this passage with established intellectual hierarchies, philosophical tradition, and political inaction—three categories that complicate, indeed almost cancel, the possibility of radical change. While the philosophical tradition of pragmatism employs irony to acknowledge the contingencies of political existence, as I later explore in connection with contemporary pragmatist Richard Rorty, Dewey in this scene seems less a model for emulation than a political cautionary tale.

The fear that irony might insulate the intellectual from the outside world motivated McCarthy's critique of her own Trotskyite circle. Indeed, seven years later in *The Oasis*, she parodied her friends so obviously that many, especially Rahv (as mentioned at the chapter's opening), were infuriated at the portrait. In this novel about an unsuccessful utopian settlement, McCarthy depicts what Alan Wald calls the "personalized dissidence" of the New York intellectuals in the 1940s.[43] The narrator links their detached and disillusioned tone with political passivity: "They had been for some time more or less inactive politically, and their materialism had hardened into a railing cynicism, yet they still retained from their Leninist days, along with the conception of history as arbiter, a notion of themselves as a revolutionary *elite* whose correctness in political theory allowed them the widest latitude in personal practice."[44] "Railing cynicism" replaces "political activity," and elitism replaces revolution. This group embraces the blasé: "there was a part of themselves which Utopia did not touch; boredom and urban cynicism had become so natural to them that an experience from which these qualities were absent seemed to be, in some way, defective."[45] The radical's desire for a better world for all is tempered by the individual's desire to prove superior to the degraded popular world. In McCarthy's view, cynicism protects the New York intellectuals from engagement.

In an interview she gave late in her life, McCarthy addressed the feared futility and defeatism of irony: "In a revolutionary situation, it may be good to be clear-minded and be radical, too. But in a non-revolutionary situation, this leads to an ironic detachment. And irony, self-irony and all the other kinds, is the present-day American curse. That is, among intelligent people."[46] Even in this brief sound bite about irony, McCarthy sets up the Catch-22 that also emerges in her stories in *The Company She Keeps*. Irony and self-ironizing provide the distinguishing signs of intelligence, yet maintaining an ironic perspective circumvents political engagement, fosters detachment, and sustains the quietism of a "non-revolutionary situation." Does the phrase "political intellectual" then constitute an oxymoron?

In his autobiography, Alfred Kazin blamed McCarthy for sowing incertitude about the political efficacy of the left. He groused: "Without the growing conviction of meaninglessness in the air, she might never have felt any authority at all. But bewilderment in the 'movement' now set her up exactly as the pathos of the 'emancipated' woman of the Twenties had made a world for Dorothy Parker."[47] Kazin's comments, reflective of his personal dislike for McCarthy, also suggest the perceived political consequences of irony. Kazin, much like Jim Barnett, sees an ironic perspective as a threat to the mission of the community. In Kazin's account, Parker and McCarthy are opportunists, taking advantage of an atmosphere of despair and doubt to encourage dissent and resignation. Kazin's anxieties about political solidarity—his implicit sense that staying with the movement is the first step to pursuing radical change—are mapped onto gender relationships. Women spoil the homosocial world of masculine intellectualism, just as irony ruptures the united political front promised by that world.

From a contemporary standpoint, however, the very individualism and pragmatism of the ironic point of view represent its greatest potential for political practice. Harvey Teres summarizes this legacy from McCarthy and her circle: "The New York intellectuals envisioned a politics that could address subjective experience, encourage diversity, accommodate spontaneity, and adjust to complexity and uncertainty." Irony's capacity to "reveal . . . the chinks in the armor of radical intellectuals whose personal lives are riven by lapses of character" prevents some risks of ideological commitment, namely "abstraction, dogmatism, and arrogance on the left."[48] Philosopher Richard Rorty also inherited the New York intellectual tradition in espousing the powers of irony. Indeed, Rorty's parents were "on the periphery of the group that would become known as the New York intellectuals."[49] In his controversial and influential defense of irony, *Contingency, Irony and Solidarity*, Rorty admits that "ironism has often seemed intrinsically hostile not only to democracy but to human solidarity," but he argues that "hostility to a particular historically conditioned and possibly transient form of solidarity is not hostility to solidarity as such."[50] Rorty thus applauds what Kazin fears: individual differentiation from a larger movement. Rorty argues that a more flexible understanding of what political solidarity could mean would expand the circle of people who could seem "one of us" instead of "one of them."[51] Rorty suggests that self-interrogation demonstrates that forms of hierarchy and affiliation are contingent, not inevitable or objectively true. When seemingly concrete bonds and barriers become elastic from this perspective, elitism could give way to a more egalitarian vision.

McCarthy explores the relationship of irony to affiliation, elitism, and political vision in the final story of *The Company She Keeps*, "Ghostly Father, I Confess." In this story, Margaret visits a psychoanalyst.[52] Margaret is skeptical of the totalizing psychoanalytic framework from the beginning of the story; she also views therapy as one cultural trend among many that defines an urban elite. Margaret, accusing her doctor of conventionality and derivative taste, speculates that he likes "the movies, and you never miss one that the *New Yorker* recommends." In Margaret's eyes, the doctor is middlebrow, and Margaret wants to establish her own cultural superiority. Margaret expresses that superiority, however, through humor that might fit in the *New Yorker*. Margaret relishes her gift for caricature and admits to her doctor, "'I've got a good eye for social types.'" She speculates about his private life and cultural tastes by supplying a list of product names, political affiliations, and literary preferences, and this caricature gives Margaret the gratification of mastery: "'She had enjoyed doing that malicious portrait'" (253). Her handiwork reveals her own milieu, however; his portrait depends upon Margaret's intimate knowledge of his bourgeois sphere. Hence the reader suspects that she too participates in circles that had "two cocktails (or was it one?) before dinner" (251). Perhaps she also reads those *New Yorker* movie reviews.

Sensitive to her cultural proximity to the good doctor, Margaret uses macabre humor to resist complicity in the therapeutic scene. Margaret insulates herself from the promise of easy happiness by imagining herself in dire, antisocial extremes: "She longed to reply in a sepulchral voice, 'Dr. James, when I was a little girl, I buried my four-year-old cousin alive.' (*Sensation in the courtroom!*) 'But don't tell anybody.' However, these miserable jokes of hers wasted a great deal of time" (255). Margaret opposes the therapeutic ethos of liberal politics and psychoanalysis by choosing miserable jokes. Wasting a great deal of time allows her to resist the illusion of progress. In her joke fantasy, the infant body is cordoned off from the compromising adult world, preserving the "little girl" body of the speaker and the buried body of her imagined cousin. Margaret embraces burial and secrecy, the opposite of display and publicity and also of the talking cure and the value it places on exposing the repressed. However, the italicized "*Sensation in the courtroom!*" that interrupts the speech in Margaret's fantasy suggests that underneath this rejection of publicity lies a flirtation with its virtues. Margaret employs this "sepulchral voice" and its capacity to shock, not just because this voice opposes therapeutic clichés but also because this voice might actually be heard. As much as Margaret wants to mock this urban elite world, she also wants to participate in it. Like Parker, she alludes to suicide as a sign of superiority, separating the morbid self from the muddled (and middlebrow) masses: "If she had any strength of character, she would commit suicide" (259).

Margaret may think Dr. James is an absurd *New Yorker* reader, but her persona, her malicious portraits and conversance in social styles, even her morbid sensibilities, echo a *New Yorker* writer. Indeed, Margaret views a witty persona as an escape from her childhood dullness: "even now, she never failed to be surprised when people laughed at her jokes because for years it had been a household axiom that poor Meg had no sense of humor" (293). Through the same cultural vehicles that Margaret mocked her doctor for accepting and embracing, she acquired her verbal style. McCarthy explained in an interview: "New Yorkers are something rather special; they have this special New York humour, and awareness, and wised-upness."[53]

This "wised-upness," however commodified or chic it might be, allows Margaret to diagnose her own limitations and contradictions in a more subtle way than her doctor who attributes Margaret's neuroses to her relationships with men. Margaret, however, confronts a political and aesthetic concern rather than a personal or familial issue: the problematic relationship of objects to her identity. Instead of making her identity into another object, as Dr. James might by defining her neurosis, Margaret examines her anxiety about class identity:

> It was not for having money that she hated herself, but (be honest, she murmured) for having some, but not enough. If she could have been very rich. . . . It was the ugly cartoon of middle-class life that she detested, Mr. and Mrs., Jiggs and Maggie, the Norths in the *New Yorker*. And the more stylish you tried to make it, smearing it over with culture and good taste, Swedish modern and Paul Klee, the more repellent it became: the cuspidors and the silk lampshades in the funny papers did not stab the heart half so cruelly as her own glass shelves with the white pots of ivy, her Venetian blinds, her open copy of a novel by Kafka, all the objects that were waiting for her at home, each in its own patina of social anxiety. (260)

McCarthy articulates the contradictions of life as a political radical in a capitalist consumer culture. Margaret acknowledges experiencing the consumer culture's attendant desires: for objects, for status, for comfort, for beauty. These desires affect not only transparent hypocrites like Jim Barnett but also complex intelligences like Margaret.

Margaret caricatures herself in this diagnosis of social and class anxiety. Jiggs and Maggie, comic strip characters from *Bringing Up Father* by George McManus, were Irish immigrants who came into wealth. In the comic strip, Maggie despaired of inducing Jiggs to behave with the proper dignity for his new lot in life. The quipping, well-tailored Norths were characters created by Richard Lockridge for the *New Yorker*. The Norths eventually starred as a crime-solving duo in a series of popular mystery novels Lockridge wrote with his wife Frances, but they debuted in *New Yorker* columns about the vagaries of such popular bourgeois pastimes as shopping and bridge for the bewildered modern husband. By associating the ethnic humor of *Bringing Up Father* with the urbane humor of the Norths, McCarthy connects immigrant assimilation and modern sophistication. She thus suggests the unexpected idea that these forms of social aspiration exist on the same spectrum. In this self-exposure, Margaret reveals that the chic urban intellectual is like an Irish bumpkin under the surface.[54] Margaret refuses the therapeutic ethos that would allow her to dismiss her hypocrisies, weakness, and culpability.[55] She is just as laughable (or potentially laughable) as Jiggs. Irony allows Margaret to hold a contradictory self in suspension and to acknowledge the opposing social pressures and political ideals that define that self and its way of being in the world. Marshall Berman argues that Marxist ideology and the marketplace require such a self-reflective balancing act: "Intellectuals must recognize the depth of their own dependence—spiritual as well as economic dependence—on the bourgeois world they despise. It will never be possible to overcome these contradictions unless we confront them directly and openly."[56] When Margaret leaves her doctor's office, she prays "preserve me in disunity," embracing rather than erasing contradiction (304).

Margaret's ironic voice resists globally explanatory narratives, whether in the traditional form of religion or the modern form of psychoanalysis. Choosing to be an ironist in Rorty's sense of a "person who faces up to the contingency of . . . her own most central beliefs and desires— someone sufficiently historicist and nominalist to have abandoned the idea that those central beliefs and desires refer back to something beyond the reach of time and chance," Margaret eschews metanarratives in favor of a probing and continuing examination of her own and her culture's contradictions.[57] This troubled acknowledgment of incertitude provides a version of irony distinct from epigrammatic wit or urban elitism. Indeed, unexpectedly given the Marxist ideologues we meet in *The Company She Keeps*, Margaret's embrace of uncertainty and contradiction echoes what Berman deems the modern quality of Marx's voice: "This voice resonates at once with self-discovery and self-mockery, with self-delight and self-doubt . . . It is ironic and contradictory, polyphonic and dialectical."[58] Perhaps Margaret's dedication to self-interrogation represents more accordance with than divergence from the spirit of Marxist inquiry.

As McCarthy established in "The Man in the Brooks Brothers Shirt" and "Portrait of the Intellectual as a Yale Man," this posture of constant inquiry and incertitude risks facilitating and justifying passivity and detachment. In her study of irony and its political potential, Linda Hutcheon lists several major objections to irony: "irony becomes a kind of surrogate for actual resistance and opposition. Even worse, irony is seen by some to have become a cliché of contemporary culture, a 'convention for establishing complicity,' a 'screen for bad faith' (Lawson 1984: 164). What was once an 'avenue of dissent' is now seen as 'a commodity in its own right' (Austin-Smith 1990, 51) . . . Almost any book or article on irony written before the last decade or so will articulate . . . the idea that irony is a conservative force, used to 'shore up the foundations of the established order' (Elliott 1960, 273)."[59] In *The Company She Keeps*, the ironic point of view is also vulnerable to the charge that it packages quietism as wit. Margaret's journey through the world of the New York intellectuals and their publications, accompanied by her alternating enchantment and disgust with politics and Marxism, leaves irony looking like a simultaneously self-congratulatory and self-excusing posture. At the conclusion of "Portrait of the Intellectual Yale Man," Jim Barnett writes for *Destiny* magazine; his ironic acceptance of the irreconcilable contradictions in both his professional and political life lulls him into complacency: "The sentry slept, relaxed, at his post, knowing that an armistice had been arranged with the enemy" (244). The New York radicals of the 1930s became the established public intellectuals of the 1940s and 1950s, and some even moved to the right. In *The Company She Keeps*, Margaret Sargent finds neither a political nor an economic theory that solves the contradictions she mulls over.

McCarthy was taken to task by critics for her reluctance to affiliate or prescribe. A *Times Literary Supplement* review on July 12, 1957, complained that "her analyses of people, ideas, ways of life are carried out from the point of view of one who is preserved, not happily, in disunity; preserved from erratic systems of belief by having no apparent beliefs at all." This book review further hints at a kinship between chic femininity and McCarthy's ironic and (the reviewer presumes) apolitical mode: "is she really no more than a most elegant cat, among the clumsy academic, political, literary pigeons?" Indeed, Lillian Hellman dismissed her rival's work as "novels by 'a lady' magazine writer" in a March 19, 1980, *New York Times* article by Michiko Kakutani entitled "Hellman-McCarthy Libel Suit Stirs Controversy." Does McCarthy simply reproduce the magazine glibness of the superficial smart girl as she seems to expose it? Is irony too smart a posture for its own good?

McCarthy employs the trope of vision in "Ghostly Father, I Confess" to suggest that the lens of irony sharpens, rather than conveniently blurs, political awareness. This "inner eye" resists blind ideology and narcissism, and Margaret "could still detect her own frauds" (303–304). McCarthy implies that irony can provide a source of political ethics for the individual by promoting clarity of vision. Margaret prays: "if the flesh must be blind, let the spirit see." Though the story begins with a description of the therapist's eyes peering at his patient with authority through a pair of glasses, in the course of the story's unfolding, we discover that Margaret was a "child with glasses" (263). Her corrective vision trumps his. In a dream sequence, McCarthy presents the unlikely pair of a Nazi and a Byronic hero as two seductive icons, political and literary, competing to woo Margaret. Through this dream, Margaret realizes that the fetishization of style links both in spite of their ideological differences.[60] Thus, she must remain vigilant: "She could still distinguish the Nazi prisoner from the English milord, even in the darkness of need" (304). Although this choice between the Nazi and the English lord is absurd, the necessity of choice that McCarthy poses is not to be taken so lightly. By confessing the charismatic appeal of snobbery and its coexistence with her egalitarian politics, Margaret dispels snobbery's enchantment and makes an ethical and political choice to reject both snobbery and in turn fascism.

McCarthy implies that the first step in becoming a responsible citizen is seeing ironically, keeping skeptical company with multiple attitudes and allegiances.[61] In Margaret's dream, McCarthy offers a version of ethics that does not entail losing oneself in the full flush of an emotional attachment to either an idea or position. Instead of being seduced by ideology, Margaret must recognize the inevitable inconsistencies within her desires, her beliefs, and her actions.[62] Rather than falling into cynical torpor as a result, Margaret playfully interrogates her own shifting vocabularies for understanding her world and their adequacy or inadequacy.[63] In this spirit, McCarthy's version of ironic vision extends the promise that meaning, identity, and even political conviction can be defined and refined by the "company it keeps."

Conclusion

In a 2008 *New York Times* editorial, Susan Faludi regretfully compared our own era to the 1920s: "Again, the news media showcases young women's 'feminist-new style' pseudo-liberation—the flapper is now a girl-gone-wild."[1] Faludi, linking the rise in modern print culture with the redirection of women's choices from politics into consumerism and sexuality, quotes a 1927 issue of *Harper's* that pitied the previous generation's political engagement, the suffragists' "zealotry." Faludi is not the only contemporary feminist to suspect that we need to look back to the modern period to understand our cultural moment of media saturation. In a 2008 lecture at Harvard University, Camille Paglia took the opposite tack on the interwar years, casting the 1920s and 1930s as "a glory period for exceptional, accomplished women, such as Dorothy Parker," who stepped into the spotlight and claimed professional status. Paglia opined that "Feminism may have dissipated as a political movement, but women's achievement and public visibility were very strong."[2] These commentaries suggest the enduring impact of the mass circulation magazines and smart feminine stereotypes that were culturally transformative in the interwar years.

The New York fantasy of feminine independence and wry humor still entrances the popular imagination. Lauren Weisberger's best-selling novel *The Devil Wears Prada* (2003), for example, follows a young woman, Andrea Sachs, who dreams of writing for the *New Yorker*: "Although I knew it was highly unlikely I'd get hired at the *New Yorker* directly out of school, I was determined to be writing for them before my fifth reunion."[3] Unfortunately, the dream trajectory to the *New Yorker* involves a detour; like Parker working for Edna Woolman Chase at *Vogue* as a caption writer, Andrea breaks into the magazine industry by taking a job as an assistant for Miranda Priestly at fictional *Runway* magazine. (Weisberger, who served in the same position for *Vogue* editor Anna Wintour, employed Mary McCarthy's unspoken strategy that the roman à clef is the best revenge.)

Unlike Parker who revels in unattractiveness or Fauset who reveals the racism of flapper iconography, Weisberger fits Andrea into the narrow contours of the fashionable female body: "Five feet ten inches and 115 pounds did not bode well for a hard night out (although, in retrospect, it boded very well for employment at a fashion magazine)."[4] This novel enforces the standards that it questions with its wry voice: "Fat was on everyone's minds, if not actually their bodies."[5] The novel's treatment of fashion is also ambivalent; Weisberger drops brand names, and Andrea marvels at her own sartorial learning curve, while the conclusion of the book sees Andrea cursing her boss and selling all of the couture she garnered from *Runway*'s closet. Weisberger's narration reflects this uncertainty: "I'd strolled into [*Runway*] . . . a clueless, poorly dressed little girl, and I'd staggered out a slightly weathered, poorly dressed semigrown-up (albeit one who now realized just how poorly dressed she was) . . . even though I'd left with nothing more concrete than a suitcase (well, OK, four Louis Vuitton suitcases) full of fabulous designer clothes—maybe it had been worth it?"[6] This tentative question mark signals the cultural ambivalence about women's professionalism ultimately expressed in such fictions. Is a "slightly weathered," "semigrown-up" feminine role the best that an ironic voice can offer?

The symbolic risks that Fauset, Powell, and McCarthy recognized in the smart woman stereotype sometimes bedevil the fictions that draw on it today; urbane humor can indirectly advocate superficiality, materialism, and apoliticism as characteristics of ideal femininity. This complicity reflects the strength of the magazine industry during the intervening years between 1942, when Powell published *A Time to Be Born* and McCarthy published *The Company She Keeps*, and today. By the early 1960s, women writers depicted magazines as a medium for confinement rather than self-expression and viewed sophistication as a pose that facilitated social control rather than rebellion. In McCarthy's novel *The Group* (1963), Vassar graduate Kay Strong reads women's magazines to improve her home-making tactics.[7] Mistrusting her own intelligence and wit, she feels resigned to inarticulacy: "If Kay could only write, she could have sold the story of it to the *New Yorker*, she thought."[8] Her husband Harald's sense of humor stands in for her own: "Kay wanted to quote it to their friends to show how witty he could be. She loved Harald's *risus sardonicus*."[9] When Harald speaks, however, McCarthy reveals his pomposity and self-centeredness: "'living with a woman is like living with an echo, a loud echo in Kay's case. That voice of hers got on my nerves. Meaninglessly repeating what it had heard. Generally from me, I admit.'"[10] Like Diogenes in Millay's "The Barrel," Harald cannot take feminine intelligence seriously. His so-called sophistication scarcely disguises his cruelty, and he commits Kay to an insane asylum.

In the mental institution, Kay's survey of her fellow inmates suggests a correspondence between attractive surfaces and self-destructive passivity: "'I saw a catatonic schizophrenic this morning. . . . She was completely rigid and had to be fed like a doll. And there was this pretty girl next to me who looked completely normal but they'd brought her in in a straight jacket."[11] Among the symbolic straitjackets that enforce pretty girls' maintenance of complete normality is magazine culture. Upon her release from the asylum, Kay dies from falling—or jumping—off a building. Suggestively, one of the women present when it happens "'was glancing through a magazine in the lounge'" when "'everything was driven from my mind by the sound of that crash.'"[12] The human costs of these feminine ideals and bourgeois distractions are high. McCarthy does speculate that an ironic perspective might productively survive in queer culture. Kay's friend Lakey, a character whom some speculated was modeled after Edna St. Vincent Millay, takes revenge on Harald by implying that she and Kay had an affair.[13] In the last lines of the novel, Lakey's cool, urbane vision triumphs over Harald's furious attempts at control: "She drove on, following the cortege, watching him in the rearview mirror as he crossed the road and stood, thumbing a ride, while cars full of returning mourners glided past him, back to New York."[14]

In *The Bell Jar* (1963), Sylvia Plath also depicts the magazine industry as a trap that places would-be women writers in a schizophrenically divided state between glamour and guts. As Parker might do, Plath describes fashion with the sardonic humor of deflating comparisons: "how stupid I'd been to buy all those uncomfortable, expensive clothes hanging limp as fish in my closet."[15] Plath's protagonist Esther Greenwood feels both claustrophobic and isolated when she imagines that "other college girls just like me all over America . . . wanted nothing more than to be tripping about in those same size-seven patent leather shoes." The duplicability of consumer identity and indeed of magazine glamour exacerbates Esther's violent feelings of detachment. Glamour is an illusion predicated on sparkle, and Esther's wit exposes its imitation and emptiness: "when my picture came out in the magazine the twelve of us were working on—drinking martinis in a skimpy, imitation silver-lamé bodice stuck on to a big, fat cloud of white tulle, on some Starlight Roof, in the company of several anonymous young men with all-American bone structures hired or loaned for the occasion—everybody would think I must be having a real whirl."[16] *The Bell Jar* plumbs the darkness behind the shiny surface of "having a real whirl." The solitary psychology of the protagonist is more important than her participation in the magazine industry. It is arguable that Esther proves her intellectual and emotional authenticity because she fails to become a magazine writer.[17]

In spite of these searing literary assessments of magazine culture's failings, witty magazine writing has continued to offer professional and literary opportunities for women since the interwar years charted in this book. Screenwriter and director Nora Ephron, for example, published humorous essays in *Esquire*, *Cosmopolitan*, and the *New Yorker* in the 1970s. In *Crazy Salad: Some Things About Women* (1975), a collection derived from her magazine writing, Ephron documented second-wave feminism and its discontents: the divisions within the women's movement, the clash of Betty Friedan and Gloria Steinem, the popularity of pornographic movie *Deep Throat* and vaginal deodorants. In the process of encapsulating this cultural moment, Ephron alluded to modern women writers—Dorothy Parker, Edna St. Vincent Millay, Zelda Fitzgerald, and Lillian Hellman—and suggested their influence on her authorial persona and her pose of witty skepticism. Indeed, Ephron described her dream to be Dorothy Parker: "All I wanted in this world was to come to New York and be Dorothy Parker. The funny lady. The only lady at the table. The woman who made her living by wit. Who wrote for the *New Yorker*. Who always got off the perfect line at the perfect moment."[18]

While this essay concludes with Ephron's reflections on Parker's limitations, the strategies that Ephron employs in the collection overlap with the style and perspective of the humor writing discussed in this book. Like Mary McCarthy's Margaret Sargent, Ephron views femininity as a troubling masquerade: "We learned that the way you sat, crossed your legs, held a cigarette, and looked at your nails—the way you did these things instinctively was absolute proof of your sex . . . I thought that just one slip, just one incorrect cross of my legs or flick of an imaginary cigarette ash would turn me from whatever I was into the other thing; that would be all it took, really."[19] Like Fauset and

McCarthy, Ephron acknowledges the tangle of motives that emerges from the conflict between ideology and feminine ideals, "women pulled between the intellectual attraction of liberation and the emotional, psychological, and cultural mishmash it's hard to escape growing up with."[20] Ephron acknowledges ruefully, in short, the problems of smartness: "In my sex fantasy, nobody ever loves me for my mind."[21]

The influence of smart women writers on Nora Ephron has not abated in recent years. She tackled their legacy directly in the 2002 musical *Imaginary Friends*, dramatizing the rivalry between Hellman and Mary McCarthy with banter and a hint of regret. "We all wanted to be one of the boys," Hellman confesses in Ephron's play.[22] In her most recent humorous essay collection, *I Feel Bad About My Neck and Other Thoughts on Being a Woman* (2006), Ephron tackles body image, materialism, political disappointments, and the dream of New York as a haven and an extension of self: "*If I can just get back to New York, I'll be fine.*" Like Millay parodying the contents of Alice in Wonderland's purse, Ephron fractures the vexed alliance of femininity and Fendi: "This is for women whose purses are a morass of loose Tic Tacs, solitary Advils, lip-sticks without tops, ChapSticks of unknown vintage, little bits of tobacco even though there has been no smoking going on for at least ten years, tampons that have come loose from their wrappings . . . scratched eyeglasses, an old tea bag, several crumpled personal checks that have come loose from the checkbook and are covered with smudge marks, and an unprotected toothbrush that looks as if it has been used to polish silver."[23]

In contemporary popular culture, the fantasy of writing for a magazine still promises fulfillment (not to mention attractiveness, sexual opportunity, and witty repartee). In *Sex and the City*, the HBO series and film, New Yorker Carrie Bradshaw is a sex columnist, a magazine writer, and a proud wit.[24] The *New York Daily News* quipped in 2001 that Edna St. Vincent Millay "didn't solely make . . . Carrie Bradshaw possible, but she played a role in making [her] plausible."[25] In the ABC series *Ugly Betty*, heroine Betty Suarez thaws the frozen assets of *Mode* magazine's icy sophistication with her warm humor and earnest professional ambitions.[26] She could be seen as a modern Vicky Haven, showing the Amanda Keelers (or in this case, the villainous Wilhelmina Slaters) of the magazine world that their versions of glamour are not all-powerful. Just as Vicky finds a "haven" downtown in the village, Betty draws support and confidence from her Latino family and community in Queens. In television shows that celebrate women's wit, modern literary forebears are sometimes acknowledged. For example, in the Warner Brothers series *The Gilmore Girls*, fast-talking betokens intimacy between a single mother and her teenage daughter. They reject the snobbery of their wealthy Connecticut origins and define community and family through quick rejoinders and cultural references. This show is littered with references to the humorists in this book. Rory Gilmore reads a biography of Edna St. Vincent Millay, *The Portable Dorothy Parker*, and *The Group*.[27] Both of the main characters in this series are named "Lorelei" (like Anita Loos's Lorelei Lee); and the television show was produced by "Dorothy Parker Drank Here" Productions.

Some of the contemporary pop cultural incarnations of the female magazine writer betray the limitations of this fantasy. While the television series *Sex and the City* celebrates friendship, humor, and sexual pleasure, the film version warns that the magazine writer should be angling for her happily-ever-after instead of her punch line.[28] Even *Ugly Betty* seems renovated by her exposure to *Mode* magazine; a new investment in body image and in strategic manipulation makes Betty worldlier and wiser, much like Andrea Sachs in *The Devil Wears Prada*. When screenwriter and director Diane English updated *The Women*, a 1936 play by Clare Boothe Luce and a famous 1939 movie by George Cukor (Anita Loos wrote the screenplay with Jane Murfin), she attempted to infuse the film with positive roles for women. English changes the Rosalind Russell villain, Sylvia, from a gossiping housewife into an ambitious magazine editor, and she dilutes her villainy.[29] Nonetheless, the film effectively advocates luxury, materialism, haute couture, and destructive female body images, even as it self-reflexively alludes to the problematic nature of those goals.

Who plays smart in our magazines today? One humorist who comes to mind is *New Yorker* writer and National Public Radio performer David Sedaris. His sardonic and self-deprecating sensibility recalls the dry self-assessments of McCarthy in her memoirs, and Sedaris alludes to Parker in *When You Are Engulfed in Flames* (2008) when he writes "Guys Look Like Asses in Euro-Style Glasses."[30] Many of Sedaris's essays in this collection and others describe the insecurities of sexual identity and the ironies of self-invention. Sedaris puts his own body on comic display in order to diagnose the marketing niches of the contemporary mass media: "today's wide selection means that in choosing a pair of frames you're forced to declare yourself a certain type of person, or, in my case, a certain type of insect."[31] When he chooses glasses, Sedaris reports that he wants to "look smart and international."[32] He thus tweaks his fashion pretensions but also reminds the reader indirectly that he writes for the

New Yorker and lives in Paris. Glasses do not make Sedaris "smart and international"; his rhetoric of self-deprecation, urbanity, skepticism, and acceptance does.

Humor writing permeates our print culture and shapes our dreams of what it might mean to be worldly, ironically aware, sophisticated, chic, independent, and, last but not least, smart. The anxiety that smartness always escapes the speaker, that it can never be achieved and held onto, reflects the persistent feelings of inadequacy associated with femininity, homosexuality, Jewishness—each an identity category commonly associated with sophistication.[33] In a recent *New Yorker* interview, Ephron remarked, "'I think people think I am much smarter than I know I am.'"[34] In "Smart Guy," Sedaris lamented, "It turns out that I'm really stupid, practically an idiot. There are cats that weigh more than my IQ score."[35] This self-deprecation cloaks the audacity of wit and the power of self-assertion that magazine writing and wise-cracking entail. Just as women writers turned to smart magazines as a vehicle for self-promotion and cultural critique in the 1920s and 1930s, so today do humor writers like Ephron and Sedaris use middlebrow venues as a platform to talk about identity, visibility, and the mass media. They play smart so that we don't have to play dumb about the costs and opportunities of embodiment and publicity.

Notes

Introduction

1. All quotations in this paragraph and the next from Nancy Hoyt, "A Very Modern Love Story," *Vanity Fair*, December 1923, 33.

2. Sigmund Freud, *Jokes and Their Relation to the Unconscious*, trans. James Strachey (New York: W. W. Norton & Company, 1960), 126.

3. Harlem Renaissance writers Jessie Fauset and Nella Larsen wrote for black press magazines, *The Crisis* and *The Brownies' Book*, and they write about the influence of white press magazines across the color-line in their fiction.

4. Ross Chambers makes the point that ironists who target the discursive system in which they participate use "wit [that] is manifestly intertextual—or, perhaps better . . . [is] palimpsestic . . . it does not efface either the system it is appropriating or the power positions produced by that system; rather, it clearly alludes to them, the better to mark the shift it is producing with respect to them." Ross Chambers, "Irony and the Canon," *Profession* 90 (1989): 22.

5. Walter Benjamin, *Illuminations* (New York: Harcourt, 1968), 153.

6. Chambers, "Irony and the Canon," 21.

7. Recent critics have begun to theorize how these female celebrities generated and exploited these celebrity roles rather than passively inhabiting them. See Jayna Brown, *Babylon Girls: Black Women Performers and the Shaping of the Modern* (Durham, NC: Duke University Press, 2008); Judith Brown, "Celebrity," in *Glamour in Six Dimensions: Modernism and the Radiance of Form* (Ithaca, NY: Cornell University Press, 2009), 97–120; and Faye Hammill, *Women, Celebrity, and Literary Culture between the Wars* (Austin: University of Texas Press, 2007).

8. Alice Kessler-Harris, *Out to Work: A History of Wage-Earning Women in the United States* (New York: Oxford University Press, 1982), 226.

9. Joan Riviere, "Womanliness as a Masquerade," in *Formations of Fantasy*, ed.

Victor Burgin, James Donald, Cora Kaplan (New York: Metheun, 1986), 39. All quotations in this paragraph from this source and page.

10. Jean Marie Lutes observes that modern women writers who began their careers as journalists to prove their professionalism ultimately "grappled with the body-conscious legacy of women's journalism." Jean Marie Lutes, *Front Page Girls: Women Journalists in American Culture and Fiction (1880–1930)* (Ithaca, NY: Cornell University Press, 2006), 11.

11. Nina Miller, *Making Love Modern: The Intimate Public Worlds of New York's Literary Women* (New York: Oxford University Press, 1998), 245.

12. Mary Douglas, *Implicit Meanings: Essays in Anthropology* (Boston: Routledge, 1975), 108.

13. Davis demonstrates that women advertising writers, situated between the categories of professionalism (coded masculine) and femininity, responded with self-conscious performances. Davis emphasizes "the irony with which adwomen generated both masculine and feminine gender stylings in their work while building their own professional lives." Simone Weil Davis, *Living Up to the Ads: Gender Fictions of the 1920s* (Durham, NC: Duke University Press, 2000), 104, 103.

14. Freud, *Jokes*, 126.

15. Henri Bergson, *Laughter: An Essay on the Meaning of the Comic*, trans. Cloudesley Brereton and Fred Rothwell (New York: Macmillan Company, 1914), 38.

16. George Douglas explains that all of these publications made an "appeal . . . to some assumed class of sophisticated readers." George Douglas, *The Smart Magazines: 50 Years of Literary Revelry and High Jinks at Vanity Fair, The New Yorker, Life, Esquire, and the Smart Set* (New York: Archon Books, 1991), 1.

17. Eli Zaretsky, *Secrets of the Soul: A Social and Cultural History of Psychoanalysis* (New York: Knopf, 2004), 106.

18. Michael Warner, *Publics and Counterpublics* (New York: Zone Books, 2002), 123.

19. Trysh Travis, "Print and the Creation of Middlebrow Culture," in *Perspectives on American Book History: Artifacts and Commentary*, ed. Scott Casper, Joanne Chaison, Jeffrey Groves (Boston: University of Massachusetts Press, 2002), 339.

20. Lisa Botshon and Meredith Goldsmith point out that "The neglected third term in the interaction between high and popular culture was *gendered*: the 'pernicious pest' that intervened between high and low was feminized and the authors of the diction that 'outrage[d] all sense and probability' were often, like Hawthorne's dreaded successfully scribbling women, female." They further note that women writers from the interwar period "successfully made transitions between literature and the burgeoning technologies of magazine publication, book clubs, advertising, radio, and film, institutions that deliberately targeted 'middle' audiences for maximum distribution and profits." Lisa Botshon and Meredith Goldsmith, *Middlebrow Moderns: Popular American Women Writers of the 1920s* (Boston: Northeastern University Press, 2003), 4.

21. Janice Radway, *A Feeling for Books: The Book-of-the-Month Club, Literary Taste, and Middle-Class Desire* (Chapel Hill: University of North Carolina Press, 1997), 152. See also Joan Shelley Rubin, *The Making of Middlebrow Culture* (Chapel Hill: University of North Carolina Press, 1992).

22. Radway, *A Feeling for Books*, 219.

23. Botshon and Goldsmith explain that modern middlebrow women writers "inhabited a space between the embrace of experimentalism and ambiguity considered the characteristic of modernism . . . and the critique of the dominant culture [Jane] Tompkins locates in the popular." Elizabeth Majerus further observes that "A number of popular magazines published during the modernist period promoted modernism and at the same time embraced a wide array of feminine culture, providing a more open forum for different kinds of modern women writers and artists than exclusively modernist venues." Botshon and Goldsmith, *Middlebrow Moderns*, 10. Elizabeth Majerus, "'Determined and Bigoted Feminists': Women, Magazines, and Popular Modernism," in *Modernism*, vol. 1, ed. Astradur Eysteinsson and Vivian Liska (Philadelphia: John Benjamins, 2007), 619.

24. Majerus, "'Determined and Bigoted,'" 623.

25. Jaime Harker, *America the Middlebrow: Women's Novels, Progressivism, and Middlebrow Authorship between the Wars* (Amherst: University of Massachusetts Press, 2007). Nicola Humble, *The Feminine Middlebrow Novel, 1920s to 1950s: Class, Domesticity, and Bohemianism* (New York: Oxford University Press, 2002), 11.

26. Nina Miller makes a strong case for the slippage between public and private in the works of modern New York women writers: "In an era of advertising and social scientific expertise, woman's private domain was permeated by a public normativity, while her person constituted a paradoxically private public display. The contemporaneous woman love poet, with her public constructions of a private self (as lover) and a private sphere (of love), was positioned in an analogously contradictory space." Miller, *Making Love Modern*, 11.

27. Lauren Berlant, *The Female Complaint* (Durham, NC: Duke University Press, 2008), 4.

28. Andreas Huyssen, *After the Great Divide: Modernism, Mass Culture, Postmodernism* (Bloomington: Indiana University Press, 1986).

29. David Savran, *A Queer Sort of Materialism: Recontextualizing the American Theater* (Ann Arbor: University of Michigan Press, 2003), 10.

30. Scholes argues that the high-low divide obscures "the way that texts we think of as belonging to one or the other of these categories often has crucial elements that our critical discourse associates with its opposite," so he proposes: "rethink[ing] the Modernist canon and curriculum, opening up both of these to accommodate texts formerly excluded." Scholes specifies literary humor as an area for further exploration: "we need to know texts that are not masterpieces—things like jokes, cartoons, and parodies—in order to grasp that fascinating lost world of Modernism." Robert Scholes, *Paradoxy of Modernism* (New Haven: Yale University Press, 2006), 26, 32.

31. Elizabeth Outka points out that "Despite modernism's recent critical rehabilitation, the growth of modernism was, in fact, often marked by nostalgia, by a disdain for mass culture, and by attempts to purify an aesthetic from any taint of commerce. . . . Both the older and the newer critics are right, even though they contradict each other." Elizabeth Outka, *Consuming Traditions: Modernity, Modernism, and the Commodified Authentic* (New York: Oxford University Press, 2009), 12.

32. Douglas, *Implicit Meanings*, 102.

33. F. Scott Fitzgerald, *The Great Gatsby* (New York: Scribner, 2004), 17.

34. Ibid., 177.

35. The biographical connections were numerous. Edna St. Vincent Millay was a

member of the Provincetown Players in their early years. Dorothy Parker was rumored to have had a fling with F. Scott Fitzgerald, and she reviewed the works of Ernest Hemingway and Dashiell Hammett. Hemingway wrote a famously nasty poem about her entitled "To a Tragic Poetess." Jessie Fauset ran the *Crisis* magazine for W.E.B. Du Bois and encouraged Langston Hughes and other Harlem Renaissance writers, while Nella Larsen counted Carl Van Vechten and Jean Toomer among her friends. Dawn Powell socialized with John Dos Passos and E. E. Cummings. Mary McCarthy married Edmund Wilson, the famous critic of modernism, while Millay was his first lover and Parker and Powell were both his friends. See Carol Brightman, *Writing Dangerously: Mary McCarthy and Her World* (New York: Harvest Books, 1994); George Hutchinson, *In Search of Nella Larsen: A Biography of the Color Line* (Cambridge, MA: Harvard University Press, 2006); Marion Meade, *Dorothy Parker: What Fresh Hell Is This?* (New York: Penguin, 1989); Nancy Milford, *Savage Beauty: The Life of Edna St. Vincent Millay* (New York: Random House, 2002); Tim Page, *Dawn Powell: A Biography* (New York: Henry Holt, 1998); Carolyn Wedin Sylvander, *Jessie Fauset: Black American Writer* (Troy, NY: Whitston Publishing Company, 1981).

36. Wayne Booth, *A Rhetoric of Irony* (Chicago: University of Chicago Press, 1974), ix. Nancy Walker, *A Very Serious Thing: Women's Humor and American Culture* (Minneapolis: University of Minnesota Press, 1988), 82.

37. Booth, *A Rhetoric of Irony*, 128.

38. Linda Hutcheon, *Irony's Edge: The Theory and Politics of Irony* (New York: Routledge, 1994), 13.

39. Alan Wilde, *Horizons of Assent: Modernism, Postmodernism, and the Ironic Imagination* (Baltimore: Johns Hopkins University, 1981), 30, 131.

40. Perhaps these writers do not register irony as loss because of what Miller and Berlant both define as the bargaining condition of women's culture and middlebrow culture. The contradictions of the middlebrow—neither high culture nor mass culture, part of the marketplace and yet literarily ambitious even though not abstruse— parallel the contradictions of the female magazine writer's position, as she negotiates between authorial persona and media-promulgated stereotype, between formal and gendered convention and literary and persona invention, between chic and cultural critique. It is a tremendous accomplishment, I would suggest, that these writers make these negotiations their topic and theme rather than their burden.

41. Davis also observes that smart is an ambiguous adjective, at once praise and patronization. "The term *smart*," she observes, "is already ambiguous . . . it means chic, of course, but embedded in this is its double valencing, a synonym simultaneously for 'intelligent' and 'saucy and presumptuous.'" Davis, *Living Up to the Ads*, 83.

42. Sarah Churchwell, "'Lost Among the Ads': *Gentlemen Prefer Blondes* and the Politics of Imitation," in *Middlebrow Moderns: Popular American Women Writers of the 1920s*, ed. Lisa Botshon and Meredith Goldsmith (Boston: Northeastern University Press, 2003), 143.

43. Carl Naether, *Advertising to Women* (New York: Prentice-Hall, 1928), 77, 78, 79.

44. George Hibbard, "The Quality of Smartness: A Modern Idea and Some of Its Devotees in the Past," *Vanity Fair*, May 1920, 120.

45. Editor Neil Harris alludes to the prominence of New York magazines in his acknowledgments to the volume: "I had never heard of the magazine before. In a first

take I concluded that this was another, lesser known version of the *New Yorker* that I had somehow missed encountering and that I would soon learn more." Neil Harris, *The Chicagoan: A Lost Magazine of the Jazz Age* (Chicago: University of Chicago Press, 2008), ix. Ann Douglas and Nina Miller both establish that New York served as a symbol of modernity, an urban space for literary, personal, and cultural experimentation, and a center for both publishing and publicity. See Ann Douglas, *Terrible Honesty: Mongrel Manhattan in the 1920s* (New York: Farrar, Straus, and Giroux, 1995), and Miller, *Making Love Modern*.

46. Thomas Bender writes eloquently about the power of the New York as an idea and an improvisation: "Whether in its physical development or its social organization, New York refuses a single logic, and it declines any notion of completeness. . . . There is not and there is not to be a final truth about itself. In this sense, New York is a pragmatic city, and as such it is necessarily an unfinished city, without final ends. Implicit in the notion of a pragmatic polity is a pluralistic conversation in search of public resolutions—a pragmatic pluralism." Thomas Bender, *The Unfinished City: New York and the Metropolitan Idea* (New York: The New Press, 2002), xii.

47. Mary McCarthy, *The Company She Keeps* (New York: Harcourt, 2003), 89. Dawn Powell, *The Happy Island* (South Royalton, VT: Steerforth Press, 1998).

48. The idea that humor builds community is not new. Booth observes that "the meaning of an irony in this view inescapably includes that engagement of person with person—in the form of peering and unmasking." So too does Freud claim that "every joke calls for a public of its own." Booth, *Rhetoric of Irony*, 33. Freud, *Jokes and the Unconscious*, 185.

49. Joseph Litvak, *Strange Gourmets: Sophistication, Theory, and the Novel* (Durham, NC: Duke University Press, 1997).

50. Rebecca Walkowitz argues that "Modernist writers influenced by the traditions of aestheticism and decadence sought to redefine the scope of international experience (by focusing on the personal, the intimate, and the artificial) and to resist the affects of heroic nationalism (by developing and analyzing marginal groups within metropolitan culture)." Rebecca Walkowitz, *Cosmopolitan Style: Modernism Beyond the Nation* (New York: Columbia University Press, 2006), 10.

51. Mary Russo, *The Female Grotesque: Risk, Excess, and Modernity* (New York: Routledge, 1995), 70.

1 / Thoroughly Modern Millay and Her Middlebrow Masquerades

1. Edna St. Vincent Millay [Nancy Boyd], *Distressing Dialogues* (New York: Harper and Brothers, 1924), 238, 3, 282, 283.

2. Donald Ogden Stewart, "'Why You Can't Afford to Miss This Number': Straight Dope on Its Contents—In the Manner of Certain of Our Popular Fiction Magazines," *Vanity Fair*, November 1921, 25.

3. Millay, *Distressing Dialogues*, vii.

4. For analysis of Millay's Nancy Boyd work in *Ainslee's*, see Deborah Woodard, "'I Could Do a Woman Better Than That': Masquerade in Millay's Potboilers," in *Millay at 100: A Critical Reappraisal*, ed. Diane P. Freedman (Carbondale: Southern Illinois University Press, 1995), 145–162.

5. Elinor Wyle, "The Doll," *Vanity Fair*, April 1923, 55. Illustrated by Rockwell Kent.

6. Anne O'Hagan, "The Doom of the Home: And What About Children? And Rubber Plants?," *Vanity Fair*, April 1915, 49.

7. Millay, *Distressing Dialogues*, 179.

8. Nina Miller, *Making Love Modern: The Intimate Public Worlds of New York's Literary Women* (New York: Oxford University Press, 1999), 91.

9. "Virile Tang," *Time*, Oct. 15, 1928.

10. On Millay and masquerade, see Sandra M. Gilbert, "'Directions on Using the Empress': Millay's Supreme Fiction(s)," in *Millay at 100: A Critical Reappraisal*, 163–181; Sandra M. Gilbert and Susan Gubar, "Female Female Impersonators: The Fictive Music of Edna St. Vincent Millay and Marianne Moore," in *No Man's Land: The Place of the Woman Writer in the Twentieth Century* (New Haven: Yale University Press, 1994), 57–120; and Woodard, "'I Could Do a Woman Better Than That,'" 145–162.

11. Such criticism attends to the dangers of feminine objectification in the mass media, but it also renders Millay passive. Gilbert and Gubar argue that "the female artist . . . was always in danger of being trapped behind the rigid mask of a self that she secretly despised as inauthentic." Cheryl Walker similarly contends that "Millay's success at exploiting her body-consciousness in her early work provided no stable persona for the poet but simply involved her in a drama of consumption." Gilbert and Gubar, "Female Female Impersonators," 61. Cheryl Walker, *Masks Outrageous and Austere: Culture, Psyche, and Persona in Modern Women Poets* (Bloomington: Indiana University Press, 1991), 145.

12. Christopher Breward, *Fashion* (New York: Oxford University Press, 1993), 37.

13. Nancy Hoyt, "The Christmas Dance: 1922," *Vanity Fair*, January 1923, 51.

14. Joan Riviere, "Womanliness as a Masquerade," in *Formations of Fantasy*, ed. Victor Burgin, James Donald, and Cora Kaplan (New York: Routledge, 1986), 35–44.

15. For a summary of the "modern love" topical and tonal conventions, see Miller, *Making Love Modern*, 108–111.

16. Millay to Norma Millay and Charles Ellis, 10 November 1922, in *Letters of Edna St. Vincent Millay*, ed. Allan Ross Macdougall (New York: Grosset & Dunlap, 1952), 165–166.

17. Millay [Nancy Boyd], "Diary of an American Art Student in Paris: Showing How She Succeeded in Going to the Louvre Every Day," *Vanity Fair*, November 1922, 44.

18. Millay to Witter Bynner, 29 October 1920, in *Letters of Edna St. Vincent Millay*, 102.

19. Millay to Allan Ross Macdougall, 11 September 1920, in *Letters of Edna St. Vincent Millay*, 100.

20. Patrick McDonnell, Karen O'Connell, and Georgia Riley de Hayenon describe Herriman's use of dialect: "His characters shifted from the highest elocution of Victorian prose to the lowest streetslang, from English to Spanish to French, from the alliteration of Navajo names to the onomatopoeia of comic-strip language." McDonnell, O'Connell, and de Havenon, *Krazy Kat: The Comic Art of George Herriman* (New York: Harry N. Abrams, 1986), 23.

21. E. E. Cummings, "Introduction," *Krazy Kat* (New York: Henry Holt & Company, 1946).

22. Millay to MacDougall, 11 September 1920, in *Letters of Edna St. Vincent Millay*, 100.

23. Ibid., 101–102.

24. Millay to Mrs. Cora B. Millay and Norma, 22 September 1917, in *Letters of Edna St. Vincent Millay*, 77.

25. "The Old Woman and the Pedlar," in *The Original Mother Goose* (Philadelphia: Running Press, 1992).

26. Millay, "Exiled," in *Collected Poems: Edna St. Vincent Millay*, ed. Norma Millay (New York: Harper & Row, 1956), 105.

27. Mary Douglas, *Implicit Meanings: Essays in Anthropology* (New York: Routledge, 1975), 98.

28. Millay, *Distressing Dialogues*, 140.

29. Douglas describes the postwar generation that "prized a histrionic truthfulness above all else, including survival. . . . Opposing every form of 'sentimentality,' they prided themselves on facing facts, the harder the better." Ann Douglas, *Terrible Honesty: Mongrel Manhattan in the 1920s* (New York: Farrar, Straus and Giroux, 1995), 33.

30. Mark Van Doren, "Women of Wit," *Nation*, 26 October 1921, 481–482.

31. One advertisement pictures a sportily clad woman walking her dog and promises that the outfit is "Smart and correct, yet permitting absolute freedom." Golflex advertisement, *Vanity Fair*, June 1921, 92. Buick promoted the feminine allure of its sedan: "Trim, smart, and graceful in general appearance . . . this Buick Sedan is also a delightfully satisfying car for women to drive." Buick advertisement, *Vanity Fair*, February 1923, 5. A perfume ad reports that the scent is in "vogue at Newport and other smart American watering places." Vivaudou's La Bohême Arly advertisement, *Vanity Fair*, July 1922, 95. A cartoon by Fish connects boxing and smart society. Fish [Anne Harriet Fish], "The Prize Fight Finally Gets Into Society: The Smartest Diversion in New York Is Now the Science of the Swat and the Slam," *Vanity Fair*, April 1920, 70.

32. "The Importance of Being Right" advertisement, *Vanity Fair*, June 1921, 13.

33. George Hibbard, "The Quality of Smartness," *Vanity Fair*, May 1920, 118.

34. Charles Hanson Towne, "Do You Believe That—? A Selection from the Convictions Most Deeply Rooted in the Average Mind," *Vanity Fair*, November 1920, 61.

35. "In Vanity Fair," *Vanity Fair*, January 1914, 13.

36. "In Vanity Fair," *Vanity Fair*, March 1914, 15.

37. Frank Wright Tuttle, "Bumping the Bumps: A Depraved Midsummer Dialogue à propos of Cerebral Love," *Vanity Fair*, August 1920, 94.

38. St. John Ervine, "The Lost Art of Conversation: Is It Possible, in the City, to Think Up Really Good Things to Say?" *Vanity Fair*, October 1920, 76.

39. W. L. George, "Latter Day Helens: The Fourth of a Series of Impressions of Modern Feminine Types: Demetra, the Woman with a Mind," *Vanity Fair*, August 1921, 33.

40. George S. Chappell, "A Defense of the Debutante: In Which One is Pursued, Wooed, and Won by Another," *Vanity Fair*, April 1921, 58.

41. Goode & Berrien Advertising Counsel advertisement, "Eve & Sir Isaac," *Vanity Fair*, February 1923, 102.

42. For an insightful consideration of the professional poses of women ad writers, see Simone Weil Davis, "'Complex Little Femmes': Adwomen and the Female Consumer," in *Living Up to the Ads: Gender Fictions of the 1920s* (Durham, NC: Duke University Press, 2000), 80–104.

43. "Careers For Young Girls: A Few Suggestions Which May Enable the Bright Ambitious Girl to Find a Life Work," *Vanity Fair*, August 1921, 76.

44. Emily Post, "Special Series on the Etiquette of Good Looks: How Does the Well-Bred Woman Dress Her Hair?" *McCall's*, October 1925, 50.

45. Millay, "The Barrel: Showing That to a Woman a Man, Even a Philosopher, is Always a Little Ridiculous, and that to a Man, Any Man, a Woman is Something More than a Nuisance," *Vanity Fair*, July 1922, 35. The quotations from this story in the following paragraphs come from this issue and page.

46. Ibid., 36.

47. Millay, *Distressing Dialogues*, 178–179. All subsequent citations from this story appear in parentheses following the quoted text.

48. Hibbard, "The Quality of Smartness," 120.

49. "For the Well-Dressed Man," *Vanity Fair*, July 1920, 79.

50. George Chauncey, *Gay New York: Gender, Urban Culture, and the Making of the Gay Male World 1890–1940* (New York: Basic Books, 1994), 115.

51. Ibid., 114.

52. Millay, *Distressing Dialogues*, 273. All subsequent citations from this story appear in parentheses following the quoted text.

53. D. Nusbaum & Co. Brooklyn Knitting Company advertisement, *Vanity Fair*, June 1923, 102.

54. Chauncey, *Gay New York*, 115.

55. Max Eastman, *Einstein, Trotsky, Hemingway, Freud and Other Great Companions: Critical Memoirs of Some Famous Friends* (New York: Collier Books, 1962), 91.

56. Millay, *Distressing Dialogues*, 113. All subsequent citations from this story appear in parentheses following the quoted text.

57. Millay, *Distressing Dialogues*, 41. All subsequent citations from this story appear in parentheses following the quoted text.

58. "The Greek Spirit Still Dominates Modern Dancing: Sculptures of Ancient Greece Serve as the Inspiration for Two Classical Dance Poses," *Vanity Fair*, March 1920, 64.

59. Edmund Wilson, "Epilogue 1952: Edna St. Vincent Millay," in *Edmund Wilson: Literary Essays and Reviews of the 1920s & 1930s* (New York: Library of America, 2007), 621.

60. Martha Bensley Bruère and Mary Ritter Beard, *Laughing Their Way: Women's Humor in America* (New York: Macmillan, 1934), 105.

61. K.D., "Rhymed Extracts from My Diaries: Unabashed Comments on Some Suitors I Might have Accepted—But Luckily Didn't," *Vanity Fair*, February 1922, 25.

62. Russell Baker, *Norton Book of Light Verse* (New York: W. W. Norton & Company, 1986), 35.

63. Alice Duer Miller, "Many Men to Any Woman," in *Redressing the Balance: Literary Humor from the Colonial Times to the 1980s*, ed. Zita Dresner and Nancy Walker (Jackson: University of Mississippi Press, 1988), 205. Line numbers appear in parentheses following the quoted text.

64. Millay, "The Penitent," in *Collected Poems*, 139–140. Line numbers appear in parentheses following the quoted text.

65. The centrality of this poem to Millay's construction of a public persona is made clear by its varied publication history. It appeared in little magazine *Poetry*, middle-

brow literary magazine *Reedy's Mirror*, and political editorial magazine *Current Opinion* in the summer of 1918. Millay, "Penitent," *Poetry*, June 1918, 130–131; "Penitant [sic]," *Reedy's Mirror*, 7 June 1918, 229; "The Penitent," *Current Opinion*, August 1918, 123–124.

66. In an oft-cited judgment, Nietzsche mused in *The Gay Science* that women were "above all . . . actresses." Friedrich Nietzsche, *The Gay Science*, trans. Thomas Common (Mineola, NY: Dover Publications, 2006), 179.

67. Millay, "Daphne," in *Collected Poems*, 141.

68. Rita Felski notes that modern texts often treat women as symbols of the "pervasive textualization of modern bodies" but also frequently assume that women were blithely unaware of the significance of their poses. "Unlike the dandy," Felski observes, women "lack the ironic self-consciousness which their presence inspires in others. They embody artifice naively, as it were, without being able to raise it to the level of philosophical reflection." Millay grants her female speaker ironic awareness of artifice and its power. Rita Felski, *The Gender of Modernity* (Cambridge, MA: Harvard University Press, 1995), 110.

69. Millay, "I shall forget you presently," in *Collected Poems*, 571.

70. Millay, "Thursday," in *Collected Poems*, 129.

71. Millay, "Love, though for this you riddle me with darts," in *Collected Poems*, 568.

72. Writing about the emergence of sexology at the turn of the century, Lawrence Birken offers an etiology of the paradox I am tracing in Millay's simultaneously feminine and self-determining persona: "the movement towards civilization and middle-class society was linked to the growing differentiation of the two sexes. But implicit in this hypothesis was a contradiction. With the process of sexual differentiation, women must become more feminine, but with the progress of individuation, they must become more active." See Lawrence Birken, *Consuming Desire: Sexual Science and the Emergence of a Culture of Abundance, 1871–1914* (Ithaca, NY: Cornell University Press, 1988), 78.

73. Wilson, "Epilogue 1952," 603–604.

74. Millay, "To the Not Impossible Him," in *Collected Poems*, 130. Line numbers appear in parentheses after the quoted text.

75. Nancy Milford, *Savage Beauty: The Life of Edna St. Vincent Millay* (New York: Random House, 2001), 200.

76. George Hibbard, "The Quality of Smartness," 120.

77. John Peale Bishop, "The Art of Living as a Feminine Institution: Expressing a Vague Hope that New Amendments Will Not Do Away with the Old Amenities," *Vanity Fair*, November 1920, 47, 116.

78. Millay, "I think I should have loved you presently, my dear," in *Collected Poems*, 571.

79. Millay, *Distressing Dialogues*, 166. All subsequent citations from this story appear in parentheses following the quoted text.

80. Ibid., 190. All subsequent citations from this story appear in parentheses following the quoted text.

81. Joan Shelley Rubin explains that popular columns offered the "continual revelation of their authors' 'untrammeled personalities.'" The readers' desire to emulate these personalities "made [columns] how-to manuals for readers anxious to achieve

distinctiveness for themselves." Joan Shelley Rubin, *The Making of Middlebrow Culture* (Chapel Hill: University of North Carolina Press, 1992), 137.

82. Roland Marchand, *Advertising the American Dream: Making Way for Modernity 1920–1940* (Berkeley: University of California Press, 1985), 200.

83. Oxford English Dictionary Online. s.v. "clever," http://dictionary.oed.com/cgi/display/50041407?keytype=ref&ijkey=T7VTtz6eDwzFU (Accessed 25 July 2009).

84. For example, a shampoo ad asserts that "Smart women nowadays are not content with merely cleansing the hair—they are particular about its sheen and luster as well." Simonson's Henna Shampoo advertisement, *Vanity Fair*, June 1921, 3. A perfume ad assures the reader that: "A Clever woman surrounds herself with the exquisite influence of a perfume—for the right perfume, carefully chosen . . . adds considerably to her poise and to her social charm." Colgate's Florient perfume advertisement, *Vanity Fair*, February 1922, 89.

85. One editorial addresses the reader as one of "those who dwell in Vanity Fair." *Vanity Fair*, January 1914, 13. Another quotes Thackeray exhorting his readers to "*step in [to Vanity Fair] for half an hour and look at the performances.*" *Vanity Fair*, March 1914, 15.

86. Millay, Distressing Dialogues, 53.

87. Millay, "III. Sonnet in Answer to a Question," "To Elinor Wyle," in *Collected Poems*, 371. Line numbers appear in parentheses in the text following the quotation.

2 / "This Unfortunate Exterior": Dorothy Parker, the Female Body, and Strategic Doubling

1. Roland Marchand notes that "the proportions of some women in the tableaux suggested a height of over nine feet." See Roland Marchand, *Advertising the American Dream: Making Way For Modernity, 1920–1940* (Berkeley: University of California Press, 1987), 182.

2. Propper stocking advertisement, *New Yorker*, 17 December 1927, 62.

3. S. Ronay, "The New York Girl," *Vanity Fair*, October 1926, 72.

4. Dorothy Parker, "Mrs. Norris and the Beast," Reading and Writing, *New Yorker*, 14 April 1928, 97.

5. Parker, "My Home Town," in *The Portable Dorothy Parker*, ed. Marion Meade (New York: Penguin Books, 2006), 459.

6. Parker, "The Flapper," in *Not Much Fun: The Lost Poems of Dorothy Parker*, ed. Stuart Y. Silverstein (New York: Scribner, 2001), 105–106.

7. Parker, "Adam and Eve and Lilith and Epigrams—Something More About Cabell," Reading and Writing, *New Yorker*, 19 November 1927, 116.

8. Parker, "Mrs. Norris and the Beast," 97.

9. Lauren Berlant, *The Female Complaint: The Unfinished Business of Sentimentality in American Culture* (Durham, NC: Duke University Press, 2008), 224.

10. Parker, "Self-Portrait from *The Paris Review*, 'Writers at Work,' 1956," in *The Portable Dorothy Parker*, 572.

11. Alexander Woollcott, *While Rome Burns* (New York: Viking, 1935), 149.

12. Faye Hammill agrees that Parker responded to this celebrity in her magazine work: "Interacting with her own celebrity image in complex ways, she became a mistress of self-satire, yet even this became a way of consolidating her trademark perso-

na." Faye Hammill, *Women, Celebrity, and Literary Culture between the Wars* (Austin: University of Texas Press, 2007), 25.

13. Parker, "How It Feels to be One Hundred and Forty-six," Reading and Writing, *New Yorker*, 29 September 1928, 86.

14. Parker, "Ethereal Mildness," in *The Portable Dorothy Parker*, 508–510. All subsequent citations from this book review come from this edition and these pages.

15. Nina Miller explains that middlebrow fiction of this period depicted "the heterosexual couple not as a private refuge but as continuous with heterosocial society, the new mingling of the sexes brought on by women's encroachment on formerly all-male turf, the public spaces of campus, office, and street." Nina Miller, *Making Love Modern: The Intimate Public Worlds of New York's Literary Women* (New York: Oxford University Press, 1999), 110.

16. Parker, "Back to the Bookshelf," Reading and Writing, *New Yorker*, 25 August 1928, 60. All subsequent citations from this book review come from this issue and this page.

17. Jessica Burstein argues that the blasé is Parker's characteristic mode as the Constant Reader and that it helps to establish her professional status: "Parker would thus pepper her work with protestations of normalcy, industry, or wallflowerishness, as compared to the urban successes of her readers. Her audience was the one having fun, and the Constant Reader . . . was the bookish sort, damned to languish in darkened interiors." Jessica Burstein, "A Few Words About Dubuque: Modernism, Sentimentalism, and the Blasé," *American Literary History* 14, no. 2 (Summer 2002), 235.

18. Parker, "Advice to the Little Peyton Girl," in *Complete Stories*, 184–190. All subsequent citations from this story appear in parentheses following the quoted text.

19. Judith Brown connects blankness with glamour's allure: "the polished surface, the stance of impenetrability . . . the suspicion of the nothing behind it all—somehow, this blankness is transmuted into something that is seductive, powerful, and often simply gorgeous." Judith Brown, *Glamour in Six Dimensions: Modernism and the Radiance of Form* (Ithaca, NY: Cornell University Press, 2009), 5.

20. Parker, "Glory in the Daytime," *Complete Stories*, 218–230. All subsequent citations from this story appear in parentheses following the quoted text.

21. P. David Marshall, *Celebrity and Power: Fame in Contemporary Culture* (Minneapolis: University of Minnesota Press, 1997), 178.

22. Simone Weil Davis finds rhetorical excess in descriptions of the body written by ad women from this period, and she observes that "the psychic economy of the commercial endeavor is always strangely shame based, but here that shame is gendered, even sexualized, via a remarkable emphasis on physical excess." Davis argues that the "unspoken association of professional women with an endangering 'filthiness' seemed to stem not only from their gendered incursion into an all-male work world, but also from the blurring of boundaries effected by the female copywriters' facility with variously gendered speech." Simone Weil Davis, *Living Up to the Ads: Gender Fictions of the 1920s* (Durham, NC: Duke University Press, 2000), 100, 102.

23. I use the phrase "women's culture," as Berlant does, to refer to publications, genres, and tones, and forms of address in popular culture pitched to a female audience. Berlant argues that "the gender-marked texts of women's popular culture cultivate fantasies of vague belonging as an alleviation of what is hard to manage in the lived real—social antagonisms, exploitation, compromised intimacies, the attrition of

life." The link between fantasy and belonging and the discrepancy between imagined intimacy and disappointing reality are emphasized in Parker's critique of women's culture in these two stories. Berlant, *The Female Complaint*, 5.

24. Kathy Peiss, *Hope in a Jar: The Making of America's Beauty Culture* (New York: Henry Holt and Company, 1998), 154.

25. Brendan Gill, *Here at the New Yorker* (New York: Da Capo Press, 1975), 203.

26. Joshua Zeitz, *Flapper: A Madcap Story of Sex, Style, Celebrity, and the Women Who Made America Modern* (New York: Random House, 2007), 87–93.

27. Lois Long, "Doldrums: The Hunted," *New Yorker*, 14 March 1931, 21. All quotations from this story are from this issue and page.

28. In 1931 when Long wrote this article, artificial eyelashes were a relatively recent innovation in feminine adornment. Lillian Gish claimed that fake eyelashes were invented in 1916 by director D. W. Griffith for his film *Intolerance*. Lillian Gish with Ann Pinchot, *The Movies, Mr. Griffith and Me* (Englewood Cliffs, NJ: Prentice-Hall, 1969), 171–172.

29. Lois Long [Lipstick], "Tables for Two," *New Yorker*, 14 November 1925, 24–25. All quotations that follow from this book review come from this issue and these pages.

30. John Limon's theoretical insights into the tactics of female stand-up comedians help me analyze this paradoxical combination of bodily presentation and disappearance. He describes comedians Paula Poundstone and Ellen DeGeneres highlighting their bodies and then "escap[ing] from audience view." John Limon, *Stand-up Comedy in Theory, or Abjection in America* (Durham, NC: Duke University Press, 2000), 5. Limon contends that this strategy of humor "works . . . not by exaggerating the body as the thing a woman most definitively has, but by depreciating the body as the sort of having that essentially entails disposing" (136n9).

31. Anita Loos, *A Girl Like I* (New York: Viking, 1966), 46.

32. Anita Loos, *Gentlemen Prefer Blondes and But Gentlemen Marry Brunettes*, ed. Regina Barreca (New York: Penguin Books, 1998), xxxvii.

33. Anita Loos, *The Talmadge Girls* (New York: Viking, 1978), 40.

34. Loos, *Gentlemen Prefer Blondes*, 8.

35. Ibid., 10, 12.

36. Ibid., 58.

37. Anita Loos, *Kiss Hollywood Good-by* (New York: Viking, 1974), 17.

38. Loos, *Gentlemen Prefer Blondes*, 123.

39. Ibid., 135.

40. Ibid., 144.

41. Cutex advertisement, *New Yorker*, 13 October 1928, 97.

42. J. H. Sears & Company advertisement, *New Yorker*, 15 October 1927, 106.

43. Parker, "In the Throes," in *The Portable Dorothy Parker*, 550–551.

44. Ibid., 552–553.

45. Parker, "The Garter," in *Complete Stories*, 99. All subsequent citations from this story appear in parentheses following the quoted text.

46. Marchand, *Advertising the American Dream*, 336.

47. Charles Dickens, *Nicholas Nickleby*, ed. Mark Ford (New York: Penguin Classics, 1999), 411–412.

48. Ibid., 411. Parker, "The Garter," 101.

49. Norris Yates explains that the Little Man is "in quest of self, or of a self-image,

all his own, in the validity of which he can believe," a quest linked to "the idea that the modern environment invades and tends to erode or to break up one's personality." Norris Yates, *The American Humorist: The Conscience of the Twentieth Century* (Ames: Iowa State University Press, 1964), 257. Nancy Walker expands upon this tension between self-blame and social critique: "The little man's sense of ineffectuality may be largely caused by global disorders, but he locates the real problems within himself." Nancy Walker, *What's So Funny?: Humor in American Culture* (Wilmington, DE: Rowman & Littlefield, 1998), 43.

50. E. B. White, "Getting Through," *New Yorker*, 28 August 1926, 13.

51. James Thurber, "A Box to Hide In," *New Yorker*, January 24, 1931, 25.

52. Parker, "The Waltz," in *Complete Stories*, 212. All subsequent citations from this story appear in parentheses following the quoted text.

53. Parker, "Men: A Hate Song," in *Not Much Fun*, 190–191.

54. Peter Stearns observes that this publication "appealed particularly to middle-class men" and that "Advertisements stressed well-muscled men, nearly nude, with large but fat-free bodies." Peter Stearns, *Fat History: Bodies and Beauty in the Modern West* (New York: New York University Press: 2002), 17.

55. Long, "Doldrums: The Swing of the Pendulum," *New Yorker*, 31 January 1931, 19.

56. Edgar Allan Poe, "Fall of the House of Usher," in *Edgar Allan Poe Selected Tales*, ed. David Van Leer (New York: Oxford World Classics, 1998), 55.

57. Litvak argues that "'mature,' 'demystified' knowledge of the world [might] *consist* in a certain untranscended juvenile delinquency, one that stops just this side of murder: more precisely, in the self-pitying, self-adoring, and above all *vindictive* . . . fantasies about the world" (italics in original). Litvak, *Strange Gourmets*, 89.

58. Hans Stengel, "Our Sermons on Sin," *New Yorker*, 12 December 1925, 22.

59. Henri Bergson, *Laughter: An Essay on the Meaning of the Comic*, trans. Cloudesley Brereton and Fred Rothwell (New York: Macmillan Company, 1914), 5.

60. Parker, "Sophisticated Poetry—And the Hell With It," in *The Portable Dorothy Parker*, 560, 562.

61. Ibid., 562.

62. Parker, "Self-Portrait," in *The Portable Dorothy Parker*, 575.

3 / "First Aid to Laughter": Jessie Fauset and the Racial Politics of Smartness

1. Jessie Fauset, "The Gift of Laughter," in *The New Negro: Voices of the Harlem Renaissance*, ed. Alain Locke (New York: Simon & Schuster, 1992), 161, 162.

2. Ibid., 167.

3. Ibid., 165.

4. Fauset, *Plum Bun: A Novel Without A Moral* (Boston: Beacon Press, 1990), 188. All subsequent citations appear in parentheses following the quoted text.

5. Werner Sollors points out that this dualistic and moralistic understanding of biracial identity inevitably denies part of a character's inheritance: "a moral condemnation of passing [rests] on the grounds that it is a form of deception, hence dishonest. Yet this only works as long as it is taken for granted that partial ancestry may have power to become totally defining." Werner Sollors, *Neither Black Nor White Yet Both: Thematic Explorations of Interracial Literature* (Cambridge, MA: Harvard University Press, 1997), 249.

6. David Leavering Lewis's description of these parties betrays his withering

appraisal of Fauset: "Evenings at Jessie Fauset's were seldom relaxed . . . guests were obliged to stretch themselves into large topics of discussion. Occasionally, Harold Jackman, the handsome bachelor, relieved an evening's formality by emptying a hip flask into the punch." David Leavering Lewis, *When Harlem Was in Vogue* (New York: Penguin Books, 1997), 123.

7. Ibid., 124.

8. Robert Hemenway reports that Hurston "entertained entire parties with tales of Eatonville," her Florida home, and she placed "a pot on the stove that visitors were expected to contribute to in order to create a common stew. At other times she fried okra or cooked Florida eel." Hemenway suggests that Hurston was self-conscious about these gestures as rejections of bourgeois affectations. At her parties, she often derisively imitated "the stuffed shirts she encountered on Park Avenue." Robert E. Hemenway, *Zora Neale Hurston: A Literary Biography* (Champaign: University of Illinois Press, 1980), 44.

9. Ann duCille, *The Coupling Convention: Sex, Text, and Tradition in Black Women's Fiction* (New York: Oxford University Press, 1993), 74.

10. Sandra M. Gilbert and Susan Gubar, "Ain't I a New Woman? Feminism and the Harlem Renaissance," in *No Man's Land: The Place of the Woman Writer in the Twentieth Century*, vol. 3, "Letters from the Front" (New Haven: Yale University Press, 1994), 136.

11. As Sollors observes, though passing was "a theme that invited serious, at times sentimental and at other times moralistic treatments," "this is not to say that comedy (let alone irony) was absent from the fiction of passing." Sollors, *Neither Black Nor White Yet Both*, 277.

12. Recent Fauset criticism has charted her thematic engagement with fashion, consumer culture, and middlebrow literature. See Jaime Harker, "Miscegenating Middlebrow: Jessie Fauset and the 'Authentic' Black Middle Class," in *America the Middlebrow: Women's Novels, Progressivism, and Middlebrow Authorship between the Wars* (Amherst: University of Massachusetts Press, 2007), 53–86; Jean Marie Lutes, "Making Up Race: Jessie Fauset, Nella Larsen, and the African American Cosmetics Industry," *Arizona Quarterly* 58, no. 1 (2002): 77–108; Cherene Sherrard-Johnson, "Jessie Fauset's New Negro Woman Artist and the Passing Market," in *Portraits of the New Negro Woman* (New Brunswick, NJ: Rutgers University Press, 2007), 49–76; and Susan Tomlinson, "'An Unwonted Coquetry': The Commercial Seductions of Jessie Fauset's *The Chinaberry Tree*," in *Middlebrow Moderns: Popular American Women Writers of the 1920s*, ed. Lisa Botshon and Meredith Goldsmith (Boston: Northeastern University Press, 2003), 227–244.

13. Harker suggests that Fauset's fiction resembles work published in white press women's magazines. Harker, *America the Middlebrow*, 84.

14. W.E.B. Du Bois, "The Browsing Reader," *Crisis*, June 1928, 202.

15. Roland Marchand, *Advertising the American Dream* (Berkeley: University of California Press, 1984), 193.

16. Lewis, *When Harlem Was in Vogue*, 109.

17. For commentary on the visual iconography of the *Crisis*, see Russ Castronovo, "Beauty Along the Color Line: Lynching, Aesthetics, and the *Crisis*," *PMLA* 121, no. 5 (October 2006): 1443–1459. For discussion of the feminine roles depicted in the *Crisis*, see Sherrard-Johnson, *Portraits of the New Negro Woman*, 55.

18. Alain Locke, "The Younger Literary Movement," *Crisis*, February 1924, 163.

19. William Albert Robinson, "As a Man Thinketh—," *Crisis*, April 1924, 276, 277.

20. W.E.B. Du Bois, "The Technique of Race Prejudice," *Crisis*, August 1923, 154.

21. Lutes notes that by 1920 "cosmetics advertising became a dominant force in white women's magazines and African American newspapers. Meanwhile, the industry developed deeply racialized patterns. Most businesses promoted a white ideal." Lutes, "Making Up Race," 80.

22. Ola Calhoun Morehead, "The Bewitched Sword," *Crisis*, February 1925, 166–167.

23. For analyses of the relationship between black middle-class femininity and the marketing of fashion and cosmetics, see Noliwe Rooks, *Ladies' Pages: African American Women's Magazines and the Culture That Made Them* (New Brunswick, NJ: Rutgers University Press, 2004), and Susannah Walker, *Style & Status: Selling Beauty to African-American Women, 1920–1975* (Lexington: University of Kentucky Press, 2007).

24. Madam C. J. Walker Hair and Skin Preparations advertisement, "The Crisis Advertiser," *Crisis*, May 1925, 51.

25. Coty advertisement, *New Yorker*, 21 January 1928, 31.

26. Ethel M. Caution, "Buyers of Dreams," *Crisis*, December 1921, 60.

27. National Training School for Women and Girls advertisement, "The Crisis Advertiser," *Crisis*, May 1921, 279.

28. Condé Nast School Service advertisement, *Vanity Fair*, July 1923, 27.

29. Eva D. Bowles, "Opportunities for the Educated Colored Woman," *Opportunity*, March 1923, 8.

30. Ibid., 10.

31. Leonard Dove, *New Yorker*, 26 October 1929, 29.

32. Judith Yaross Lee notes that "race and dialect often served as convenient or shorthand class markers" and that this cartoon "establishes a series of other contrasts, some more amusing than others: the multiribboned head of the child against the elegantly coiffed mannequin, curly hair against smooth fur, real vs. fake, big vs. small, white vs. black, rich vs. poor." Judith Yaross Lee, *Defining New Yorker Humor* (Jackson: University Press of Mississippi, 2000), 24.

33. Lutes explains that "Fauset simultaneously evokes the pleasures of department stores and clarifies their racialized nature." Lutes, "Making Up Race," 92.

34. Al Jolson advertisement, *New Yorker*, October 26, 1928, 90.

35. [Anne Harriet] Fish cartoon, *New Yorker*, October 26, 1928, 76.

36. Bermuda advertisement, *New Yorker*, October 26, 1929, 70.

37. Langston Hughes, *The Big Sea* (New York: Hill and Wang, 1993), 272.

38. Ibid., 248.

39. Lewis calls these parties "a stock exchange for cultural commodities, where interracial contacts and contracts were sealed over bootleg spirits and the verse or song of some Afro-American who was then the rage of New York." Lewis, *When Harlem Was in Vogue*, 136.

40. Ibid., 136.

41. Nella Larsen, *Quicksand* (New York: Penguin Classics, 2002), 46. All subsequent citations appear in parentheses following the quoted text.

42. In his biography of Larsen, George Hutchinson writes, "With a sensibility embracing artifice, naïve exaggeration, and pleasure at unintended irony, Van Vechten

was the king of camp before anyone else knew what camp was." George Hutchinson, *In Search of Nella Larsen* (Cambridge, MA: Harvard University Press, 2006), 178.

43. Hazel Carby also stresses Larsen's ambivalent representation of urban anonymity: "[Helga's] initial identification was with the anonymity of the city, where she had the appearance of freedom but no actual home or friends. This anonymity brought brief satisfaction and contentment . . . but she discovered her vulnerability as an object of exchange." Hazel Carby, *Reconstructing Womanhood: The Emergence of the Afro-American Woman Novelist* (New York: Oxford University Press, 1987), 172.

44. Thelma E. Berlack, "New Author Unearthed Right Here in Harlem," *Amsterdam News*, 23 May 1928.

45. "There Is Confusion," *The Crisis Advertiser*, April 1924, 284.

46. Gilbert and Gubar note that "the most widely distributed photograph of Fauset presents her decorously garbed in black, decorated with a string of cultured pearls, and her Phi Beta Kappa key." Gilbert and Gubar, "Ain't I A New Woman," 125.

47. Hughes, *The Big Sea*, 94.

48. Hutchinson observes that "Larsen almost certainly attended these 'teas' on occasion, but she would leave a remarkably unflattering description based on them in her first novel, in a passage that Fauset could well have taken personally." Hutchinson, *In Search of Nella Larsen*, 165. Larsen writes that "The tea to which [Helga] had so suddenly made up her mind to go she found boring beyond endurance, insipid drinks, dull conversation, stupid men." Larsen, *Quicksand*, 54.

49. "The Horizon," *Crisis*, November 1924, 29.

50. Marchand observes: "A few black women did make an appearance as maids or cleaning ladies, but they were outnumbered more than ten to one by young white women in immaculate caps and aprons." Marchand, *Advertising the American Dream*, 202.

51. Laura Wheeler, "Once more we exchange adieu," *Crisis*, May 1928, 19.

52. Fauset, "Dark Algiers the White," in *The Chinaberry Tree and Selected Writings* (Boston: Northeastern University Press, 1995), 386.

53. Ibid., 387.

54. Ibid., 294.

55. Hughes laments that these were "literary soirées with much poetry but little to drink." Hughes, *The Big Sea*, 244.

56. Fauset, "La Vie C'est La Vie," *Crisis*, July 1922, 124.

57. Fauset, "Here's April!" *Crisis*, April 1924, 277. Millay was also a client of Fauset's first literary agent, Brandt & Brandt. Harker, *America the Middlebrow*, 70.

58. Louis Untermeyer, "Versed Aid to the Injured: How to Become a Popular As Well As a Publishable Poet Over the Week-End," *Vanity Fair*, July 1921, 41.

59. Gwendolyn B. Bennet, "To Usward," *Crisis*, May 1924, 19.

60. Fauset, "The 13th Biennial Meeting of the N.A.C.W.," *Crisis*, October 1922, 260.

61. Fauset, "Mary Elizabeth," in *Honey, Hush!: An Anthology of African American Women's Humor*, ed. Daryl Cumber Dance (New York: W. W. Norton & Company, 1998), 307. All subsequent citations from this story appear in parentheses following the quoted text.

62. In her consideration of Fauset's novels, Carby notes the vexed relationship between the modern black middle class and history: "The new middle class both emerged from and changed previous history and its interpretations; the forces of previous his-

tory alone could not provide a basis for its future." Carby suggests that Fauset's novels obviate this problem by rejecting history through romance plots that emphasize the future in their happy endings: "Fauset constructed a chaotic and irrelevant history to which the heroes, not the heroines, brought a new order and meaning." Fauset's ironic treatment of middle-class amnesia about the traumatic history of slavery in "Mary Elizabeth" suggests a more skeptical authorial perspective on bourgeois progress. Carby, *Reconstructing Womanhood*, 168.

63. Nina Miller also argues for the importance of publicity in the representation of gender and racial roles in this novel. Nina Miller, "Femininity, Publicity, and the Class Division of Cultural Labor: Jessie Redmon Fauset's *There Is Confusion*," *African American Review* 30, no. 2 (1996): 205–220.

64. Fauset, *There Is Confusion* (Boston: Northeastern University Press, 1989), 75. All subsequent citations appear in parentheses following the quoted text.

65. For a history of the treatment of African American soldiers during World War I, see Arthur E. Barbeau and Florette Henri, *The Unknown Soldiers: African-American Troops in World War I* (Cambridge, MA: Da Capo Press, 1996).

66. There is some speculation about the character of Fauset's relationship with Du Bois. Harker refers to "Fauset's affair with the married W. E. B. Du Bois," and Du Bois biographer David Leavering Lewis explains that she was his "protégée, collaborator, and soon his lover." Harker, *America the Middlebrow*, 3. David Leavering Lewis, *W.E.B. Du Bois, 1868–1919: Biography of a Race* (New York: Henry Holt & Company, 1993), 464.

67. Fauset's biographer Carolyn Wedin Sylvander writes: "many duties were handled by Fauset. She corresponded with subscribers, with the NAACP Board, with authors. She handled contest judging details. She managed the office when Du Bois made his frequent and extended lecture tours and trips to Europe and Africa." Carolyn Wedin Sylvander, *Jessie Redmon Fauset* (Troy, NY: Whitson, 1981), 27.

68. DuCille writes: "Fauset was a source of encouragement, support, and exposure for both burgeoning black talents and more established writers . . . the magazine's preeminent position in the realm of African American letters was due in large measure to the efforts of Jessie Fauset." duCille, *The Coupling Convention*, 77.

69. Cheryl Wall describes the testy Du Bois: "[Fauset] took pains to defend him from the charge that he was embittered. . . . Yet she acknowledged that Du Bois was arrogant, even haughty, and irascible. Moreover, in an essay replete with references to his personal accomplishments, she credited *The Crisis*, rather than its editor-in-chief, as having been 'the greatest single contributing factor in the growth of significant Negro writers.' In so doing, she retained some well-deserved credit for herself." Cheryl Wall, *Women of the Harlem Renaissance* (Bloomington: Indiana University Press, 1995), 73.

70. Lutes also views Melissa's narcissism as the result of her "absorption in mass-market beauty culture." Lutes, "Making Up Race," 90.

71. Fauset, *The Chinaberry Tree & Selected Writings* (Boston: Northeastern University Press, 1995), 93. All subsequent citations appear in parentheses following the quoted text.

72. Dorothy Parker, "Arrangement in Black and White," in *Dorothy Parker: Complete Stories*, ed. Colleen Breese (New York: Penguin Classics, 1995), 77.

73. Ibid., 79.

74. Fauset, "The Gift of Laughter," 166.

4 / The Indestructible Glamour Girl: Dawn Powell, Celebrity, and Counterpublics

1. Edmund Wilson, "Dawn Powell: Greenwich Village in the Fifties," *New Yorker*, 17 November 1962, 233.

2. Tyrus Miller defines late modernism as a response to these very historical and cultural changes: "shifting hierarchies within the arts, intensive development of the mass media, and traumatic events of social and political history—historical trends that were incipient for high modernist writers, yet not so ineluctably part of the 'weather' as they would become during the 1930s." Tyrus Miller, *Late Modernism: Politics, Fiction, and the Arts between the World Wars* (Berkeley: University of California Press, 1999), 24.

3. Tim Page, *Dawn Powell* (New York: Henry Holt & Co., 1998), 271.

4. Ibid., 180.

5. Page includes several discussions of her friendships with these literary luminaries, including Powell's friendship with John Dos Passos, Edmund Wilson, E. E. Cummings, and Ernest Hemingway. Ibid., 59–60, 160, 58.

6. Dawn Powell, *The Diaries of Dawn Powell: 1931–1965*, ed. Tim Page (South Royalton, VT: Steerforth Press, 1995), 209.

7. Ibid., 178.

8. Andreas Huyssen, "Mass Culture as Woman: Modernism's Other," in *After the Great Divide: Modernism, Mass Culture, Postmodernism* (Bloomington: Indiana University Press, 1986), 44–62.

9. Powell, *Diaries*, 93.

10. Douglas contends that the modern generation symbolically committed matricide and embraced a masculine style: "Urban women writers of the 1920s specialized in matricidal texts as surely as their male peers did." Ann Douglas, *Terrible Honesty: Mongrel Manhattan in the 1920s* (New York: Farrar, Straus, and Giroux, 1995), 249.

11. Powell, *Diaries*, 93.

12. Ibid., 31.

13. Ibid., 33.

14. Walter Benjamin, *Illuminations: Essays and Reflections*, ed. Hannah Arendt (New York: Schocken, 1969), 221, 231.

15. Dawn Powell, *Turn, Magic Wheel* (South Royalton, VT: Steerforth Press, 1999), 177. All subsequent citations appear in parentheses following the quoted text.

16. Warren Susman, *Culture as History: The Transformation of American Society in the Twentieth Century* (New York: Pantheon, 1984), 277.

17. P. David Marshall points out that "familiarity and intimacy are much more central to the construction of a female celebrity than to the construction of a male celebrity." P. David Marshall, *Celebrity and Power: Fame in Contemporary Culture* (Minneapolis: University of Minnesota, 1997), 144.

18. Marshall explains that in the 1920s "the private lives of the stars provided a public discourse on intimacy and a constructed narrative or morality tale that implicitly expressed where the normative center of that discourse should be." In this light, Effie's self-invention indicates the proper relationship of a devoted wife as a support and helpmeet to her genius husband no matter his infractions. Ibid., 106.

19. Roland Marchand, *Advertising the American Dream: Making Way for Modernity (1920–1940)* (Berkeley: University of California Press, 1986), 149–150.

20. Benjamin, *Illuminations*, 228.

21. Fredric Jameson describes claustrophobic and surveilled space as a characteristic of postmodern city life: "the suppression of distance (in the sense of Benjamin's aura) and the relentless saturation of any remaining voids or empty places." The body is "exposed to a perceptual barrage of immediacy from which all sheltering layers and intervening mediations have been removed." Fredric Jameson, *Postmodernism, or the Cultural Logic of Late Capitalism* (Durham, NC: Duke University Press, 1991), 412–413.

22. For an illuminating discussion of the "face-object," stardom, and the mask, see Roland Barthes, "The Face of Garbo," in *Mythologies*, trans. Annette Lavers (New York: Hill & Wang, 1972), 56–57.

23. In her study of female reporters, Jean Marie Lutes discusses the cultural potency of "the image of a fraternity of newsmen, manly reporters who cast a cynical look at the world around them." Jean Marie Lutes, *Front Page Girls: Women Journalists in American Culture and Fiction, 1880–1930* (Ithaca, NY: Cornell University Press, 2007), 5.

24. Robert Scholes argues that anxiety about middlebrow cultural production motivates modernist formal experimentation: "An attempt to exclude the middle can be seen as the engine driving Modernist paradoxy itself." Robert Scholes, *Paradoxy of Modernism* (New Haven: Yale University Press, 2006), 26.

25. Joan Shelley Rubin explains that "In the three decades following the First World War, Americans created an unprecedented range of activities aimed at making literature and other forms of 'high' culture available to a wide reading public." Joan Shelley Rubin, *The Making of Middlebrow Culture* (Chapel Hill: University of North Carolina Press, 1992), xi.

26. These advertisements include such warning questions as: "Are We a Nation of Low-Brows?"; "Are people ready to read these 25 books?"; "Where would we be anyway if it weren't for advertising?"; and "Do *You* Know How to Behave?" Advertisement for 25 Books, Haldeman-Julius Company, *McClure's*, November 1922, 5. Advertisement by *McClure's Magazine* "in cooperation with The American Association of Advertising Agencies," *McClure's*, November 1922, 6. Advertisement for the Book of Etiquette by Nelson-Doubleday Inc., *McClure's*, November 1922, 7.

27. Pelman Institute advertisement, *McClure's*, November 1922, 9.

28. Mathew Thomson, *Psychological Subjects: Identity, Culture, and Health in Twentieth-Century Britain* (New York: Oxford University Press, 2006), 25.

29. Effie's costume resembles Edna St. Vincent Millay's preferred attire for readings. Millay wrote to her family early in her career: "I *must* have long dresses, trailing ones." Edna St. Vincent Millay to the Millay Family, September 3, 1917, in *Letters of Edna St. Vincent Millay*, ed. Allan Ross Macdougall (New York: Grosset & Dunlap, 1952), 76. The gray smocks also reflect the stereotyped bohemian wardrobe described in *Vanity Fair*: "she goes in for smocks and soft shades of soot-grey and bright flaming soulmates." "Greenwich Villagers: Who Are Not Yet Able to Forget the Village from Which They Came," *Vanity Fair*, June 1922, 68.

30. Rita Felski analyzes this strategy in her consideration of the modern dandy:

"the aesthete's playful subversion of gender norms and adoption of feminine traits paradoxically reinforce his distance from and superiority to women, whose nature renders them incapable of this kind of free-floating semiotic mobility and aesthetic sophistication." Felski, *Gender of Modernity*, 106.

31. For an insightful study of the relationship between modernist style and celebrity, see Aaron Jaffe, *Modernism and the Culture of Celebrity* (Cambridge: Cambridge University Press, 2005).

32. Loren Glass, *Authors Inc.: Literary Celebrity in the Modern United States, 1880–1980* (New York: New York University Press, 2004), 143.

33. With this insight, Powell anticipates recent criticism of modernism and its relationship to print culture and publicity. Lawrence Rainey argues that, in spite of its mythos of independence and loftiness, modernism was characterized not by stark division but by negotiation: "Modernism marks neither a straightforward resistance nor an outright capitulation to commodification but a momentary equivocation that incorporates elements of both in a brief, necessarily unstable synthesis." Lawrence Rainey, *Institutions of Modernism: Literary Elites and Public Culture* (New Haven: Yale University Press, 1998), 3. Jaffe tweaks the modernist's pretense of literary independence: "Modernist authorial immanence starts to seem worryingly indistinguishable from the forms of publicity and promotion best left to secondary literary work." Jaffe, *Modernism and the Culture*, 16. Patrick Collier agrees that "the journalistic and literary worlds were so intertwined that it was impossible for writers to escape entanglement with the newspaper press." Patrick Collier, *Modernism on Fleet Street* (Burlington, VT: Ashgate Publishing Company, 2006), 3–4.

34. Dawn Powell, *Happy Island* (South Royalton, VT: Steerforth Press, 1998), 9.

35. For analyses of 1930s gangster films, see Jonathan Munby, *Public Enemies, Public Heroes: Screening the Gangster from Little Caesar to Touch of Evil* (Chicago: University of Chicago Press, 1999), and Eugene Roscow, *Born to Lose: The Gangster Film in America* (New York: Oxford University Press, 1978). Munby observes: "[The gangsters] all attempt to execute those otherwise deferred promises of upward mobility." Munby, *Public Enemies, Public Heroes*, 50.

36. Eli Zaretsky suggests that the symbolic modern significance of women and gay men was parallel: "Debates over the implications of modernity for gender relations revolved around the cultural roles of two new dramatis personae: the 'new woman' and the public male homosexual. Both of them pioneered personal life in the sense of life outside of, or at least not defined by, the family." Eli Zaretsky, *Secrets of the Soul: A Social and Cultural History of Psychoanalysis* (New York: Knopf, 2004), 43.

37. Michael Warner, *Publics and Counterpublics* (New York: Zone Books, 2005), 63.

38. Marshall contends that "Celebrities represent subject positions that audiences can adopt or adapt in their formation of social identities. Each celebrity represents a complex form of audience-subjectivity that, when placed within a system of celebrities, provides the ground on which distinctions, differences, and oppositions are played out." Marshall, *Celebrity and Power*, 65.

39. The shame linked with sophistication is its unavoidable shadow, Joseph Litvak teaches us: "even the most celebratory invocations of sophistication as worldliness remain haunted by the guilty sense of sophistication as a deviation from, even a crime against, nature." Litvak further points out that "while sophistication cannot be reduced simply to homosexuality, gay, lesbian, and queer critics have a particularly

vital interest in the analysis of sophistication—which is to say, in the analysis of so-phistophobia." Joseph Litvak, *Strange Gourmets: Sophistication, Theory, and the Novel* (Durham, NC: Duke University Press, 1997), 4.

40. Warner, *Publics and Counterpublics*, 119.

41. Powell, *A Time to Be Born*, 788.

42. James Baughman explains: "Until the late 1930s, Luce's publications could convey contradictory points of view. . . . Starting in 1940, Time Inc. publications at times deliberately presented the news in ways that revealed Luce's preoccupations. The magazines continued to summarize events in typical *Time* fashion, but after 1939 they regularly ridiculed opponents of certain policies Luce advocated." James Baughman, *Henry R. Luce and the Rise of the American News Media* (Baltimore: Johns Hopkins University Press, 2001), 3.

43. Sylvia Jukes, *Rage for Fame: The Ascent of Clare Boothe Luce* (New York: Random House, 1997), 161–175.

44. Powell, *Diaries*, 213.

45. Powell viewed humor as the sacred weapon of the powerless, a force begrudged by the powerful, as she explained in a 1961 diary entry:

Smug people feel their smugness shaken when they cannot pity someone—that the pitiable objects should joke or have fun among themselves is not proper. Be sad, damn you—they want to say when they see children of the poor having fun with some old boards and cans. It is the great pleasure of the poor, the crippled, the doomed—laughter when they can—and the Haves are furious because their laughter-means are so limited. Look, they say, what are you laughing at? *We* are the ones in the Mercedes with the Sarasota tan and our jet tickets to Rome and our lists of Hilton hotels and our latest TV sets and our legs we seldom use and our educations laid on our heads like Man Tan—what are you people in wheelchairs, in hovels, in institutions, in debt, in a beat-up old car or shack, how can you laugh? How can you do anything but wail and weep and beg? See how pitiful, how unlucky you are. So if you aren't lucky—even if you aren't rich, maybe you love your tiny security of laughter so much you are smugger than the rich. (Ibid., 423)

46. Nancy Walker sees this approach as a major tactic in the tradition of American women's humor: "while superficially accepting the assessment of the dominant culture—e.g., women are frivolous, gossipy, inept—on a deeper level women's humor calls into question the values that have led to these assessments." Nancy Walker, *A Very Serious Thing: Women's Humor and American Culture* (Minneapolis: University of Minnesota Press, 1988), 36.

47. Baughman, *Henry R. Luce*, 3–5.

48. Mary Douglas, *Implicit Meanings: Essays in Anthropology* (London: Routledge, 1975), 104.

49. Miller, *Late Modernism*, 54, 52.

50. Ibid., 64.

51. Diana Trilling, "Four Recent Novels," *Nation*, September 19, 1942, 244.

5 / "Scratch a Socialist and You Find a Snob": Mary McCarthy, Irony, and Politics

1. Harvey Teres observes that McCarthy's novel *The Oasis* "mocks habits of mind such as abstraction, idealism, rigidity, and unprovoked combativeness which, if they

202 / NOTES TO PAGES 141-147

are not necessarily shown to originate in male prerogative, nonetheless enhance it."
These "habits of mind" also serve as the object of satire in *The Company She Keeps*.
Harvey M. Teres, *Renewing the Left: Politics, Imagination, and the New York Intellectu-als* (New York: Oxford University Press, 1996), 192.

2. Carol Brightman, *Writing Dangerously: Mary McCarthy and Her World* (New York: Harcourt Brace & Company, 1994), 314.

3. William Barrett, *The Truants: Adventures Among the Intellectuals* (Garden City, NY: Anchor Books, 1982), 67.

4. Mary McCarthy, *How I Grew: A Memoir of the Early Years* (New York: Harcourt Books, 1987), 214, 62.

5. Ibid., 111–112.

6. Ibid., 209. McCarthy treats her early affection for Millay's verse as symptoms of adolescent sentimentalism: "Among these same Annie Wright [boarding school] relics, I find entire poems—Edna Millay, Margaret Widdemer, unidentified others—written out as though for commonplacing." Ibid., 101.

7. McCarthy, *Intellectual Memoirs: 1936–1938* (New York: Harvest Books, 1993), 17.

8. McCarthy, *A Bolt from the Blue and Other Essays*, ed. A. O. Scott (New York: New York Review Books, 2002), 3–4.

9. McCarthy, *The Company She Keeps* (New York: Harvest/HBJ Books, 2003), 112. All subsequent citations appear in parentheses following the quoted text.

10. Joseph Litvak trenchantly describes this process of Other-ing sophisticates: "the bold infractions of elite criticism have to get recoded as *pathological* . . . so that what might seem an enviable cosmopolitanism can take on instead the horrifying, abject alterity of what one avoids like the plague." Joseph Litvak, *Strange Gourmets: Sophistication, Theory, and the Novel* (Durham, NC: Duke University Press, 1997), 31.

11. For more on the *Partisan Review* circle, see Terry Cooney, *The Rise of the New York Intellectuals: Partisan Review and Its Circle, 1934–1945* (Madison: University of Wisconsin Press, 2004); Teres, *Renewing the Left*; Alan M. Wald, *The New York In-tellectuals: The Rise and Decline of the Anti-Stalinist Left from the 1930s to the 1980s* (Winston-Salem: University of North Carolina Press, 1987); and Hugh Wilford, *The New York Intellectuals: From Vanguard to Institution* (New York: Manchester Univer-sity Press, 1995).

12. Dawn Powell, *The Diaries of Dawn Powell 1931–1965* (South Royalton, VT: Steerforth Press, 1995), 316.

13. Mary McCarthy interview by Elisabeth Niebuhr, in *Writers at Work: The Paris Review Interviews, Second Series*, ed. by George Plimpton (New York: Penguin, 1977), 297.

14. A.O. Scott, "Introduction," in *A Bolt from the Blue and Other Essays*, ix.

15. Cooney, *Rise of the New York Intellectuals*, 246.

16. Quoted in Brightman, *Writing Dangerously*, 146.

17. Cooney, *Rise of the New York Intellectuals*, 13.

18. Barrett stresses her exceptional status: "For the popular imagination, of course, this figure of the New York Intellectual . . . was always definitely of the male sex . . . if one . . . dared to imagine the typical intellectual as a woman . . . there could only be one person on whom one's choice could light—Mary McCarthy." Barrett, *The Truants*, 65.

19. McCarthy, *A Bolt from the Blue*, 341.

20. Cooney explains that the editors of the *Partisan Review* rejected the *Southern Review*'s celebration of regionalism and New Criticism's inattention to social-political context, but he notes that "the *Partisan Review* critics found much that was positive among the southerners as their own concern shifted toward the defense of literary sophistication and cultural modernism." Cooney, *The Rise of the New York Intellectuals*, 208.

21. Clement Greenberg defined kitsch as the adoption of avant-garde styles for commercial uses. He called the *New Yorker* "fundamentally high-class kitsch for the luxury trade, [that] converts and waters down a great deal of avant-garde material." Clement Greenberg, in *The Collected Essays and Criticism*, Vol. 1: *Perceptions and Judgments, 1939–1944*, ed. John O'Brien (Chicago: University of Chicago Press, 1986), 13.

22. Alfred Kazin, *Starting Out in the Thirties* (Boston: Little, Brown, 1965), 155.

23. Quoted in Ben Yagoda, *About Town: The New Yorker and the World It Made* (New York: Da Capo Press, 2001), 38.

24. Susan Hegeman, *Patterns for America: Modernism and the Concept of Culture* (Princeton, NJ: Princeton University Press, 1999), 134.

25. Ibid., 137.

26. The modern period was distinguished by the new broad availability of high cultural artifacts, whether summarized in magazines or delivered to the doorstep by Book-of-the-Month clubs. Joan Shelley Rubin in *The Making of Middlebrow Culture* (Chapel Hill: University of North Carolina Press, 1992) and Janice Radway in *A Feeling for Books: the Book-of-the-Month Club, Literary Taste, and Middle Class Desire* (Chapel Hill: University of North Carolina Press, 1999) argue for the importance of analyzing middlebrow literature and the way it constitutes, refracts, and sometimes challenges middle-class and feminine identities. Their work has led to several recent feminist considerations of women writers and middlebrow literature. See Lisa Bosthon and Meredith Goldsmith, eds., *Middlebrow Moderns: Popular American Women Writers of the 1920s* (Boston: Northeastern University Press, 2003); Faye Hammill, *Women, Celebrity, and Literary Culture between the Wars* (Austin: University of Texas Press, 2007); Jaime Harker, *America the Middlebrow: Women's Novels, Progressivism, and Middlebrow Authorship between the Wars* (Amherst: University of Massachusetts Press, 2007); and Nicola Humble, *The Feminine Middlebrow Novel: 1920s to 1950s: Class, Domesticity, and Bohemianism* (New York: Oxford University Press, 2002).

27. Bourdieu points out that "the distinctive power of cultural possessions or practices—an artifact, a qualification, a film culture—tends to decline with the growth in the absolute number of people able to appropriate them" and that intellectuals are "divided between their interest in cultural proselytism" and "concern for cultural distinction, the only objective basis of their rarity." Pierre Bourdieu, *Distinction: A Social Critique of the Judgment of Taste*, trans. Richard Nice (Cambridge, MA: Harvard University Press, 1984), 229–230.

28. Greenberg, "Avant-Garde and Kitsch," 12.

29. *Oxford English Dictionary Online*, s.v. "muster," http://dictionary.oed.com/cgi/display/00319591?keytype=ref&ijkey=zrP5AavoWhqq (accessed September 20, 2009).

30. McCarthy, *A Bolt from the Blue*, 277.

31. Ibid., 278.

32. Foucault's observations about exercise could apply to Margaret's painful self-

improvement regimen: "Exercise, having become an element in the political technology of the body and of duration, does not culminate in a beyond, but tends towards a subjection that has never reached its limit." Michel Foucault, *Discipline and Punish: The Birth of the Prison*, trans. Alan Sheridan (New York: Vintage, 1977), 162.

33. Jill Wacker views McCarthy's depiction of consumer discourse as "a specifically female and American idea of intellect," and she traces "the tension that McCarthy sensed between the mass-produced nature of the commodity and society's claim that it could represent or express a unique subjectivity for women." Jill Wacker, "'*Knowing* Concerns Me': The Female Intellectual and the Consumer Idiom" in *Twenty-four Ways of Looking at Mary McCarthy*, ed. Eve Swertka and Margo Viscusi (Westport, CT: Greenwood Press, 1996), 44.

34. Dorothy Parker, "The Garter," in *Dorothy Parker: Complete Stories*, ed. Colleen Breese (New York: Penguin Books, 2003), 101.

35. Hegeman, *Patterns for America*, 191.

36. Bourdieu, *Distinction*, 230.

37. McCarthy recognizes a contradiction in Margaret's status that is more generally true of Marxist intellectuals, as Marshall Berman observes: "The networks and ambiguities of the market are such that everybody is caught up and entangled in them." Indeed, "radical intellectuals encounter radical obstacles: their ideas and movements are in danger of melting into the same modern air that decomposes the bourgeois order they are working to overcome." Berman argues that this entanglement provides all the more reason that the intellectual should be self-aware about this inevitable complicity. Marshall Berman, *All That Is Solid Melts into Air: The Experience of Modernity* (New York: Simon & Schuster, 1982), 119.

38. The *Oxford English Dictionary* offers two definitions of the noun form of "travesty": "a grotesque or debased imitation or likeness; a caricature" or "(dressing in) the attire of the opposite sex." *Oxford English Dictionary Online*, s.v. "travesty," http://dictionary.oed.com/cgi/display/50256842?keytype=ref&ijkey=TYwMcpqce8j52 (accessed 20 September 2009).

39. Joan Riviere suggested that for women in white-collar professions, "Womanliness could . . . be assumed and worn as a mask, both to hide the profession of masculinity and to avert the reprisals . . . as a thief will turn out his pockets and ask to be searched to prove that he has not the stolen goods." Joan Riviere, "Womanliness as a Masquerade," in *Formations of Fantasy*, ed. Victor Burgin, James Donald, and Cora Kaplan (New York: Routledge, 1986), 38. In this scene, Margaret flaunts the stolen goods.

40. Analyzing the ramifications of Riviere's theory, Stephen Heath notes that the masquerade of womanliness also undermines the stability of masculine power: "she puts on a show of femininity as they demand . . . and returns masculinity to them as equally unreal, another act, a charade of power." Stephen Heath, "Joan Rivière and the Masquerade," in *Formations of Fantasy*, 56. Margaret's imitation of Trotsky vexes the primacy and authority of masculine intellectualism.

41. Brightman, *Writing Dangerously*, 223.

42. Sabrina Abrams Fuchs argues that McCarthy's outsider status as a woman and a Catholic within a predominantly male and Jewish circle enabled her satirical vision. Sabrina Abrams Fuchs, *Mary McCarthy: Gender, Politics, and the Postwar Intellectual* (New York: Peter Lang, 2004).

43. Alan Wald, "The Politics of Culture: The New York Intellectuals in Fiction," *The Centennial Review* 29, no. 3 (Summer 1985): 354.

44. Mary McCarthy, *The Oasis* (New York: Random House, 1949), 221.

45. Ibid., 112.

46. Carol Gelderman, *Conversations with Mary McCarthy* (Jackson: University Press of Mississippi, 1991), 110.

47. Kazin, *Starting Out in the Thirties*, 156.

48. Teres, *Renewing the Left*, 13, 180.

49. Neil Gross, *Richard Rorty: The Making of An American Philosopher* (Chicago: University of Chicago Press, 2008), 29.

50. Richard Rorty, *Contingency, Irony, and Solidarity* (New York: Cambridge University Press, 1989), xv.

51. Ibid., 190.

52. Rorty argued that the Freudian framework helps the intellectual retrain attention "from the universal to the concrete, from the attempt to find necessary truths, ineliminable beliefs, to the idiosyncratic contingencies of our individual pasts." Ibid., 34.

53. Gelderman, *Conversations with Mary McCarthy*, 89.

54. McCarthy was not the only one to make this connection. In Dawn Powell's assessment of McCarthy's authorial persona, she pigeonholed her ethnic identity and class aspiration: "She has her two manners—her lace-curtain Irish, almost unbelievably genteel lady scholar torn between desire to be Blue Stocking without losing her Ladyship; and then her shanty Irish where she relaxes, whamming away at her characters like a Queen of the Roller Derby, groin-kicking, shin-knifing, belly-butting, flailing away with skates and all arms at her characters and jumping on them with a hoarse whoop of glee when they are felled." Powell, *Diaries*, 354.

55. Morris Dickstein also notes that McCarthy's emphasis on self-examination resists the promise of self-improvement: "far from being healing and therapeutic in the manner of popular fiction, this bolt of self-knowledge brings us harsh news of our own limitations, the iron cage of personality." Morris Dickstein, *A Mirror in the Roadway: Literature and the Real World* (Princeton, NJ: Princeton University Press, 2005), 98.

56. Berman, *All That Is Solid Melts into Air*, 119.

57. Rorty, *Contingency, Irony, and Solidarity*, xv.

58. Berman, *All That Is Solid Melts into Air*, 23. This description of Marx parallels Dickstein's description of McCarthy's aesthetic and philosophy: "For McCarthy, self-awareness and lucidity, the very things that descend like a plague on Jim Barnett, are nearly absolute values." Dickstein, *Mirror in the Roadway*, 98.

59. Linda Hutcheon, *Irony's Edge: The Theory and Politics of Irony* (New York: Routledge, 1994), 29.

60. Rorty posits that irony resists manipulation and seduction because it acknowledges the ease of translation; by treating the Byronic hero and the fascist as the same man, McCarthy anticipates Rorty's point that "anything can be made to look good or bad by being redescribed." Rorty, *Contingency, Irony, and Solidarity*, 73.

61. McCarthy thus draws upon a political philosophy shared by others in the *Partisan Review* circle. Hegeman explains that Greenberg feared the proximity of professed affiliation to fascism: "Not only was it important to be politically detached, but to be otherwise was implicitly to be *totalitarian*, hence a political threat." While Hegeman

is skeptical about the validity of this argument, both McCarthy and Greenberg made this connection between intellectual independence from political parties and resisting fascism. Hegeman, *Patterns for America*, 174.

62. Berman views those conflicts as fertile ground for Marxist inquiry: "The great gift [Marx] can give us today, it seems to me, is not a way out of the contradictions of modern life but a surer and deeper way into these contradictions.... He knew we must start where we are: psychically naked, stripped of all religious, aesthetic, moral haloes and sentimental veils, thrown back on our individual will and energy." Berman, *All That Is Solid Melts into Air*, 129.

63. Here I follow Rorty in his premise that the ironist recognizes that her final vocabulary, a set of premises and terms for understanding her place in the world and political convictions, is forever contingent, reflective of historical context and life experiences. Rorty's description of the ironist's position fits Margaret's resolve to remain in disunity: "[the] renunciation of the attempt to formulate criteria of choice between final vocabularies, puts [ironists] in the position which Sartre called 'meta-stable': never quite able to take themselves seriously because always aware that the terms in which they describe themselves are subject to change, always aware of the contingency and fragility of their final vocabularies, and thus of their selves." Rorty, *Irony, Contingency, and Solidarity*, 73–74.

Conclusion

1. Susan Faludi, "Second-Place Citizens," *New York Times*, 26 August 2008.

2. Camille Paglia, "Feminism Past and Present: Ideology, Action, and Reform," *Arion: A Journal of the Humanities and the Classics* 16, no. 1 (Spring/Summer 2008): 8–9.

3. Lauren Weisberger, *The Devil Wears Prada* (New York: Doubleday, 2003), 11.

4. Ibid., 12.

5. Ibid., 174.

6. Ibid., 351–352.

7. Mary McCarthy, *The Group* (New York: Harcourt, 1963), 96.

8. Ibid., 90.

9. Ibid., 91.

10. Ibid., 484.

11. Ibid., 425–426.

12. Ibid., 467.

13. Daniel Mark Epstein, *What Lips My Lips Have Kissed: The Loves and Love Poems of Edna St. Vincent Millay* (New York: Henry Holt and Company, 2001), 94.

14. McCarthy, *The Group*, 487.

15. Sylvia Plath, *The Bell Jar* (New York: HarperCollins, 2003), 2.

16. Ibid., 3.

17. For an analysis of magazine culture in *The Bell Jar*, see Garry M. Leonard, "'The Woman Is Perfected. Her Dead Body Wears the Smile of Accomplishment': Sylvia Plath and *Mademoiselle* Magazine," *College English* 19, no. 2 (June 1992): 60–82.

18. Nora Ephron, *Crazy Salad: Some Things About Women* (New York: Random House, 1975), 134.

19. Ibid., 3.

20. Ibid., 17.

21. Ibid., 15.

22. Nora Ephron, *Imaginary Friends* (New York: Vintage, 2003).

23. Nora Ephron, *I Feel Bad About My Neck and Other Thoughts on Being a Woman* (New York: Alfred Knopf, 2006), 10.

24. *Sex and the City* (HBO, 1998); *Sex and the City* (HBO, 2008).

25. Sherryl Connelly, "Just a Touch of the Poet: A Biography of Edna St. Vincent Millay Focuses on the Work, Not the Woman," *New York Daily News*, 9 September 2001.

26. *Ugly Betty* (ABC, 2006).

27. Rory is seen reading *The Group* and reports reading *The Portable Dorothy Parker* in *Gilmore Girls*, "Rory's Dance," Season 1, Episode 9, 2000. She reads *Savage Beauty* by Nancy Milford in "Like Mother, Like Daughter," Season 2, Episode 7, 2001.

28. *Sex and the City* (HBO, 2008).

29. *The Women* (TimeWarner, 2008).

30. David Sedaris, *When You Are Engulfed in Flames* (New York: Little, Brown and Company, 2008), 52.

31. Ibid., 52.

32. Ibid., 53.

33. Sander Gilman points out that modern and contemporary American mass culture aligns Jewishness with masculine sexual insecurity and feminine dominance so these three categories are not as separate in their vexed relationship to smartness as my list might suggest. Sander Gilman, *Smart Jews* (Lincoln: University of Nebraska Press, 1996), 175–206.

34. Ariel Levy, "Nora Knows What to Do: The Filmmaker Foodie Pays Homage to Julia Child," *New Yorker*, 6 and 13 July 2009, 62.

35. David Sedaris, *Me Talk Pretty One Day* (New York: Back Bay Books, 2000), 246.

Selected Bibliography

Anderson, Amanda. *The Powers of Distance: Cosmopolitanism and the Cultivation of Detachment*. Princeton, NJ: Princeton University Press, 2001.

Barreca, Regina. "Introduction." In *Dorothy Parker: Complete Stories*, ed. Colleen Breese, vii–xix. New York: Penguin Books, 1995.

———. *They Used to Call Me Snow White . . . But I Drifted: Women's Strategic Use of Humor*. New York: Penguin Books, 1991.

Barrett, William. *The Truants: Adventures among the Intellectuals*. Garden City, NY: Anchor Books, 1982.

Baughman, James. *Henry R. Luce and the Rise of the American News Media*. Baltimore: Johns Hopkins University Press, 2001.

Benchley, Robert. *The Benchley Round-Up*. Chicago: University of Chicago Press, 1983.

Bender, Thomas. *New York Intellect: A History of Intellectual Life in New York City, from 1750 to the Beginnings of Our Own Time*. Baltimore: Johns Hopkins University Press, 1987.

———. *The Unfinished City: New York and the Metropolitan Idea*. New York: The New Press, 2002.

Benjamin, Walter. *Illuminations: Essays and Reflections*. Trans. Harry Zohn. New York: Schocken Books, 1968.

Berlant, Lauren. *The Female Complaint: The Unfinished Business of Sentimentality in American Culture*. Durham, NC: Duke University Press, 2008.

Berman, Marshall. *All That Is Solid Melts into Air: The Experience of Modernity*. New York: Penguin, 1982.

Bergson, Henri. *Laughter: An Essay on the Meaning of the Comic*. Trans. Fred Rothwell. New York: Macmillan, 1914.

Biers, Jesse. *The Rise and Fall of American Humor*. New York: Holt, Rinehart and Winston, 1968.

Blair, Walter, and Hamlin Hill. *America's Humor: From Poor Richard to Doonesbury*. New York: Oxford University Press, 1978.

Booth, Wayne. *A Rhetoric of Irony*. Chicago: University of Chicago Press, 1974.

Botshon, Lisa, and Meredith Goldsmith, ed. *Middlebrow Moderns: Popular American Women Writers of the 1920s*. Boston: Northeastern University Press, 2003.

Bourdieu, Pierre. *Distinction: A Social Critique of the Judgement of Taste*. Trans. Richard Nice. Cambridge, MA: Harvard University Press, 1984.

Brightman, Carol. *Writing Dangerously: Mary McCarthy and Her World*. New York: A Harvest Book, 1992.

Brown, Dorothy. *Setting a Course: American Women in the 1920s*. Boston: Twayne Publishers, 1987.

Brown, Judith. *Glamour in Six Dimensions: Modernism and the Radiance of Form*. Ithaca, NY: Cornell University Press, 2009.

Burstein, Jessica. "A Few Words about Dubuque: Modernism, Sentimentalism, and the Blasé." *American Literary History* 14, no. 2 (Summer 2002): 227–254.

Carby, Hazel. *Reconstructing Womanhood: The Emergence of the Afro-American Woman Novelist*. New York: Oxford University Press, 1987.

Carpio, Glenda. *Laughing Fit to Kill: Black Humor in the Fictions of Slavery*. New York: Oxford University Press, 2008.

Chauncey, George. *Gay New York: Gender, Urban Culture, and the Making of the Gay Male World 1890–1940*. New York: Basic Books, 1994.

Cooney, Terry. *The Rise of the New York Intellectuals: Partisan Review and Its Circle, 1934–1945*. Madison: University of Wisconsin Press, 2004.

Davis, Simone Weil. *Living Up to the Ads: Gender Fictions of the 1920s*. Durham, NC: Duke University Press, 2000.

DiBattista, Maria. *Fast-Talking Dames*. New Haven: Yale University Press, 2001.

Dickstein, Morris. *A Mirror in the Roadway: Literature and the Real World*. Princeton, NJ: Princeton University Press, 2005.

Douglas, Ann. *Terrible Honesty: Mongrel Manhattan in the 1920s*. New York: Farrar, Straus, and Giroux, 1995.

Douglas, George H. *The Smart Magazines: 50 Years of Literary Revelry and High Jinks at Vanity Fair, the New Yorker, Life, Esquire, and the Smart Set*. Hamden, CT: Archon, 1991.

Douglas, Mary. *Implicit Meanings: Essays in Anthropology*. Boston: Routledge, 1975.

duCille, Ann. *The Coupling Convention: Sex, Text, and Tradition in Black Women's Fiction*. New York: Oxford University Press, 1993.

Dumenil, Lynn. *The Modern Temper: American Culture and Society in the 1920s*. New York: Farrar, Straus, and Giroux, 1995.

Ephron, Nora. *Crazy Salad: Some Things about Women*. New York: Modern Library, 2000.

———. *I Feel Bad about My Neck and Other Thoughts on Being a Woman*. New York: Alfred A. Knopf, 2006.

———. *Imaginary Friends*. New York: Vintage, 2003.

Epstein, Daniel Mark. *What Lips My Lips Have Kissed: The Loves and Love Poems of Edna St. Vincent Millay*. New York: Henry Holt and Company, 2001.

Fass, Paula. *The Damned and the Beautiful: American Youth in the 1920s*. New York: Oxford University Press, 1979.

Fauset, Jessie. "The 13th Biennial Meeting of the N.A.C.W." *Crisis*, October 1922, 260.

———. *The Chinaberry Tree & Selected Writings*. Boston: Northeastern University Press, 1995.

———. "The Gift of Laughter." In *The New Negro*, ed. Alain Locke, 161–167. New York: Simon & Schuster, 1992.

———. "Here's April!" *Crisis*, January 1924, 277.

———. "La Vie C'est la Vie." *Crisis*, July 1922, 124.

———. "Mary Elizabeth." In *Honey, Hush!: An Anthology of African American Women's Humor*, ed. Daryl Cumber Dance, 307–314. New York: W. W. Norton & Company, 1998.

———. *Plum Bun: A Novel Without A Moral*. Boston: Beacon Press, 1990.

———. *There Is Confusion*. Boston: Northeastern University Press, 1989.

Felski, Rita. *The Gender of Modernity*. Cambridge, MA: Harvard University Press, 1995.

Fitzgerald, F. Scott. *The Great Gatsby*. New York: Scribner, 2004.

Freedman, Diane P., ed. *Millay at 100: A Critical Reappraisal*. Carbondale: Southern Illinois University Press, 1995.

Freud, Sigmund. *Jokes and Their Relation to the Unconscious*. Ed. and trans. James Strachey. New York: W. W. Norton & Company, 1960.

Fuchs, Sabrina Abrams. *Mary McCarthy: Gender, Politics, and the Postwar Intellectual*. New York: Peter Lang, 2004.

Gaines, James. *Wit's End: Days and Nights of the Algonquin Round Table*. New York: Harcourt Brace Jovanovich, 1977.

Gelderman, Carol. *Conversations with Mary McCarthy*. Jackson: University Press of Mississippi, 1991.

———. *Mary McCarthy: A Life*. New York: St. Martin's Press, 1990.

Gilbert, Sandra M., and Susan Gubar. *No Man's Land: The Place of the Woman Writer in the Twentieth Century*, vol. 3: "Letters from the Front." New Haven: Yale University Press, 1994.

Gill, Brendan. *Here at the New Yorker*. Cambridge, MA: Da Capo Press, 1997.

Gilman, Sander. *Smart Jews*. Lincoln: University of Nebraska Press, 1996.

Glass, Loren. *Authors Inc.: Literary Celebrity in the Modern United States, 1880–1980*. New York: New York University Press, 2004.

Greenberg, Clement. "The Avant-Garde and Kitsch." In *The Collected Essays and Criticism*, Vol. 1: *Perceptions and Judgments, 1939–1944*, ed. John O'Brien, 5–22. Chicago: University of Chicago Press, 1986.

Hammill, Faye. *Women, Celebrity, and Literary Culture between the Wars*. Austin: University of Texas Press, 2007.

Harker, Jaime. *America the Middlebrow: Women's Novels, Progressivism, and Middlebrow Authorship between the Wars*. Amherst: University of Massachusetts Press, 2007.

Hegeman, Susan. "Taking Blondes Seriously," *American Literary History* 7, no. 30 (Autumn 1995): 525–554.

———. *Patterns for America: Modernism and the Concept of Culture*. Princeton, NJ: Princeton University Press, 1999.

Hibbard, George. "The Quality of Smartness." *Vanity Fair*, May 1920, 118, 120.

Hoyt, Nancy. "A Very Modern Love Story." *Vanity Fair*, December 1923, 33.

Hughes, Langston. *The Big Sea*. New York: Hill and Wang, 1993.

Humble, Nicola. *The Feminine Middlebrow Novel, 1920s to 1950s: Class, Domesticity, and Bohemianism*. New York: Oxford University Press, 2002.

Hutcheon, Linda. *Irony's Edge: The Theory and Politics of Irony*. New York: Routledge, 1994.

Hutchinson, George. *In Search of Nella Larsen*. Cambridge, MA: Harvard University Press, 2006.

———. *The Harlem Renaissance in Black and White*. Cambridge, MA: Harvard University Press, 1995.

Huyssen, Andreas. *After the Great Divide: Modernism, Mass Culture, Postmodernism*. Bloomington: Indiana University Press, 1986.

Jaffe, Aaron. *Modernism and the Culture of Celebrity*. Cambridge: Cambridge University Press, 2005.

Jameson, Fredric. *Postmodernism, or the Cultural Logic of Late Capitalism*. Durham, NC: Duke University Press, 1991.

Kazin, Alfred. *Starting Out in the Thirties*. Boston: Little, Brown, 1965.

Kessler-Harris, Alice. *Out to Work: A History of Wage-Earning Women in the United States*. New York: Oxford University Press, 1982.

Kitch, Carolyn. *The Girl on the Magazine Cover: The Origins of Visual Stereotypes in American Mass Media*. Chapel Hill: University of North Carolina Press, 2001.

Larsen, Nella. *Quicksand*. New York: Penguin Classics, 2002.

Lee, Judith Yaross. *Defining New Yorker Humor*. Jackson: University Press of Mississippi, 2000.

Lewis, David Leavering. *When Harlem Was in Vogue*. New York: Penguin Books, 1997.

Limon, John. *Stand-up Comedy in Theory, or, Abjection in America*. Durham, NC: Duke University Press, 2000.

Litvak, Joseph. *Strange Gourmets: Sophistication, Theory, and the Novel.* Durham, NC: Duke University Press, 1997.

Long, Lois. "Doldrums: The Hunted." *New Yorker,* 14 March 1931, 21–23.

———. "Doldrums: The Swing of the Pendulum." *New Yorker,* 31 January 1931, 18–20.

———. [Lipstick] "Tables for Two." *New Yorker,* 14 November 1925, 24–25.

Loos, Anita. *Gentlemen Prefer Blondes and But Gentlemen Marry Brunettes.* Ed. Regina Barreca. New York: Penguin Books, 1998.

———. *A Girl Like I.* New York: Viking Press, 1966.

———. *Kiss Hollywood Good-by.* New York: Viking Press, 1974.

———. *The Talmadge Girls.* New York: Viking Press, 1978.

Lutes, Jean Marie. *Front Page Girls: Women Journalists in American Culture and Fiction, 1800–1930.* Ithaca, NY: Cornell University Press, 2006.

———. "Making Up Race: Jessie Fauset, Nella Larsen, and the African American Cosmetics Industry." *Arizona Quarterly* 58, no. 1 (2002): 77–108.

Majerus, Elizabeth. "'Determined and Bigoted Feminists': Women, Magazines, and Popular Modernism." In *Modernism,* vol. 1, edited by Astradur Eysteinsson and Vivian Liska, 619–636. Philadelphia: John Benjamins, 2007.

Marchand, Roland. *Advertising the American Dream: Making Way for Modernity, 1920–1940.* Berkeley: University of California Press, 1986.

Marshall, P. David. *Celebrity and Power: Fame in Contemporary Culture.* Minneapolis: University of Minnesota Press, 1997.

McCarthy, Mary. *A Bolt from the Blue and Other Essays.* Ed. A. O. Scott. New York: New York Review Books, 2002.

———. *The Company She Keeps.* New York: Harvest/HBJ Books, 2003.

———. *The Group.* New York: Harcourt, 1963.

———. *How I Grew: A Memoir of the Early Years.* New York: Harcourt Books, 1987.

———. Interview by Elisabeth Niebuhr. In *Writers at Work: The Paris Review Interviews, Second Series,* ed. by George Plimpton. New York: Penguin, 1977.

———. *Intellectual Memoirs: 1936–1938.* New York: Harvest Books, 1993.

———. *The Oasis.* New York: Random House, 1949.

Meade, Marion. *Dorothy Parker: What Fresh Hell Is This?* New York: Penguin, 1989.

Milford, Nancy. *Savage Beauty: The Life of Edna St. Vincent Millay.* New York: Random House, 2002.

Millay, Edna St. Vincent. "The Barrel: Showing That to a Woman a Man, Even a Philosopher, Is Always a Little Ridiculous, and that to a Man, Any Man, a Woman Is Something More than a Nuisance." *Vanity Fair,* July 1922, 35.

———. *Collected Poems: Edna St. Vincent Millay.* Ed. Norma Millay. New York: Harper & Row, 1956.

———. [Nancy Boyd]. "Diary of an American Art Student in Paris: Showing

How She Succeeded in Going to the Louvre Every Day." *Vanity Fair*, November 1922, 44.

———. [Nancy Boyd]. *Distressing Dialogues*. New York: Harper & Row, 1924.

———. *Letters of Edna St. Vincent Millay*. Ed. Allan Ross Macdougall. New York: Grosset & Dunlap, 1952.

———. *The Selected Poetry of Edna St. Vincent Millay*. Ed. Nancy Milford. New York: Modern Library, 2002.

Miller, Alice Duer. "Many Men to Any Woman." In *Redressing the Balance: Literary Humor from the Colonial Times to the 1980s*, ed. Zita Dresner and Nancy Walker, 205. Jackson: University of Mississippi Press, 1988.

Miller, Nina. "Femininity, Publicity, and the Class Division of Cultural Labor: Jessie Redmon Fauset's *There Is Confusion*," *African American Review* 30, no. 2 (1996): 205–220.

———. *Making Love Modern: The Intimate Public Worlds of New York's Literary Women*. New York: Oxford University Press, 1999.

Miller, Tyrus. *Late Modernism: Politics, Fiction, and the Arts between the World Wars*. Berkeley: University of California Press, 1999.

Morehead, Ola Calhoun. "The Bewitched Sword." *Crisis*, February 1925, 166–167.

North, Michael. *The Dialect of Modernism: Race, Language, and Twentieth-Century Literature*. New York: Oxford University Press, 1994.

———. *Machine Age Comedy*. New York: Oxford University Press, 2009.

Page, Tim. *Dawn Powell*. New York: Henry Holt and Company, 1998.

Parker, Dorothy. "Adam and Eve and Lilith and Epigrams—Something More about Cabell." Reading and Writing, *New Yorker*, 19 November 1927, 116.

———. "Back to the Bookshelf." Reading and Writing, *New Yorker*, 25 August 1928, 60.

———. *Dorothy Parker: Complete Stories*. Ed. Colleen Breese. New York: Penguin Classics, 2003.

———. "How It Feels to Be One Hundred and Forty-six." Reading and Writing, *New Yorker*, 29 September 1928, 86.

———. "Mrs. Norris and the Beast." Reading and Writing, *New Yorker*, 14 April 1928, 97.

———. *Not Much Fun: The Lost Poems of Dorothy Parker*. Ed. Stuart Y. Silverstein. New York: Scribner, 1996.

———. *The Portable Dorothy Parker*. Ed. Marion Meade. New York: Penguin Classics, 2006.

Peterson, Theodore. *Magazines in the Twentieth Century*. Urbana: University of Illinois Press, 1956.

Pettit, Rhonda. ed. *The Critical Waltz: Essays on the Work of Dorothy Parker*. Madison, NJ: Fairleigh Dickinson University Press, 2005.

———. *A Gendered Collision: Sentimentalism and Modernism in Dorothy Park-*

er's Poetry and Fiction. Madison, NJ: Fairleigh Dickinson University Press, 2000.

Plath, Sylvia. *The Bell Jar.* New York: HarperCollins, 2003.

Powell, Dawn. *Dawn Powell: Novels 1930–1942.* Ed. Tim Page. New York: Library of America, 2001.

———. *The Diaries of Dawn Powell 1931–1965.* Ed. Tim Page. South Royalton, VT: Steerforth Press, 1995.

———. *The Happy Island.* South Royalton, VT: Steerforth Press, 1998.

Radway, Janice. *A Feeling for Books: the Book-of-the-Month Club, Literary Taste, and Middle Class Desire.* Chapel Hill: University of North Carolina Press, 1999.

Rice, Marcelle Smith. *Dawn Powell.* New York: Twayne, 2000.

Riviere, Joan. "Womanliness as a Masquerade." In *Formations of Fantasy,* ed. Victor Burgin, James Donald, and Cora Kaplan, 35–44. New York: Routledge, 1986.

Rooks, Noliwe. *Ladies' Pages: African American Women's Magazines and the Culture That Made Them.* New Brunswick, NJ: Rutgers University Press, 2004.

Rorty, Richard. *Contingency, Irony, and Solidarity.* New York: Cambridge University Press, 1989

Rourke, Constance. *American Humor: A Study of the National Character.* New York: New York Review Books, 2004.

Rubin, Joan Shelley. *The Making of Middlebrow Culture.* Chapel Hill: University of North Carolina Press, 1992.

Russo, Mary. *The Female Grotesque: Risk, Excess, and Modernity.* New York: Routledge, 1994.

Scholes, Robert. *Paradoxy of Modernism.* New Haven: Yale University Press, 2006.

Sedaris, David. *Me Talk Pretty One Day.* New York: Back Bay Books, 2000.

———. *When You Are Engulfed in Flames.* New York: Little, Brown and Company, 2008.

Sherrard-Johnson, Cherene. *Portraits of the New Negro Woman.* New Brunswick, NJ: Rutgers University Press, 2007.

Showalter, Elaine. "Women Writers between the Wars." In *Columbia Literary History of the United States,* ed. Emory Elliott, 822–841. New York: Columbia University Press, 1988.

Sollors, Werner. *Neither Black Nor White Yet Both: Thematic Explorations of Interracial Literature.* Cambridge, MA: Harvard University Press, 1997.

Stearns, Peter. *Fat History: Bodies and Beauty in the Modern West.* New York: New York University Press, 2002.

Stengel, Hans. "Our Sermons on Sin." *New Yorker,* 12 December 1925, 22.

Stewart, Donald Ogden. "'Why You Can't Afford to Miss This Number': Straight

Dope on Its Contents—In the Manner of Certain of Our Popular Fiction Magazines." In Vanity Fair, *Vanity Fair*, November 1921, 25.

Susman, Warren. *Culture as History: The Transformation of American Society in the Twentieth Century*. New York: Pantheon, 1984.

Swertka, Eve, and Margo Viscusi, ed. *Twenty-four Ways of Looking at Mary McCarthy: The Writer and Her Work*. Westport, CT: Greenwood Press, 1996.

Sylvander, Carolyn Wedin. *Jessie Redmon Fauset*. Troy, NY: Whitson, 1981.

Tebbel, John, and Mary Ellen Zuckerman. *The Magazine in America 1741–1990*. New York: Oxford University Press, 1991.

Teres, Harvey. *Renewing the Left: Politics, Imagination, and the New York Intellectuals*. New York: Oxford University Press, 1996.

Thurber, James. *The Thurber Carnival*. New York: Harper Collins, 1999.

Wald, Alan M. *The New York Intellectuals: The Rise and Decline of the Anti-Stalinist Left from the 1930s to the 1980s*. Winston-Salem: University of North Carolina Press, 1987.

Walker, Cheryl. *Masks Outrageous and Austere: Culture, Psyche, and Persona in Modern Women Poets*. Bloomington: Indiana University Press, 1991.

Walker, Nancy A. *A Very Serious Thing: Women's Humor and American Culture*. Minneapolis: University of Minnesota Press, 1988.

Walker, Susannah. *Style & Status: Selling Beauty to African-American Women, 1920–1975*. Lexington: University of Kentucky Press, 2007.

Walkowitz, Rebecca. *Cosmopolitan Style: Modernism Beyond the Nation*. New York: Columbia University Press, 2006.

Wall, Cheryl. *Women of the Harlem Renaissance*. Bloomington: Indiana University Press, 1995.

Warner, Michael. *Publics and Counterpublics*. New York: Zone Books, 2002.

Weisenberger, Lauren. *The Devil Wears Prada*. New York: Doubleday, 2003.

White, E. B. "Getting Through." *New Yorker*, 28 August 1926, 13.

Wicke, Jennifer. *Advertising Fictions: Literature, Advertisement, and Social Reading*. New York: Columbia University Press, 1988.

Wilford, Hugh. *The New York Intellectuals: From Vanguard to Institution*. New York: Manchester University Press, 1995.

Wilson, Edmund. "Epilogue 1952: Edna St. Vincent Millay." In *Edmund Wilson: Literary Essays and Reviews of the 1920s & 1930s*, 601–640. New York: Library of America, 2007.

———. "Dawn Powell: Greenwich Village in the Fifties." *New Yorker*, 17 November 1962, 233.

Wood, James Playsted. *Magazines in the United States*. New York: Ronald Press Company, 1956.

Yagoda, Ben. *About Town: The New Yorker and the World It Made*. New York: Da Capo, 2001.

Yates, Norris. *The American Humorist: The Conscience of the Twentieth Century*. Ames: Iowa State University Press, 1964.

INDEX

Adams, Franklin Pierce, 37–38; "The Conning Tower," 38

advertisements, 29, 44, 46–47, 66–67, 84, 86–87, 101, 121, 187n31, 190n84

Advertising to Women (Naether), 14

"Advice to the Little Peyton Girl" (Parker), 56–57

African Americans: and class mobility, 80, 84, 97, 98; and consumer culture, 85–86, 87–88, 92, 101; and domesticity, 80, 86–87, 96–101, 109; and earnestness, 80, 86–87; and feminine roles, 80, 83, 86–87, 94, 100; and magazine industry, 83–89, 101, 182n3; and middle-class culture, 80, 84, 85–86, 92, 96, 98; and professional identity, 82, 97–100; and stereotypes, 79–80; wit of, 81, 89. *See also* Harlem Renaissance; race

Ainslee's, Millay in, 21, 40

Algonquin Round Table, 53, 63, 66, 81, 89, 112

"Are Women People?" (A. Miller), 39

"Arrangement in Black and White" (Parker), 89, 106–108

Art Deco, 27, 51, 64, 88

"The Avant-Garde and Kitsch" (Greenberg), 149, 151, 158

Baker, Russell, 38

banter: and counterpublics, 15, 19, 130–131, 136; and femininity, 43, 80, 160–161; and interracial communication, 89, 97–98, 105; in romance plots, 102; in television series, 177–178

"The Barrel" (Millay), 29–31

Barrett, William, 141–142, 202n18

Baughman, James, 201n42

Beard, Mary Ritter, 38

The Bell Jar (Plath), 175–176

Benchley, Robert, 71–72, 87; "The Noon Telephone Operator," 72

Bender, Thomas, 16, 185n46

Benjamin, Walter, 3, 114–115, 117–118, 126

Bennett, Gwendolyn B., 96; "To Usward," 96

Bergson, Henri, 5, 7, 75

Berlant, Lauren, 9–10, 53, 184n40, 191n23

Berman, Marshall, 168, 204n37, 206n62

"The Bewitched Sword" (Morehead), 85

Birken, Lawrence, 189n72

Bishop, John Peale, 43

Bodenheim, Maxwell, 112

body-mind divide, 13–15, 44, 56, 72–75

Bogan, Louise, 112

Bonaparte, Pauline, 14–15, 32

Booth, Wayne, 12

Botshon, Lisa, 182n20, 183n23

Bourdieu, Pierre, 151, 157, 203n27

Bowles, Eva D., 87; "Educated Colored Women," 87

Douglas, Mary, 4–5, 11, 139
Du Bois, W.E.B., 79–80, 84, 85, 99, 100, 184n35, 197n66; "The Technique of Race Prejudice," 85
duCille, Ann, 83

earnestness, 77, 80, 84–87, 96, 129–130
"Educated Colored Women" (Bowles), 87
elitism, 145–160; in advertisements, 47; and feminine ideal, 143; and irony, 166; and politics, 146, 147, 160, 164; and smartness, 6; woman as symbol of, 147
English, Diane, 178
Ephron, Nora, 176–177, 179; Crazy Salad: Some Things About Women, 176; I Feel Bad About My Neck and Other Thoughts on Being a Woman, 177; Imaginary Friends, 177
Esquire, Ephron in, 176

"The Fall of the House of Usher" (Poe), 74
Faludi, Susan, 173
fascism, 111, 114, 131–132, 137, 139, 170, 205–206n61
fashion: and alienation, 175; and consumer culture, 136; and female body, 23, 53–54, 153, 159, 174; and masculine desire, 61, 65; and McCarthy, 143; and Millay's personae, 20, 23, 25; and narcissism, 100, 121; and New York intellectuals, 147; and professionalism, 174; and smartness, 6
Fauset, Jessie, 18, 79–109; The Chinaberry Tree, 100–103, 131; "Dark Algiers the White," 95; femininity and humor in works of, 94–103; "The Gift of Laughter," 18, 79, 80, 108–109; "Here's April!", 95–96; "La Vie C'est la Vie," 95; "Mary Elizabeth," 96–97; and Parker, 104–108; Plum Bun, 80–82, 88, 103, 104–109, 111; There Is Confusion, 84, 97–99
Felski, Rita, 189n68, 199–200n30
femininity: African American, 83, 86, 97–99; and body, 60–68, 153; and celebrity, 125; and humor, 6, 94–103, 170; and masculine insecurities, 68–78, 122, 161–163; roles and stereotypes of, 3, 51–52, 56, 69, 112–13, 128, 130, 143, 152, 159. See also flappers; gender roles; masquerade

A Few Figs from Thistles (Millay), 27, 37, 38, 44
"First Fig" (Millay), 38
Fiske, Dwight, 112
Fitzgerald, F. Scott, 11, 184n35; The Great Gatsby, 11
Fitzgerald, Zelda, 176
flapper, 5, 7: and Fauset, 80, 103, 106, 107, 174; humor of, 13, 80, 109; and Long, 61, 62, 63; and Millay, 25–26, 32–33; narcissism of, 18, 86; and Parker, 52, 54, 67
"For the Well-Dressed Man" (Vanity Fair column), 32
Fortune: Chamberlain in, 163; and Luce, 132, 137
Freud, Sigmund, 2, 5, 7
Friedan, Betty, 176
The Front Page (Hecht), 31
Fuchs, Sabrina Abrams, 204n42

"The Garter" (Parker), 69–71, 75, 156
gender roles: and African Americans, 80, 83, 93, 97; anxiety about, 9, 31, 32, 35, 122, 129, 165; and humor, 30–31, 80, 160–62; in magazines, 2, 5–6, 32; normative, 10, 39, 53, 69; and professionalism, 31–32, 68–78; and publicity, 10; theatricality of, 31, 34–47. See also femininity; masculinity; masquerade
Gentlemen Prefer Blondes: The Illuminating Diary of a Professional Lady (Loos), 11, 63–66
"Getting Through" (E. B. White), 72
"Ghostly Father, I Confess" (McCarthy), 166–169, 170
"The Gift of Laughter" (Fauset), 18, 79, 80, 108–109
Gilbert, Sandra, 83, 94, 186n11, 196n46
Gill, Brendan, 61
Gilman, Sander, 207n33
The Gilmore Girls (television series), 178
A Girl Like I (Loos), 63
Gish, Lillian, 192n28
glamour: Fauset on, 83, 88; Millay on, 36, 47; Parker on, 56, 57, 60, 68, 74; Plath on, 175–176; Powell on, 18, 110, 133–140
Glass, Loren, 124
"Glory in the Daytime" (Parker), 57–60
Goldsmith, Meredith, 182n20, 183n23

Larsen, Nella, 18, 83, 89–94, 184*n*35;
    Quicksand, 18, 83, 84, 89–94, 102
Laughing Their Way (anthology), 38
"La Vie C'est la Vie" (Fauset), 95
Lee, Judith Yaross, 195*n*32
leftist ideology, 141, 144, 165–168. *See also*
    Marxist ideology
Lewis, David Leavering, 82, 84, 195*n*39
Life: and Luce, 132; Parker in, 52, 68
light verse, 3–4, 15, 37–43, 76, 96
Limon, John, 192*n*30
"Lipstick." *See* Long, Lois
"Little Man" humor, 71–72, 76
Litvak, Joseph, 16, 193*n*57, 200*n*39, 202*n*10
Locke, Alain, 79, 84; *The New Negro*, 79
Lockridge, Richard, 168
Long, Lois, 15, 17, 60–63, 73–74, 78; "On
    the Avenue," 61; "Tables for Two," 61
Loos, Anita, 11, 17, 21, 60–61, 63–67, 75, 78,
    178; *But Gentlemen Marry Brunettes*,
    63, 66; *Gentlemen Prefer Blondes: The
    Illuminating Diary of a Professional
    Lady*, 11, 63–66; *A Girl Like I*, 63; *Kiss
    Hollywood Good-by*, 65
Luce, Clare Boothe, 132, 137, 178; *The
    Women*, 178
Luce, Henry, 132, 137
Lutes, Jean Marie, 182*n*10, 195*n*21

Macdougall, Allan Ross, 24
MacFadden, Bernarr, 73
"Madame A Tort!" (Millay), 44–46, 49
magazines: advice columns in, 57; black vs.
    white press, 83–89; female readership
    of, 28; feminine stereotypes in, 51–52;
    gender roles in, 2, 5–6, 32; and humor, 83;
    illustrations in, 6, 11, 23, 51–52, 67, 88, 95,
    101, 117; industry expansion in 1910s and
    1920s, 52–53; influence of, 6–7, 111, 142;
    as medium for confinement, 174–175;
    and modernity, 8–9; photography in,
    117–118. *See also* advertisements; smart
    magazines; *and specific publications*
Majerus, Elizabeth, 9
"The Man in the Brooks Brothers Shirt"
    (McCarthy), 148–160, 169
Marchand, Roland, 47, 190*n*1, 196*n*50
Marshall, P. David, 58, 128, 129, 198*nn*17–
    18, 200*n*38
Marxist ideology, 147, 148, 162, 168–169.
    See also leftist ideology

"Mary Elizabeth" (Fauset), 96–97
masculinity: and body-building, 73; and
    cross-gender identification, 123; and
    disenchantment, 125; femininity
    vs., 68–78; and humor, 99; and
    intellectualism, 144–145, 160, 165;
    and leftist ideology, 148; and literary
    identity, 113, 116, 122, 123, 161–162;
    and magazine writers, 119–120, 121;
    as masquerade, 34–35; and normative
    gender roles, 129; and political
    identity, 161–162; and professional
    identity, 71; and sexual sovereignty,
    41–42, 43; and smartness, 32, 33. *See
    also* gender roles
masquerade, 4, 18; Ephron on, 176; Fauset
    on, 80; Loos on, 64, 66, 78; McCarthy
    on, 152, 157–158; Millay on, 22, 34–35,
    40, 42; Powell on, 113, 116, 119, 122,
    124, 126, 129–130. *See also* Riviere, Joan
McCarthy, Mary, 19, 141–171; *A Charmed
    Life*, 146; *The Company She Keeps*, 19,
    141–171; "Ghostly Father, I Confess,"
    166–169, 170; *The Group*, 141, 174–175;
    Groves of Academe, 146; Hellman
    rivalry with, 170, 177; *How I Grew*,
    145; *Intellectual Memoirs: New York
    1936–1938*, 143; irony in works of, 160–
    171; "The Man in the Brooks Brothers
    Shirt," 148–160, 169; *Memories of a
    Catholic Girlhood*, 145; *The Oasis*, 141,
    146, 164; and *Partisan Review*, 141, 143,
    144, 148; "Portrait of the Intellectual as
    a Yale Man," 160–164, 169; and Wilson,
    184*n*35
McDonnell, Patrick, 186*n*20
McManus, George, 168; *Bringing Up
    Father*, 168
Memories of a Catholic Girlhood
    (McCarthy), 145
"Men: A Hate Song" (Parker), 73
Mencken, H. L., 66, 92
middlebrow culture, 7–13; African
    American, 80, 84, 85–86, 96; and
    celebrity, 56–60; class identity and
    aspiration in, 10–11, 84, 151–153;
    elitism and, 145–160; expansion
    of, 8–9, 150–151; and humor, 2, 11;
    and intellectualism, 145–160; and
    modernism, 8–9, 10–11, 112, 124, 126,
    147, 150

American, 81, 89; as commodity,
132–133; and detachment, 9; Fauset
on, 105; and intellectualism, 145; and
modern women, 80; and politics, 146;
as smartness, 43–44, 50
The Women (C.B. Luce), 178
"Women of Wit" (Van Doren), 27
Woodard, Deborah, 21

Woollcott, Alexander, 53
Wylie, Elinor, 1, 21, 49; "The Doll," 21

Yates, Norris, 192n49

Zaretsky, Eli, 5, 200n36
Zeitz, Joshua, 61

ABOUT THE AUTHOR

Catherine Keyser is an assistant professor of English at the University of South Carolina. A feminist scholar of American literature, she has previously published on Hannah Crafts, Edna St. Vincent Millay, and Dorothy Parker. Her essay "Girls Who Wear Glasses" about New York women humorists of the 1920s is included in *A New Literary History of America*, edited by Greil Marcus and Werner Sollors. She lives in Columbia, South Carolina, with her husband, Paul Famolari. Among their pets is a cat named Dorothy Parker.

Breinigsville, PA USA
11 April 2011
259533BV00001BA/1/P